PENGUIN BOOKS

CATHOLICS IN CRISIS

Jim Naughton was formerly a reporter at *The Washington Post* and *The New York Times*. He lives with his wife and two sons in Washington, D.C.

CATHOLICS
IN
CRISIS

*The Rift Between American Catholics
and Their Church*

JIM NAUGHTON

PENGUIN BOOKS

PENGUIN BOOKS
Published by the Penguin Group
Penguin Putnam Inc., 375 Hudson Street, New York, New York 10014, U.S.A.
Penguin Books Ltd, 27 Wrights Lane, London W8 5TZ, England
Penguin Books Australia Ltd, Ringwood, Victoria, Australia
Penguin Books Canada Ltd, 10 Alcorn Avenue, Toronto, Ontario, Canada M4V 3B2
Penguin Books (N.Z.) Ltd, 182–190 Wairau Road, Auckland 10, New Zealand

Penguin Books Ltd, Registered Offices: Harmondsworth, Middlesex, England

First published in the United States of America by
Addison-Wesley Publishing Company, Inc. 1996
Published in Penguin Books 1997

1 3 5 7 9 10 8 6 4 2

Many of the designations used by manufacturers and sellers to distinguish their
products are claimed as trademarks. Where those designations appear in this book
and the publisher was aware of a trademark claim, the designations have been
printed in initial capital letters.

Grateful acknowledgment is made to the following for reprinted material:
"Psalm 42 (As the Deer Longs)," by Donna Harkin. Copyright 1975 by World Music
Company, a division of Word, Inc. All rights reserved. Used by permission.
"We Shall Rise Again," by Jeremy Taylor. Copyright GIA Publications,
Chicago, Illinois. All rights reserved. Used by permission.
"When Love Is Found," by Brian Wren. Copyright 1983 by Hope Publishing
Company, Carol Stream, Illinois. All rights reserved. Used by permission.

THE LIBRARY OF CONGRESS HAS CATALOGUED THE HARDCOVER AS FOLLOWS:
Naughton, Jim.
Catholics in crisis: an American parish fights for its soul / Jim Naughton.
p. cm.
ISBN 0-201-62458-3 (hc.)
ISBN 0 14 02.6818 9 (pbk.)
1. Holy Trinity Church (Washington, D.C.)—History—20th century.
2. Washington, D.C.—Church history—20th century. I. Title.
BX4603.W32N38 1996
282'.753—dc20   96–14880

Printed in the United States of America
Set in Bembo
Designed by Karen Savary

FOR MY SONS,

BENJAMIN *and* CHRISTOPHER

INTRODUCTION

The Roman Catholic Church in the United States is a disputatious communion. Riven by the same issues—abortion, homosexuality, sex education and the role and rights of women—that set Left against Right in this country's "culture wars," it is, nonetheless, united by the faithful's belief in the redemptive passion and resurrection of Jesus Christ, and in his "real presence" in the sacraments.

Polls illustrating the gulf between the teachings of Pope John Paul II and the beliefs of his American flock have appeared with a frequency sufficient to make them a journalistic cliché. Yet the Catholic Church, with roughly 60 million members, remains by far the largest religious denomination in the United States. And despite abundant differences with Rome, American Catholics remain loyal to their faith. Roughly three-quarters of American Catholics attend mass at least once a month, and among those who seldom cross the threshold of a church, two-thirds continue to count themselves as Catholic.

This book is an effort to explore, in narrative form, the tensions inherent in this situation; to examine the issues that set much of the American laity against the Vatican and to elucidate the effect of these divisions on Catholics as they struggle, individually and communally, to reconcile their own moral perceptions with the teachings of their Church.

It is also an account of one community's quest for a deeper appreciation of its faith and a more sustained encounter with its God. It is a story about sexual ethics and ecclesial power, but it is also an examination of contemporary Catholics' commitment to prayer, service and what the Second Vatican Council called the "preferential option for the poor."

Finally, this book is an attempt to help redress an imbalance in the telling of the American Catholic story. The turmoil that engulfs the Church in the United States has been probed with sociological distinction by George Gallup and James Castelli, by Father Andrew Greeley and his colleagues at the National Opinion Research Center, and by Dean Hoge and others at the Catholic University of America. The arguments of ecclesial liberals and conservatives have been articulated with clarity and passion in journals such as *America, Commonweal, First Things,* the *National Catholic Reporter,* the *National Catholic Register* and the *New Oxford Review.* But the story of the upheavals that have shaken the American Church since the Second Vatican Council has only occasionally been rendered as a story. As a result, the reading public may have a clearer picture of American Catholics as a population than as a people, and a stronger sense of the Church as a debating society than as a family of faith.

I wrote this book, in part, to supplement the rich, if rather abstracted literature on the recent history of American Catholicism with a work informed by concerns of time, place and character. My hope in doing so was to make the American Catholic story more emotionally and intellectually accessible, so that the anguish of American Catholics, and the complexity of the issues they are struggling with might be more readily understood.

I nursed a small theological aspiration as well: to persuade readers, through my choice of the narrative form, that God is active everywhere; that the great work of the Church is interpreting and responding to this activity; and that the essential text for this enterprise is the lived experience of ordinary Christians.

The book focuses on a single parish: Holy Trinity, in Washington, D.C. The Jesuit-staffed church has long enjoyed a reputation as a place where post–Vatican II Catholicism is at its most vital. It is also a community in which the American dissent from Vatican teaching is clearly articulated and quietly advanced.

For eight years, beginning in 1987, I was a parishioner at Holy Trinity. Initially, to avoid possible conflicts between duty and affection, I intended to set this book in a different church. But Holy Trinity's history, I soon discovered, was uniquely illustrative of the forces that have sundered and sustained American Catholicism over the last three decades. And the events which began unfolding there in the spring of 1992 captured in microcosm the struggle for control of the American Church.

I remained active in the parish during my research and writing, but aside from asking a question at an open forum, making several retreats and participating in an offertory procession, my role in the events recounted here was strictly journalistic.

The book is based on more than four hundred hours of interviews with roughly two hundred subjects, and on the proceedings of scores of meetings, lectures and forums which I attended over an eighteen-month period. Several people, most notably Cardinal James Hickey, Bishop Alvaro Corrada and Father Peter Vaghi, declined to be interviewed or did not return phone calls. I have reported their activities through other sources.

There are no composite characters or conflated events in this story. On a few occasions, remarks made during separate interviews are presented as though part of a single conversation. Several persons are identified by pseudonyms to protect their privacy or that of their families. These individuals are designated by an asterisk (*) on first reference; details which might identify them have been altered.

PRELUDE

The bells rang all over Holy Hill, from the rickety steeple of the parish church to the blunt belfry of the cloister chapel, and from the campus courtyard to the modest convent near the Catholic hospital. Three times each day—at nine, noon and six—they washed the neighborhood in a clamorous tide, summoning the faithful to prayer.

In pious pockets amid the din, activity ceased. Housewives and shop clerks paused at their labors; Jesuit scholars turned from their research and children folded their hands over textbooks, lunches or homework to recall the words of the Angelus: *The angel of the Lord declared unto Mary, and she conceived of the Holy Ghost. . . .*

The western edge of Georgetown, in Washington, D.C., was a distinctively Catholic piece of real estate in the years after World War II, an insular world in which all authority flowed from the Church. Within five blocks stood Holy Trinity Church, its rectory, convent and schools; Georgetown University and the residence of the Jesuits who taught there; the cloister of the Sisters of the Visitation and their prep school; and the convent of the Sisters of the Good Shepherd, who shared their home with the Magdalenes, a community of women, some former prostitutes, who had embraced a penitential life to atone for past sins.

It was a world that moved to an ecclesial rhythm as regular and pervasive as the sound of the bells. On the first Friday morning of each month, children rose early and eddied through the streets, the boys in dark pants, white shirts, navy blazers and clip-on ties; the girls in blue pleated jumpers, white shirts with Peter Pan collars, dark cardigans and white ankle socks—all on their way to mass. After half an hour of silent prayer, policed by ever watchful nuns, they processed down the aisles of the nave, out the rear doors and up the precipitous stairs of the school buildings which stood on either side of the church.

By that time college students and their black-caped Jesuit professors were hurrying across the grassy campus to classes. Tradesmen and shop owners were coursing along the sidewalks of Georgetown, and cars were filing through the brick gate of the convent school, bearing suburban girls whose parents still cherished this cozy corner of Catholic America.

When the children were safely in school, a fitting silence stole over the neighborhood as the parish buried its dead. Several mornings each week, a procession of black Cadillacs cruised slowly down Wisconsin Avenue, crept through the cramped side streets and pulled up in front of the church, where one of the DeVol brothers waited to help the mourners from their cars and direct the pallbearers in hoisting the casket and carrying it into the sanctuary. By the time the children started home for lunch, the Cadillacs would be gone, flying small purple flags emblazoned with the word FUNERAL and the sign of the cross, bound for the archdiocesan cemeteries in the suburbs.

Dismissal from the parish school came at three o'clock, and sometimes, in the calm that followed, the Sisters of Mercy, who taught at the school in those years, would come out to stroll along Thirty-sixth Street, wearing their heavy blue habits and holding their hands as though in a muff. They were strict, serene, and at times seemed utterly unknowable. Yet they were often spotted bearing food to some of the poor families who lived in Georgetown before the neighborhood became synonymous with wealth and power.

The Jesuits, dressed in their black cassocks and birettas, were more frequently abroad on the cobblestone streets, and their neighbors regarded them with the deferential fascination they might have shown exotic birds.

One Jesuit, some years earlier, spent so much time sipping Cokes on a packing crate in Tom Jenkins's father's store that he converted the proprietor. Another had played checkers with a little girl named Hattie Wise, and persuaded her older brother to join the order. And then there was Father Righy, who remained a fisher of fish long after he had become a fisher of men, and once brought home a sea bass so big that it took two of the Kuhn boys to carry it down O Street and into their mother's kitchen.

It was an easy community in which to find one's place. The men belonged to the Holy Name Society, which prayed and kept the church solvent. The women belonged to the Mothers' Club, which mended the priests' vestments. The boys served on the altar, and came to know a smattering of Latin and the smell of incense on their surplices. And the girls belonged to the Blessed Virgin's Sodality, and on Holy Thursday, resplendent in white gloves and dresses, they scattered petals in the path of the Virgin as their fathers bore her statue through the church.

Obedience was synonymous with salvation on Holy Hill, and rules were rigorous and far-reaching. Catholics did not read volumes listed on the Index of Forbidden Books or see films proscribed by the Legion of Decency. They did not eat meat on Fridays or practice artificial contraception. Some would not even brush their teeth on Sunday mornings for fear of swallowing water, ruining their fasts and leaving themselves unable to receive Communion.

They were taught that the moral tenor of one's life counted for little compared with the state of one's soul at the moment of death, and so, each Saturday, they lined up in the rear of the church, waiting to step into the darkened confessional and enumerate their failings to a priest who could not see them but often recognized their voices. ("Tell your mother I'm coming for dinner," one girl's Jesuit uncle told her after she had confessed some particularly embarrassing sins.) After absolution they were once again in a "state of grace," but only until their next impure thought.

Because their God was such a rigorous judge, the people of Holy Hill often approached him through intermediaries, especially the Blessed Mother, to whom they offered such an array of devotions—rosaries, litanies and novenas—that Protestants accused them of making her a god. But she was not a god in their eyes. Her they loved; Him they feared.

Hence the turgid solemnity of each Sunday morning when they

came into His presence and knelt in the burgundy and gilt church, as a priest at the white marble altar offered the sacrifice of the Mass. They could not see what he was doing because he stood with his back to them, and they could not understand what he was saying because he spoke in Latin. But every so often a somber-faced altar boy would ring a bell and they would look up from their rosaries or prayer books and softly beat their breasts.

Then, when the prayers had been concluded and the last bell had been rung, they professed their unworthiness, processed to the altar and knelt at the Communion railing, waiting for the priest to raise the body of their Savior from the ciborium and place it upon their tongues.

The brittle wafer dissolving against the roofs of their mouths was their promise of life in a world beyond Holy Hill. What they could not know was how quickly a new world was coming, and how suddenly the world that they and so many other American Catholics had known would pass.

CHAPTER ONE

On the Sunday after Easter, a bearded man in a dark suit walked into Holy Trinity Church for the 9:15 mass, slipped into a pew near the front of the assembly and stood with upturned hands as though receiving a gift—or offering one. His eyes were closed behind thick glasses, and his expression was prayerful and vaguely pained.

For perhaps ten minutes he was the only person standing in the church, aside from the growing number clustered in the rear who had arrived after every seat was filled. Soon, however, the strains of the opening hymn filled the sanctuary and the congregation rose as Father Joe Sobierajski and his party processed to the altar.

Like everyone else in the throng, the bearded man contemplated his sins, prayed for forgiveness and sang God's glory. But when the others sat for the Scripture readings, Ray McGovern remained upright in their midst, provoking wariness and speculation.

Gayle Garrett wondered if her friend had hemorrhoids. Margaret Costello assumed he had wrenched his back. Brian Depenbrock, a clinical

1

social worker who sang in the choir, thought the man might be disturbed, and made plans to subdue him if he began to babble or gesticulate.

McGovern, however, was the picture of composure. He stood silently through Father Sobierajski's homily and remained on his feet while the others knelt for the Eucharistic prayer and the elevation of the host and chalice. Ray took Communion, which dispelled some people's fears that he was in a trance, but afterward he remained standing while others knelt in private thanksgiving.

By the time Mass ended, the hiss of whispered questions filled the church. "Go in peace," Father Sobierajski told them, though he must have realized that peace was unlikely. The final note of the concluding hymn had barely faded when a knot of parishioners surrounded McGovern. Was he all right? What was going on?

Ray was seldom inclined to be succinct, and he gave his interrogators the full benefit of his thinking.

A few weeks earlier in the late winter of 1992, the National Conference of Catholic Bishops had released the third draft of its pastoral letter on the role of women in the American Church. It was a more conservative document than its predecessors and no longer suggested that the Church discuss ordaining women as deacons. On returning from Rome, where he had been summoned for consultations, Bishop Matthew Clark of Rochester, New York, told reporters that Pope John Paul II was irrevocably opposed to women's ordination and had decided that further conversation would only breed dissent and disillusionment.

McGovern heard "the voice of the oppressor" in these words. It was a voice he had heard repeatedly in his previous line of work, monitoring the Soviet bloc for the Central Intelligence Agency. And though the pope had played an essential role in the crusade against Communism, Ray viewed him as a repressive force within the Church.

Believing that Rome was in the wrong on women's ordination and a welter of other issues did not distinguish McGovern from the majority of American Catholics. In a Gallup survey released that year, nearly 90 percent of the Catholic respondents said they believed couples could morally disregard the Church's ban on artificial birth control; 70 percent said priests should be allowed to marry; 68 percent believed that premarital sex could be morally acceptable in some circumstances and two-thirds supported ordaining women to the priesthood.

In the same survey a solid majority supported allowing divorced Catholics to remarry in the Church. Fifty-two percent said abortion should be legal in many or all instances. Respondents backed equal rights for gays and lesbians, but they were about evenly split on the morality of homosexual relationships.

Dissent was probably even more widespread at Holy Trinity, which is among the more liberal parishes in the country. But until that morning, disagreement had never escalated into protest.

Several Sundays earlier, however, McGovern's daughter, Christin, the youngest of his five children, had come home angry from religious instruction, which Catholics call CCD, an acronym for the Confraternity of Christian Doctrine. The sophomores had been studying the sacraments, and when the teacher began to explain Holy Orders, the sacrament of priestly ordination, Christin interrupted. If she couldn't receive the sacrament, she said, she didn't want to hear about it. A few of the other girls supported her, and they brought the class to a halt.

Ray had taught CCD himself for several years and had never heard of an incident like this one. But the more he reflected on it the more he came to admire what his daughter had done. He and his wife, Rita, had raised Christin and her two sisters to believe that God had created them the equal of any man. And in all that time, he suddenly felt, the Catholic Church had been working against them.

"I felt I should not sit still for this," McGovern told people that Sunday morning. "So I stood up."

News of Ray's protest spread quickly through the crowd that gathered after mass in the basement of the parish's upper school for coffee, doughnuts and conversation. Reaction was vigorously mixed. Most of the volunteers who helped plan the 9:15 liturgy were angered that the mass had been disrupted, but most of the women of the parish staff were pleased that someone had called attention to Rome's intransigence on women's issues. There was amusement among those who took a tolerant view of Holy Trinity's penchant for controversy, and indignation among those who did not.

Underlying all these reactions, however, was a communal sense of foreboding, for the people of Holy Trinity understood that their parish was already vulnerable to the resurgent conservatism that John Paul II had breathed into the Church and that McGovern's protest might intensify the precariousness of its position.

That Holy Trinity is different from most Catholic parishes is evident at a glance. The church is neither Gothic, like the parishes of so many Catholic childhoods, nor modernist, like the brick piles that jut from sprawling parking lots in the suburbs. Rather it is neoclassical, and resembles a lyceum more than a church.

Graceful, narrow arches supported by Corinthian columns flank its altar and frame its windows. A hand-carved likeness of the Blessed Virgin, which stands against a wall near the front of the church, is the only statue. The richly colored windows bear no devotional imagery, and the dominant piece of artwork is not a crucifix but a huge brass "Cross of Glory," augmented by a sunburst and bearing no corpus. Suspended from the ceiling just behind the white marble altar, the cross is backed by a swath of deep purple fabric.

Despite the prominence of the cross, the church's most distinctive aesthetic quality is the way in which sunlight takes on the color of the faint blue walls. If the old Gothic sanctuaries, with their flickering candles and sacred crannies, suggested the journey into a somber and unfathomable mystery, this one hints at a distant, abstracted radiance shining through from the other side.

Through either grace or happenstance, the architecture of the 140-year-old building embodies the spirit of the contemporary parish. The church was constructed as the young American republic was rediscovering the political and artistic virtues of ancient Greece—the primacy of reasoned discourse and the right of the individual to bring his views before the community chief among them. The people of Holy Trinity espouse similar values in the face of an unpersuaded Catholic hierarchy.

Few parishes take lay participation in the liturgy so seriously. Each mass is prepared by volunteer planning teams coordinated by the parish's Worship Committee. Trinity employs a full-time director of liturgy, a full-time director of music, several part-time choir directors and a full-time liturgical aide. All are lay people. Lay people design and oversee the decoration of the sanctuary. They read from the Scriptures and give one another Communion. On rare occasions, they preach.

This inclusive approach has helped make Holy Trinity the most popular parish in the Archdiocese of Washington, D.C. In the thirty years since the close of the Second Vatican Council the parish has grown fivefold, though the population of its Georgetown neighborhood has increased barely at all. More than forty-four hundred households are currently on its rolls. Nearly 40 percent come from the neighboring diocese of Arlington, Virginia, and some parishioners live as far as forty-five miles away.

The enthusiasm generated by the liturgy at Holy Trinity is such that the church, its two elementary school buildings and its crumbling parish center cannot hold it all. Nearly seven hundred students are enrolled in the Sunday morning CCD program. They fill every room on the campus and a few more in a building across the street that is owned by Georgetown University. Holy Trinity also sponsors ambitious programs in adult education, Jesuit spirituality and social outreach. Meeting rooms on its campus are in such demand that several groups convene at 8:30 on Saturday mornings.

To many of the laity who crowd its pews each Sunday, and to a handful of the diocesan priests who watch from an envious distance, Holy Trinity is the model of what a contemporary parish should be: liturgically vibrant, theologically sophisticated, spiritually enriching and socially aware, a place where Catholics gather to encounter their God in the pages of Scripture, the sacrament of the Eucharist, and in their fellowship with one another.

But for officials of the Archdiocese of Washington, Holy Trinity is a problem. In their eyes the parish's popularity has come at too great a price. For at the core of its success lies a willingness to trust the spiritual integrity and moral judgment of its parishioners. And this, the archdiocese believes, is sometimes done at the expense of Catholic doctrine.

On an average Sunday morning Holy Trinity either directly violates or implicitly challenges a number of the Church's rubrics and teachings. Its liturgy director rewrites prayers and Scripture readings to make the language more inclusive. The parish occasionally prays publicly for homosexuals and others "marginalized by the Church." It does not deny Communion to non-Catholics, sexually active gays and lesbians or those whom its priests know have remarried without benefit of an annulment.

Nor does it emphasize orthodoxy on the issues which have driven many Catholics from the Church. There is a paucity of antiabortion activity and almost no preaching on sexual ethics. In the marriage-preparation program the Church's ban on artificial birth control is stated but not insisted upon. The CCD program has traditionally concentrated

on "community-building," "moral decision-making," and fostering a relationship with Jesus rather than on dogma and devotions.

All this led one disgruntled former parishioner to say that "the place
just wasn't very Catholic," and an amused visitor to describe it as
"R.C. Lite."

Most Holy Trinity parishioners see matters somewhat differently.
They believe that with the exception of certain core teachings, doctrine
can be "developed"—which is to say, altered—to reflect new insights
and understandings. Such an outlook dictates that questioning and challenging be respected as acts of faith, and that the hand of authority rest
lightly on the pilgrims.

That may be why Holy Trinity is often the place where alienated
Catholics take their first steps back into the Church, and why it is also
the parish of last resort for those who find Catholic teaching on sex roles
and sexual ethics to be oppressive. It was certainly the reason Cardinal
James Hickey, the archbishop of Washington, and his advisors were becoming increasingly concerned about the direction of the parish. For
by the spring of 1992, Holy Trinity was dramatically out of step with
the Vatican.

Unlike most parishioners at the Georgetown church, Cardinal Karol
Wojtyla, who became pope in 1978, believes that the "renewal" catalyzed by the Second Vatican Council is degenerating into anarchy, and
that the truths of the faith are being lost in a mist of relativity. As
John Paul II, he has devoted himself to reasserting Roman authority
by disciplining dissenting theologians, appointing authoritarian bishops,
promoting the cause of conservative organizations such as Opus Dei, and
insisting with frequency and eloquence that some of the Church's most
hotly contested moral teachings are perfect expressions of the divine will.

These exhortations have done little to persuade most American
Catholics, but they have inspired Cardinal Hickey and other conserva-
tive-minded clerics, intellectuals and lay people to undertake the pope's
campaign at home.

During the 1980s and 1990s, a peculiar dynamic has taken hold.
Neither John Paul nor most of his supporters have the appetite for the
kind of wholesale crackdown that would be necessary to rid the Church
of its dissident majority. By the same token, even John Paul's most outspoken American critics cling to their Catholic faith rather than seeking—
or creating—a more hospitable church. The result is a circumscribed

combat in which each camp schemes to subdue the other while not unduly damaging the Church in the process.

Curiously, this struggle seldom publicly manifests itself in the lives of American Catholics. They might follow the latest controversy in the newspapers, but there is peace, and often lethargy, in their parishes. As for themselves, they do not so much *oppose* the Vatican as selectively ignore its teachings. And their bishops and pastors are powerless to halt this silent and passive dissent.

But the tensions that are invisible in other parishes have a way of becoming public at Holy Trinity. In October of 1992 Cardinal Hickey and his staff, in conjunction with the Jesuits of the Maryland province, were to begin the search for Holy Trinity's next pastor. And many parishioners understood immediately that Ray McGovern's protest, if it continued, might deliver their church into the hands of its ecclesial opponents. There was even speculation that if a suitable Jesuit were not found, the cardinal might expel the Society of Jesus from a church its missionaries had founded more than two centuries earlier.

For many of them, that would mean the demise of the only church in which they felt truly comfortable, and perhaps the slow deterioration of their faith as well. Afraid of finding themselves nomads in a spiritual desert, they turned to their pastor, hoping that somehow he could save Holy Trinity from becoming another front in the struggle for control of the American Church.

CHAPTER TWO

Through the spring of 1992 Father Jim Maier had nursed the modest hope that his last year as pastor of Holy Trinity would be quieter than his first five. He had survived a series of painful parish disputes on issues from the financial to the musical and was looking forward to a period in which he could contemplate his future. He thought he might like to teach science to students from poor backgrounds at the Jesuit college in Detroit, or Appalachia, or El Salvador.

But when word of Ray McGovern's protest reached the rectory that morning, Jim sensed that his meditation on his future would have to wait. For he knew his fractious parish well enough to imagine what would unfold. A handful of parishioners would demand that he deliver Ray an ultimatum: sit down or get out. Ray, in all likelihood, would refuse. If matters dragged on, the archdiocese would become involved and, in the end, he would be expected to prevail upon McGovern to leave the parish, or perhaps have him carried from the church.

Carried from the church! Now that would send parish children a wonderful example of how conflict was handled within the family of the faith.

The situation was all the more difficult for Father Maier because exercising authority was neither an interest nor a strength, a fact evident to anyone who visited his office on the second floor of the decaying parish center. The tiny room was jammed with bookcases, papers, posters, an aquarium and a computer. It looked like the carrel of an overworked divinity student. Though crosses, icons and mementos of his pilgrimages to El Salvador were plentiful, nothing in the room suggested its inhabitant was a person of ecclesial power.

Jim had come to Holy Trinity after seven years as master of novices at the Maryland province's formation house in Wernersville, Pennsylvania. In that role he had guided scores of young Jesuits through a two-year period of prayer, counseling and instruction, and helped them determine whether they had a priestly vocation. Though he enjoyed being a pastor, he missed the long, intense conversations he shared with his novices as they tried to discover where God was leading them. This spiritual "discernment" was central to the Jesuit tradition and Jim believed in it so strongly that he felt it could be used to mediate conflicts within the Church. At times he conceived of his role at Holy Trinity as less a pastor than a communal spiritual director.

To parishioners who saw him in the pulpit each Sunday, Father Maier looked the part of a spiritual guide, at least in a late-twentieth-century sort of way—an Old Testament prophet by way of *Gentleman's Quarterly*. He was tall, slender and vigorous. His thick, once-dark hair was streaked with steel and silver, and his closely trimmed beard had turned the color of snow. Yet he looked younger than his fifty-three years.

He had deep brown eyes and a reassuring expression. In conversation he focused so intently on the face of whomever stood before him that it seemed unlikely he would have noticed had that person's clothing caught fire. Yet when he spoke of himself, his gaze frequently wandered, as though in search of visual ballast. To watch him enter a room was to see a man at war with his own magnetism.

Though Jim sometimes projected a commanding presence, he was suspicious of charisma, particularly his own, and often seemed deliberately subdued.

This had not prevented him from becoming an immensely popular pastor. He was beloved for his openness to new ideas, his generosity with his time and what one parishioner called his willingness to "struggle in public." The air of prayerful consideration that he brought to the Eucharist remained with him throughout the working day—as though attending meetings, answering mail and hanging out on the schoolyard were a continuation of the sacrament. Several otherwise sober people said knowing him was as close as they were likely to come to knowing Jesus.

The comparison tickled Jim's friends. Did Jesus have a goofy, edgeless sense of humor? A touch of physical vanity? Was He ruthless on the racquetball court?

Father Maier suspected that if parishioners knew him better they would admire him less. But they were more familiar with his shortcomings than he supposed. Jim was uninterested in learning the kind of ecclesial footwork that would have made life easier for himself and his parish. He was unwilling to articulate clear and comprehensive goals, and gave little direction to his staff. In the face of conflict, he was paralyzed by impartiality.

"I have a curse of being very balanced," he said one morning in his office. "People tell me I'm not passionate enough or angry enough. It takes a great deal to push me into fire."

Father Maier liked to describe his style as "servant leadership," the kind Jesus practiced when he washed the feet of his Apostles and told them that the first among them must become like the least. But the degree to which he shared his pastoral authority with the laity alarmed the archdiocese. "They would like me to be more *directive*," he said. "I know that. But I prefer colleagueship."

It was a preference born in his childhood, when Jim's parents wrestled with the same question that now beset Holy Trinity and the rest of the American Church: how to proceed in love when there is no unity.

James T. Maier, Sr. didn't realize that he would have to sign his unborn offspring over to the Roman Catholic Church until after he and Dorothy Storch got engaged. Jim, Sr. was a Lutheran, which, in the mid-1930s, meant that most of Dorothy's family assumed he was going straight to hell when he died. This, of course, was his own business, but the Storchs were not about to let him take the children along with him.

Jim, Sr.'s preference was for compromise. Let the boys be raised in his religion and the girls in their mom's. But the Archdiocese of Pittsburgh had no interest in negotiation. Either he pledged to raise the children as Catholics or Dorothy's marriage would not be recognized by the Church.

Jim Sr. believed deeply in the truths of his own faith. He believed even more deeply that no church should insinuate itself into the sacred bond between a husband and a wife. But he believed most deeply that the greatest of Christian virtues was love, and he and Dorothy were powerfully in love. He signed the pledge, and he and Dorothy were married on August 10, 1937. Within a year, they moved to Charleston, West Virginia.

Sundays were a complicated affair in the Maier household, particularly after the three children were born. Jim, Sr. and the kids would drive Dorothy to St. Anthony's, drop her off and return home, where Jim, Sr. would fix the kids breakfast. Once he had the dishes in the sink, he would pack the kids back into the car, pick up his wife and return to the house where he would shower and dress for church himself.

When the children—Jim, Jr., John and Jane—were old enough, they began attending mass, too. Then Jim, Sr. would eat his breakfast and worship alone. Jim, Jr. felt sorry for his father and wanted to accompany him to services, but the Church and his parents forbade it. Jim, Sr. was so scrupulous about his pledge that he allowed the kids to be educated in Catholic schools, where the probable fate of his immortal soul was raised more than once.

The Church exerted a powerful influence on Jim Jr. and during his junior and senior years in high school he began to wonder whether he had a vocation to the religious life. The men who taught at his school were members of the Capuchin branch of the Franciscan order, and he was impressed by their spirituality and the simplicity of their lifestyle. Perhaps he might join them as a brother, he thought, for he considered himself unworthy to become a priest.

For two years Jim was alternately exhilarated and terrified by the prospect of dedicating his life to the Church. Men and women who enter Catholic religious orders take vows of poverty, obedience and chastity, and while the first two didn't strike him as particularly onerous, the last one sounded excruciating. He had a steady girlfriend. He had dreams of raising a family. And yet he kept hearing his nettlesome call.

In ordinary circumstances, Jim would have sought his father's guidance. But he was afraid the choice he was considering would set them against each other, afraid that Jim, Sr. would feel he had lost his son to

Rome. As months went by, however, and he became more certain of his vocation, Jim realized he would have to open up.

His father's reaction surprised him. Jim, Sr. had a brother in the ministry whom he greatly admired, and if his son wanted to follow a similar course, he said that was all right with him.

Jim, Jr. entered the seminary in the summer of 1958 at the age of nineteen. By that time the particulars of his plan had changed. Rather than joining the Capuchins as a brother, he entered the Jesuit novitiate at Wernersville and began the fourteen-year course of studies that would culminate with his ordination as a priest.

Among his only regrets that day was the certainty that he would never be able to minister to his father, the man whose faith had so nourished his own. But four years later, Pope John XXIII convened the Second Vatican Council, and during its four historic sessions the barrier that once separated Catholics from other Christians became suddenly permeable. For the first time, Jim, Sr. was welcome in his family's church. And for the first time, his wife and children could allow themselves to feel welcome in his.

When the Council decreed that the Mass could be celebrated in English, Jim, Sr. joked with his son that after four hundred years, Catholics were finally getting the message. And not only that, they were getting it in a language they could understand.

In the spring of 1984, as he lay dying, Jim, Sr. asked his son to give him the last rites.

Jim thought of his parents' marriage at times when his parish or his Church seemed determined to tear itself apart over less than what had separated the faith of his mother from the faith of his father.

⟨∞⟩

The sentiment against the Vatican's teaching on the role of women in the Church was particularly strong at Holy Trinity, and parishioners were inventive in advancing their dissent. Not long after Jim became pastor, the 11:30 liturgy planning team asked him if he would allow women to assist the priest at the altar at Mass.

Jim's predecessor had turned down a similar request because he didn't feel passionately enough about the issue to risk a run-in with the archdiocese. Father Maier didn't feel passionately about it either, but he couldn't think of a logical reason to say no.

After the Second Vatican Council, many parishes had begun to allow girls to assist at the altar. Most bishops overlooked this minor transgression of Church rubrics (including the bishop of Rome, Pope John Paul II, who lifted the ban on altar girls in 1994). But Catholics had started down a slippery slope. If girls could serve at the altar, why not women?

Jim gave the liturgy planning team his tentative approval and waited to see how the community and the archdiocese would react.

Most of those who attended the 11:30 mass held liberal views on women's issues, but a significant minority liked things done by the book. Among these were the people who had notified Cardinal Hickey when someone at Holy Trinity mixed a little honey into the recipe for Communion bread. In that case the archdiocese had fired off a letter demanding an end to confectionery unorthodoxy, so Jim was not optimistic about the longevity of women altar servers.

But that first Sunday passed without a complaint, and in the weeks ahead the archdiocese was silent. This small victory had given Father Maier a sense that he and the vast majority of his parish were in synch on women's issues, and he resolved to pursue a policy that was prudent but progressive.

In his first five years as pastor, he had instituted a variety of "non-Eucharistic liturgies"—rituals such as vespers and reconciliation services at which lay people, including women, under existing Church rubrics, were allowed to "offer reflections." (Only the ordained can give a homily.) He had also hired women to the pastoral staff, approved the selection of women as leaders of the Parish Council and its various committees, and continued the practice of including women spiritual directors on the parish retreat team.

If there was something more he could have done to advance the status of women in the Church, he did not know what it was. And that meant he had nothing to offer Ray McGovern by way of a compromise, no means of inducing him to sit down before the archdiocese got wind of the protest and used it as an excuse to impose a pastor who would try to crush the spirit that he and four predecessors had nursed for thirty years.

Perhaps, he told himself that morning, the parish would prove his forecast wrong. Perhaps Ray would relent, or the community would ignore him.

But before the afternoon was out his friend Kathy Hartley called to warn him that a few prominent members of the 9:15 congregation were outraged that the mass had been disrupted, and to suggest that he call a meeting for the following Saturday at which Ray, the parish staff and the liturgy planning team could talk matters through.

Lacking a better alternative, Father Maier fell back on his bottomless faith in discernment and agreed.

CHAPTER THREE

The long, narrow enclosure on the second floor of the parish center was jokingly known as the Upper Room, for the site where Jesus appeared to his disciples after the Resurrection. It was a cramped space, cluttered with wobbly, contact-paper-topped tables and uncomfortable chairs with orange upholstery. Black and white photographs of long-dead pastors hung crookedly on the walls beside class pictures from Holy Trinity School circa 1940. At one end of the room a dusty, little-used chalkboard stood in front of discarded stained-glass depictions of the Annunciation and the Nativity, giving the place the feel of a large ecclesial closet.

As he looked around the long, oval assemblage of tables that Saturday morning, Father Maier took a cold moment's comfort in the irony of his situation. The room was rapidly filling up with women.

Across the table, near the windows that looked out over the schoolyard, sat Margaret Costello, who trained CCD teachers and helped run the program that prepared young men and women to receive the sacrament of Confirmation. Beside her stood Anna Thompson, the director of religious education. Arrayed elsewhere around the room were Ellen Crowley, who directed the program that brought converts into the Church; Shannon Jordan, who organized the Sunday morning lecture series; Linda Arnold, a member of the parish's retreat team, and Kathy Hartley, former chair of the Social Concerns Committee. Jim had hired, appointed or promoted every one of them, and now he couldn't help feeling that they had assembled to blame him, as the representative of the Church, for its sins against their gender.

As he scanned the room for potential defenders his eyes fell on Father Ed Dougherty. Ed had come to Holy Trinity following his ordination four years earlier. He was a thin man, perhaps thirty-five years old, with fine auburn hair, a pale Irish complexion and a dark mustache that gave his choirboy features a vaguely rakish gravity.

Of the four priests on the parish staff and the three others in residence at the rectory, Ed was the most committed to elevating the stature of women in the Church. Early in his tenure he had apprenticed himself to Anna Thompson, and she had helped develop his nascent distrust of the "Father Knows Best" decision-making style so prevalent in Catholicism. Together they argued at staff meetings for greater lay involvement in the parish's power structure, bolder action on behalf of women in the Church and a more forceful articulation of the Gospel's teaching on issues of wealth, privilege and social justice.

Father Maier understood that if he came under fire that morning he could not expect support from Ed, even though he was the younger man's religious superior and they shared a real affection for one another.

Perhaps he could count on Paul Quinn, a stalwart of the 9:15 liturgy planning team. Paul, a dark-eyed, heavyset man with courtly manners and an unruly beard, was profoundly disturbed by Ray's protest. Perhaps too disturbed, Jim feared, to speak judiciously.

As Father Maier fretted over the course of the meeting, Ray McGovern reveled in his momentary success. Besides the two Jesuits and several members of the parish staff, the group in the Upper Room included a handful of the most influential lay people in the parish—all gathered to hear his reasons for standing during mass.

The turnout was, in part, a tribute to McGovern's commitment to the church. While teaching CCD he had earned a certificate in theology by attending night school at Georgetown University. He had been active for almost two decades in Cursillo, a lay men's prayer movement, and also served as president of Bread for the City, a charity that provided food and medical care to impoverished residents of the District of Columbia. However bothersome his critics found his protest, they knew he could not easily be dismissed.

Figuring he owed his audience "five minutes of cogent explanation," Ray had prepared a brief statement, and after the opening prayer, he laid it on the table and began to read. Though not a forceful presence, McGovern projects a tortured decency and he speaks with great sincerity, no matter how casual the conversation. He told the group gathered that morning that the issue of women's equality had been much on his mind in recent months, and that he yearned to hear Church leaders remind the nation that every human being was created in the image of God. But the new draft of the pastoral letter had confirmed his fears that John Paul II would never recognize and repent the Church's historic repression of Catholic women.

He spoke of his daughter's growing alienation from the Church and the Vatican's meddling in the pastoral letter. He quoted St. John Chrysostom, who taught that Christians must not be complicit in evil. Acceptance was a form of complicity, he said, and standing at the liturgy was his way of renouncing what he saw as an evil in the Church.

There was a respectful silence when Ray finished, and then a slow outpouring of personal testimony from the women around the tables. It was as though McGovern had punctured a balloon filled with frustration, and the anger and resentment were whistling out into the room. One by one most of the women present spoke of the contempt they encountered in theology schools, the mistrust and condescension manifest in their dealings with the archdiocese, and the intellectual poverty and pastoral callousness of the Vatican's teachings on women. When it was Margaret Costello's turn to speak, she simply burst into tears.

A warm and reflexively empathic woman, with a round face, dark eyes and short, honey-colored hair, Margaret had friends among the most progressive people in the parish as well as among the most traditional. Her experience at Holy Trinity had begun ten years earlier when she was elected to the parent board that oversaw the CCD program. One of the board's tasks was sorting through textbooks and curriculum guides to choose the ones most appropriate for Holy Trinity's children. As she pored over these materials, Margaret was struck by the great variety of approaches and emphases. She wanted to know more about the theological principles that informed these approaches, and so began her transformation, from a "Martha" to a "Mary."

Martha and Mary, the sisters of Lazarus, are central figures in a Gospel story with particular resonance for Catholic women. When Jesus and his disciples visited their home, Martha spent her time alone in the kitchen preparing a meal for her guests, while Mary sat at the master's feet taking instruction. Martha asked Jesus to command her sister to help her, but Jesus replied that Mary had "chosen the better portion" and would not be denied.

For centuries Catholic women were denied the "better portion." Theological education, even among nuns, was minimal at best. But in the wake of the Second Vatican Council, many Church ministries were opened to the unordained, and Catholic women poured into graduate programs in theology, spirituality and religious education. By the early 1990s there were more lay people in graduate theology programs in this country than there were young men studying for the priesthood, and most of those lay students were women.

During this period, the number of active American priests dropped precipitously, from almost sixty thousand in 1968 to barely fifty thousand in 1992. At the same time, the American Catholic population surged from roughly forty-eight million to more than 55 million, and the priest shortage was born.

By 1992, nearly ten percent of the roughly 19,300 parishes in the United States were without resident pastors. Many of these "priestless" communities were led by nuns who acted as administrators and presided at non-Eucharistic liturgies. The sacramental functions these women could not perform were executed by circuit-riding priests.

Sometimes, however, these priests could not be present, and that raised a troubling question: if the Mass were the central expression of the Catholic faith and there were too few priests to celebrate it, then why not expand the pool of potential candidates? Why not drop the discipline of *mandatory* celibacy? Why not open the priesthood to the women who were already doing much of the work? Or was enforcing these contested teachings more important than making the Lord's Supper available to all his people?

Pope John Paul II had done everything in his considerable power to preserve the clerical status quo. In public statements he drew a sharp distinction between those who "ministered" in the Church, meaning the ordained, and those who did "apostolic work," meaning nuns and lay people. He asserted that women, though equal to men in the eyes of God, were, by nature, a different kind of being, and entitled to different treatment. The Church's decision to ban them from the ordained ministry and to emphasize the virtues of their traditional roles as mothers and helpmates was not, therefore, a manifestation of patriarchal arrogance but of love and reverence, an affirmation of the intended place of women in God's creation and in his Church.

This argument failed to persuade most American theologians, who didn't believe that these "natural" differences, assuming they existed, justified excluding women from the priesthood and the hierarchy. Nor did it impress the majority of American Catholics, many of whom extended the logic of the civil rights movement to the question of women's role in the Church.

Realizing that rhetoric alone would not halt the progress of the women's movement within the Church, a group of American bishops, led by James Hickey of Washington, had founded the Consortium Perfectae Caritatis, as a counterweight to the Leadership Conference of Women Religious, a progressive organization which, among its other duties, lobbied for an increase in the ecclesial stature of nuns.

By the spring of 1992 a rumor current in clerical circles suggested that John Paul was so troubled by the gathering momentum of the women's ordination movement that he was preparing an encyclical forbidding further discussion of the issue, and that he might declare his position infallible, thereby making it almost impossible for a future pontiff to reverse. While this news was comforting to traditionalists who believed that what Catholics refer to as the "deposit of faith" was being contaminated by Western feminism, it offered little hope to faithful Catholics who, because of the priest shortage, could not participate fully in the life of the Church.

With seven Jesuits living in the rectory and a small battalion living in a large residence hall on the Georgetown University campus just one block away, Holy Trinity had no shortage of priests. But Jim Maier believed that "inviting women into ministry" was a matter of simple justice, and his policies had created opportunities for women like Margaret Costello.

Margaret took her first steps into more Mary-like work by becoming a catechist, or teacher, in the CCD program after her term on the parent board ended in 1986. As part of her duties, she attended the East Coast Conference on Religious Education in Washington, where religious educators gathered for lectures, workshops, conversation and prayer. For three years she studiously avoided the information booth of the Washington Theological Union, a Catholic graduate school where laity, priests, nuns and seminarians took classes together.

"I knew if I made any move toward ministry in this Church I would be buying into a whole hell of a lot of pain," she once said. "And I didn't want to be another middle-aged woman growing old and bitter in this Church."

But in 1989, the youngest of her three children had just entered the first grade, and for the first time in 15 years, Margaret had time on her hands. After an eight-day silent retreat at the Jesuit spirituality center in Wernersville, she came home knowing she wanted to study theology.

It was not an entirely welcome realization. Though she had a master's degree in counseling, she worried about the rigors of returning to graduate school. Would her studies consume time better spent with her children? And how would her husband regard this deepening commitment to a faith he did not fully share? Tom was a Presbyterian, but one of several dozen Protestants who worshiped at Holy Trinity. "If I had wanted to marry a minister," he told Margaret at one point, "I would have married a minister."

But once her academic work began, Margaret felt the faith of her childhood unfolding in all its richness. She began her studies with the intention of earning a thirty-six-credit master's in theology, but soon decided on a one-hundred-credit master of divinity—the same degree traditionally taken by candidates for the priesthood.

She felt particularly drawn to the study of the liturgy and its elegant encapsulation of the Christian mystery. But she believed that the wonders of the Mass were insufficiently explored. The Gospels, she knew, held meaning for women, for parents and for working people that celibate men with no financial worries could neither fully understand nor adequately convey. Her hope was to share these insights with the people of her parish, and to help them share their insights with one another.

Though she aspired to become a professional liturgist, Margaret made it clear that morning that working in the Church was a constant source of strain for most women because the Vatican taught that they were not "fit matter" for the priesthood. This meant that no woman, regardless of how profoundly she understood and how brilliantly she elucidated the mysteries of the liturgy, would ever be granted the privilege of consecrating the bread and wine that Catholics believe becomes the body and blood of Christ. And whether a woman yearned for ordination or not, Margaret said, she could not help but be wounded by this exclusion.

One morning she was working at home on an assignment for her class in theological reflection. Her task was to write a meditation on one of the Eucharistic prayers the priest recites at Mass. In her bedroom she had a chalice that a friend who believed Margaret had a calling to the priesthood had given her as a gift, and it occurred to Margaret that her reflection might be more fruitful if she held it as she prayed.

After retrieving the chalice she sat at a table in her living room and began to speak the words. Soon she found tears rolling down her face. Whether they were tears of joy or sorrow, she could not say.

When she understood the significance of Ray's actions the previous Sunday, Margaret had had two almost simultaneous reactions: "Oh damn!" and "Thank God!" She recognized that his protest might spawn a movement and that supporting such a movement might jeopardize her position as a part-time staff member. But she was so grateful for what McGovern was doing that she had all but determined to take that risk. She assumed that most of the other women in the room would take it with her.

In this she was mistaken. Not everyone was thankful for the protest. Among the most eloquent of Ray's opponents was Ellen Crowley, a blond, blue-eyed woman in her early fifties whose personality was equal parts steel and sensitivity. Ellen's road into church work had been similar to Margaret's, and her theological credentials were much the same. But she was less conflicted than many of her female colleagues about her position in a male-dominated church.

In part, this was because she had fulfilled her ministerial ambitions. Ellen directed the Rite of Christian Initiation of Adults (RCIA), a nine-month program of instruction and reflection that brings non-Catholics into the Church. She was also a member of the parish's retreat team and gave individual spiritual direction. None of these roles would have been open to her thirty years earlier, but by 1992 her ministry was in no way controversial.

In the wake of the Second Vatican Council the Church had opened itself to women with Ellen's gifts, removing the barriers that still stymied women who wanted to preach at mass, administer the sacraments and shape the teachings of the Church. Where Margaret met intransigence, Ellen had encountered flexibility, and it gave her hope that the Vatican would one day recognize its error and accept women into the priesthood. In the meantime, however, there was rewarding work for women like herself in the household of the faith.

Ellen's moderation was deepened by fear. For more than twenty years, Holy Trinity had been the center of her family's life. Her husband, Jack, was a past president of the Parish Council. Her two children had been educated in the CCD program. She saw in Ray's protest the beginnings of a movement that might splinter the congregation, and she desperately wanted him stopped.

None of her anxiety was evident that morning, however, as she expressed her theological conviction that the liturgy should never be politicized. It had to remain the forum in which Catholics transcended their differences, she said. Or else the promise of being one in Christ was lost.

Ray would later counter that such unity could never be attained until the Church accepted women as full partners in its communion. But at that first meeting there were no arguments, just quietly passionate though vaguely conflicting statements of conscience and concern.

As the morning drew to a close, Father Maier promised that he would continue to do whatever he could to increase the visibility and influence of women in the parish. But as he watched his parishioners filing out of the Upper Room, he was uncertain where things stood. Having registered his protest, would Ray be content to sit down? Or would others join him? If so, how many? And what was he as the pastor of Holy Trinity supposed to do to satisfy them?

In the months ahead, Jim would be forced to contemplate that last question at length.

CHAPTER FOUR

❦

The following morning, worshipers at the 9:15 mass once again found Ray McGovern upright in their midst. Standing elsewhere around the church were Margaret Costello, Anna Thompson, Kathy Hartley and four others. They accounted for barely one percent of the congregation, but their presence, and their prominence within the parish, utterly altered the nature of the mass.

On that Sunday, amid the liturgical rejoicing of Eastertide, parishioners at Holy Trinity sensed that they might be witnessing the birth of a movement. The Standing, as it came to be known, graduated from a curiosity to a crisis, and many felt compelled to choose sides.

Brian Depenbrock watched the protest unfold from the risers at the front of the church, where he and the rest of the choir stood. Though he had eyed McGovern suspiciously the week before, he and his teenage daughter Keara were elated when they learned what Ray was doing, and eager to embrace his cause. Like McGovern they believed that the Church's teaching on women's ordination was sinful and had to be changed. Unlike Ray, they had seen the anguish it created firsthand.

One year earlier Brian's wife, Martha Manning, had left the Catholic Church and become an Episcopalian to explore a future in the priesthood. After several months, Martha had decided against entering the seminary, but she remained an Episcopalian. At roughly the same time, Keara was preparing to receive Confirmation—the sacrament in which young Catholics recommit themselves to their faith.

Her daughter's deepening engagement with the Church filled Martha with ambivalence and inspired her to write a column that was later published in *U.S. Catholic* magazine. The question she asked herself was the one that priests pose to parents at the beginning of the Rite of Baptism: "What do you ask of the Church?"

Once, Martha wrote, she had asked for the opportunity to follow God's call wherever it led her. But when the Vatican denied that request, she left the Church and, for a time, she asked nothing. But Keara's impending Confirmation changed all that.

"Now in my daughter's name, I ask plenty," she wrote. "I ask that you continue to provide her with an unerring commitment to the gospels and to show her the great variety of ways in which Christ comes alive in this world each day.

"I ask you to continue to provide her with the great reassurance of ritual, the constancy of community and the paths to a prayerful life.

"But I ask something else. I ask you to change. I ask you to take the opportunity to really see this woman-child in her gifts as well as her needs. I ask you to cherish her unbridled passion for ideas and to tolerate her tenacity in following questions to satisfying conclusions. I ask that you savor her energy for change in herself; her family; her community and, yes, even in her church. I ask you to stop holding women at arm's length and open your arms to my child. Embrace her as fully as she embraces you."

But after having their liturgy disrupted for the second successive Sunday, many people in the 9:15 community were in no mood to embrace anyone. Paul Quinn, perhaps the most prominent member of the community, was also among the most upset. He was a former seminarian who now owned an antique shop, and he had once directed the CCD program. Paul and his wife, Cathy, a nurse practioner, had served on innumerable parish committees and organized countless social events, but they were proudest of their involvement in the family mass, the 9:15 service, which they had helped nurse from its infancy into one of the most popular liturgies in the archdiocese.

To the Quinns and their many friends, the primary spiritual function of a parish was to foster community among its members, to help them find Christ in one another. They viewed Ray McGovern as a vandal and women's ordination as a secondary issue.

"I think it is wrong. I think it is sacrilegious. It might even be blasphemous," Paul told people. "Jim Maier needs to be ready to call the police. He needs to tell Ray that he is not welcome, and that if he continues he will be arrested and removed."

But Jim was uncertain how to proceed and took no immediate action, so the protest's opponents employed private channels to make their displeasure felt.

Margaret Costello was the first to feel their ire. After standing for two Sundays, she received a phone call from one of her best friends, Pam Hall, who sang in the 9:15 choir. The two women had been friends for more than a decade, and their families were planning a cruise together that summer. But in recent months, as Margaret's ministerial ambitions had deepened, her relationship with Pam had become strained.

Pam neither understood her friend's desire to become an ecclesial pioneer nor saw the need for such pioneering at Holy Trinity. She and her husband, Mike, a former Navy pilot who served on the Parish Council and the 9:15 liturgy team, had discovered the parish after a long and dispiriting search through the neighboring diocese of Arlington, and they saw no reason to disturb its status quo.

Margaret had not discussed the Standing with Pam, and she could sense immediately, from the anger in her friend's voice, that this had been a mistake. They had barely greeted one another when Pam demanded to know what Margaret thought she was doing. How could she jeopardize the future of the parish just to make a political point?

"*You* are ruining everything *we* worked for," Pam said, articulating each word with bristling precision and leaving little doubt that the second pronoun no longer included the first.

Parishioners were more diplomatic in expressing their displeasure to Father Maier, but he too understood that the 9:15 community was roiling, and he sat in the rectory after the third Sunday of protest contemplating his unsatisfying options.

He was not about to have Ray McGovern and the others carried from the church. That might provide a few people with a moment of vengeful pleasure, but what happened if others rose to protest the presence of the police in their assembly? Should he empty the building to prove his authority?

Besides, he wasn't sure that removing McGovern was entirely legal. The Standing might constitute a breach of sacramental etiquette, but it was hardly a breach of the peace.

Members of the 9:15 liturgy team wanted him to denounce the standers from the pulpit, but he thought that would only alienate those who supported women's ordination but were ambivalent about the protest. Ray's allies, on the other hand, wanted Jim to authorize a liturgical lamentation of sexism in the Church. Jim did not know whether to laugh or wince when he imagined how news of such a service would be received by the archdiocese.

It occurred to him that he might have had an easier time dealing with the Standing had he not agreed with its aims. In his seven years as a novice master he had become confident of his ability to discern priestly vocations, and he knew several women at Holy Trinity whom he believed had one.

"If it walks like a duck and talks like a duck it's probably a duck," he liked to say. But Rome did not believe in the existence of female ducks. And the future of Holy Trinity might depend on him persuading parishioners to suppress their dissent.

Jim did not want to be remembered as the pastor who lost Holy Trinity, but neither did he relish asking people to be silent about their convictions. Perhaps the Standing would simply run out of energy. This was not entirely wishful thinking, he told himself, because two of the protestors had already decided to sit down.

The most prominent of these was Anna Thompson, the director of religious education. Anna was a fiercely idealistic woman whose prematurely white hair flared like flame from her freckled face. She was, perhaps the most liberal member of the Trinity staff, and the gulf between what her parish was and what she wished it to be drove her to overwork and frustration.

Yet Anna had been ambivalent about the Standing from the start. On the first Sunday, while most of the protestors stood in the midst of the assembly, she had remained in the back of the church and might easily have been mistaken for someone who had arrived too late to find a seat.

One year earlier, she had been at the center of another parish controversy, this one over the way the Church's sexual teachings were presented in the CCD program. Through months of contentious discussions, she had defended her methods and her vision of what religious education should be against a vigorous attack by a small band of conservative parishioners. Now she was weary of feeling as though she were on trial, and after two weeks of protest had decided to sit down.

Margaret Costello, who had received a second angry phone call from another close friend, had also decided to abandon the protest because she believed the Standing might irrevocably sunder the 9:15 community. But even without these two widely respected parishioners, Ray McGovern's movement was growing. By the fifth Sunday after Easter, the standers numbered 10.

Father Maier had written to several of the protestors telling them that their behavior was inappropriate at the Eucharist, and requested that they sit down. But these letters had thus far gone unheeded. Jim heard through the clerical grapevine that Cardinal Hickey was monitoring the situation at Holy Trinity and expected him to make short work of it. But the cardinal seemed unaware that the laity was no longer as compliant as it had once been.

ᏩᎻᏩ

For most of its history, the Catholic Church in the United States was a church of immigrants—displaced peasants who made their living as miners, housekeepers and industrial workers and depended on the Church to ease their assimilation into American life. But with the passage of the G.I. bill in 1944, American Catholics began an educational and economic ascent which continues today. By the early 1990s they had attained levels of income and education higher than any Christian denomination in this country save Episcopalians.

With the election of a Catholic president, they had also overwhelmed their political opponents who still believed that the Vatican was bent on world dominion. This was a special joy to the people of Holy Trinity, for John F. Kennedy had worshiped at their parish during his years in the U.S. Senate, and attended mass there on the morning of his inauguration.

But worldly achievement had altered American Catholics' relationship with their Church and made them restive under its restrictive discipline, suspicious of its more pietistic practices and skeptical about the authority of the clergy. In many cases, Father's theological sophistication, psychological acumen and managerial abilities now seemed inferior to their own.

The men and women of this new generation found themselves in a paradoxical position. Aggressive and analytical on the job, they were to be docile and unquestioning in their faith. Trained to perform and to demand performance, they were to support a Church that offered them neither influence nor accountability. Skilled at solving problems and devising alternatives, they were told that there was only one route to heaven and that certain insuperable obstacles, such as an unsanctioned marriage, could block the path.

The election of John Kennedy may have settled whether Protestants would accept Catholics as loyal Americans, but now the Vatican had reason to wonder whether Americans could remain loyal Catholics.

The United States is the only country with a heresy named after it. "Americanism" is a vaguely defined transgression promulgated in the late nineteenth century to correct the excesses of bishops like John Ireland of Minneapolis–St. Paul who were supposedly too earthly in their pastoral concerns and too lenient in enforcing doctrine and liturgical standards. But the Church's historical antipathy toward this country is rooted more deeply.

The founding documents of the United States are fruits of the Enlightenment, which ranks just behind Communism as an intellectual calamity in the eyes of the Church. The American Revolution helped trigger the French Revolution, which resulted in the sack and seizure of Church property, the prosecution of the clergy and the virtual disestablishment of the Church in France. The success of democracy in this country fueled similar movements throughout Europe, precipitating the fall of the Vatican's monarchical allies, the unification of Italy and the demise, in 1861, of the Papal States.

The Church and democracy had fought a war for temporal power, the Church had lost, and the antagonism lingered. Until 1965, despite having been rescued from fascism by the Allied democracies, the Church still taught that the ideal human society required a Catholic government and a Catholic head of state.

Lay Catholics in Western Europe and North America disagreed. They had given husbands, brothers and sons to the proposition that democracy was the great guarantor of human liberty, only to be plunged into a terrifying cold war against another brand of dictatorship. It was difficult for them to feel that the democracy so many died for was anything short of sacred, and natural to wonder that if God willed democracy for the world, might God not also will it for the Church?

Or, more bluntly, if the concentration of power in the hands of a small secretive coterie was evil in Germany and evil in the Soviet Union, was it not also potentially evil in Rome?

Pope John XXIII was asking himself a similar question. In 1962 he convened the historic Second Vatican Council and altered, perhaps forever, the course of Catholicism.

Even a few years earlier, the prospect of radical change in the Roman Catholic Church was virtually unimaginable. Since the Council of Trent, which ended in 1563, the Church had defined itself in reaction to the modern world. In response to the intellectual challenge of the Enlightenment and the theological challenge of the Reformation, the Tridentine fathers taught that the Church was an institution that existed outside of history, a divinely ordered society in full possession of as much truth as the human mind could comprehend. Change in its structure or its teaching was not only undesirable, it was evil.

Unfortunately the Church codified this essentially medieval worldview at the dawn of the modern age. The scientific revolution was already chipping away at the Vatican's claim of a complete understanding of the universe. The development of mercantilism was empowering a new class to challenge the Church's monarchical allies for political primacy, and the rise of democratic nationalism would soon loosen its hold on the moral imagination of ordinary men and women.

The Church battened its doors against each of these storms, and trundled through four centuries crying "No!" at most of what came along. There was no room in the Catholic mind for the discoveries of Darwin or the insights of Freud. At the dawn of the space age the Vatican had yet to rehabilitate Galileo. So certain was the Church of its right to command assent that in the wake of the Holocaust, it still held that there was no right to religious freedom.

This view of the Church as a divinely ordered hierarchy came under renewed scrutiny beginning in the middle of the nineteenth century. A new generation of Scripture scholars found no clear evidence that Jesus imparted an institutional framework to his disciples, and church historians demonstrated that early apostolic communities bore little resemblance to their modern counterpart.

Theological difficulties were emerging as well. To say that the Church was the sole conduit of divine revelation was to dictate terms to the Almighty. To say it was perfectly ordered was to make an idol of the institution. To suggest its leaders enjoyed special access to God ignored that in its two-thousand-year history the Church had occasionally been led by murderers, pederasts, adulterers and thieves.

Despite these flaws, the vision of the Church as a perfect institution, a bulwark against relativism and a refuge from worldly evil was enormously popular among the laity. The formidable challenge for progressive bishops and theologians who dominated the Second Vatican Council was to formulate a compelling alternative. This they accomplished through the sheer power of pent-up creativity.

During the four years of the Council, a four-hundred-year-old dam broke and a flood tide of intellectual, political and cultural change poured forth. Church historians began to explain how the faith had been co-opted and corrupted during the fifteen hundred years in which the Church struggled for temporal power, how the sacraments had developed over time rather than springing fully formed from the pages of Scripture, and how ecclesial power had shifted from local bishops and congregations to the autocratic curia in Rome.

Moral theologians outlined an ethic based less on observing prohibitions than on doing good, and less on leading a blameless life than on leading a redemptive one. Ecumenists focused Catholic attention on what the Church shared with other Christian denominations and catalyzed a rapprochement. And, in political theology, John Courtney Murray, a Jesuit theologian who had taught many of the priests in the Maryland province, persuaded the Council to recognize the right to religious freedom.

Perhaps most significantly, in the Constitution on the Church in the Modern World (Gaudium et Spes), the Council fathers affirmed a "universal call to holiness." There was no pyramid of sanctity with the pope on the top, the clergy in the middle and the laity on the bottom.

The Church had redefined itself as "the people of God," and all God's people were on pilgrimage.

Above all these particulars hovered one central fact: the Church had changed. Theologians whose work had once been banned were now celebrated. Disciplines which the Church said it would never relax had disappeared. And if the Church had changed once, then it could change again.

As the council ended in December 1965, many progressive American Catholics looked forward to the day when priests could marry and women could be ordained, when artificial birth control would no longer be banned, when remarriage within the Church would not be left to the whim of a clerical tribunal, when the laity would exercise greater governing power and when the Church would make full disclosure of its financial affairs.

But sober analysts of the Council's accomplishments understood the dangers that lay ahead. The bishops had showered Catholics with new and liberating insights about themselves, their Church and their God, but they had also retained a hierarchical structure which vested absolute power in the pope. Such an arrangement could only work if the pontiff and his people remained in absolute accord.

As it was, the accord lasted less than three years. On July 29, 1968, Pope Paul VI released *Humanae Vitae*, reiterating the Church ban on artificial birth control and throwing the Church into a confusion from which it has yet to recover.

At Holy Trinity, Father Tom Gavigan, who was then pastor, disputed the encyclical publicly and was deprived of his right to hear confessions. But most of the parish rallied around its dissident priest. To many minds, it was Father Gavigan's courage that established Holy Trinity as a place where Catholics could remain in the Church even as they rejected some of its less persuasive teachings.

Ray McGovern and the other protestors at the 9:15 liturgy were laying claim to this legacy of principled dissent. And in the process they were forcing Jim Maier to examine his deepest loyalties. For aside from his father, no one had done more to shape Jim's vocation than Tom Gavigan.

CHAPTER FIVE

In the rainy spring that Ray McGovern began his protest, Father Tom Gavigan was ensconced in the infirmary on the third floor of the Jesuit residence at Georgetown University, just a few blocks from the church. Though he had been in failing health since a stroke in December of 1988, the priest whom some parishioners referred to as "the second founder of Holy Trinity" still received a steady trickle of visitors, one of whom was Jim Maier.

Tom had been Jim's novice master, the man who had introduced him to Jesuit life, and the two had had almost identical careers. Both began their ministries at Loyola College in Baltimore, became master of novices at Wernersville and left for the pastorate at Holy Trinity, where they tangled with the archdiocese on behalf of their flocks.

On some days Jim found his old mentor in a dense mental fog, like a lost ship slipping in and out of radio contact. But on others Tom was his barbed but solicitous self, a playfully crotchety man who never stopped asking his visitors what he could do for them. On those days,

Tom liked to sit in a bedside chair with a blanket over his knees and his chin sunk deep into the collar of a flannel shirt and gossip about the church he had transformed thirty years earlier.

When Father Gavigan arrived in Georgetown in the fall of 1964, Holy Trinity was a spiritually lethargic community, and he had set out to revive it by breathing life into its moribund liturgy. Disappointed by the sluggishness of his own staff, he invited two of the brightest young theologians in Washington—Regis Duffy, a Franciscan, and William McFadden, a Jesuit—to preach at the 11:30 mass. Next he recruited an insurance-agent-cum-organist named Dick Lucht, and a singer-turned-educator named Mary Barnds, to teach the parish how to sing. Then he persuaded Jim English, one of his former novices and a man of great theatrical flair, to turn the soporific children's mass into a family celebration.

By 1969 the parish was renowned for its vibrant liturgies, lusty singing and excellent preaching. That spring, Father Joseph Champlin of the U. S. Bishops' Committee on the Liturgy chronicled Tom's success in *Our Sunday Visitor,* a weekly bulletin supplement with a national audience. "People came to pray, sing, worship that day at Trinity, not out of obligation, but as a free choice," he wrote. The mass was "a small miracle," and a model of what the new liturgy could be.

In five short years a new parish had been born at Holy Trinity. It drew worshipers from northern Virginia, suburban Maryland and all over northern D.C. If the Second Vatican Council had approved an innovation, Holy Trinity gave it a try. There were communal penance services, a rapidly expanding CCD program and a popularly elected parish council that included Senator Edward M. Kennedy, who attended the 9:15 mass; he had finished second in the balloting behind the funeral director Don DeVol.

Tom was an ardent supporter of the budding ecumenical movement and once, during the Octave of Christian Unity, he gave Communion to Angus Dun, the retired Episcopal bishop of Washington. "It was almost the eighth deadly sin," one of his assistants remembers. "And I think they both wept."

In this long season of Christian renewal, Pope Paul VI released *Humanae Vitae.*

The Second Vatican Council had seemingly cleared the way for a change in the Church's teaching on birth control by recognizing that

God intended sexual intercourse not simply for procreation, but for the "mutual consolation" of the spouses. In his encyclical, however, Paul decreed that the "unitive" and "procreative" aspects of intercourse could not be separated. And because artificial contraception caused such a separation, it was inherently sinful.

The Church's ban on birth control stood.

Many Catholics viewed *Humanae Vitae* as a betrayal of the collegial spirit of the Council, for the pope had overruled his own advisory panel. Others simply saw it as evidence that the Church, despite changes, was still primarily interested in preventing people from having sex.

The pope had not helped matters by adopting a position which only a minority of theologians found plausible. If God intended every act of intercourse to be open to procreation, Paul's critics asked, then why were women not always fertile? And if it was moral to conspire against conception by gauging the rhythm of a woman's cycle, then why was it sinful to improve the odds by wearing a condom?

In Washington, a rift over the encyclical opened between Cardinal Patrick O'Boyle, who was then archbishop, and some of his most respected priests. Tom Gavigan was among them.

Tom believed that the encyclical was poorly reasoned, but his objections were more pastoral than they were doctrinal. He understood that the same people who had been energized by Vatican II would be outraged by *Humanae Vitae*, and that they would oppose the teaching of the pope with the same ardor that they supported the reforms of the Council. His fear was that this would trap the Church in a self-defeating dynamic, and that the hierarchy would come to equate vitality with dissent and lethargy with loyalty.

After Tom and forty other dissenters published an open letter in *The Washington Post*, the cardinal called each of the renegade priests to a private meeting and pressured them to recant. The great majority refused and were disciplined. Some were removed from teaching positions. Others were deprived of the right to preach. Most—including Tom— were forbidden to hear confessions.

After the sanctions were announced, O'Boyle sent a letter to every parish in the archdiocese excoriating the dissidents. A cover letter instructed pastors around the archdiocese that the missive was to be read at every mass with neither introduction nor comment. But at Holy Trinity, a young Jesuit named Larry Madden attempted to set the dispute into context.

"I simply reiterated the classic teaching that if a teaching is not designated as dogma, and if a significant number of moral theologians hold a contrary opinion, the Catholic is not conscience-bound to follow the teaching of the magisterium," he said.

It was perhaps the only instance in which an explanation of the teaching known as "probabilism" was greeted by sustained applause.

Though most of his parishioners cheered Tom's stand, few understood the turmoil he was in. "He was right between two worlds," says Father Jim English. "There was the world he had always lived in, and to which he had given his life, and this new world which may or may not have been the future.

"Nowadays you look back and say, 'What a great thing to do! How obvious! How clear!' But it wasn't. And it wasn't inside him. I think there was a great conflict as to whether he could be doing this, should be doing this. Whether he was breaking obedience, what he was doing."

Father Gavigan's pastorate ended late the following summer, and the Jesuits rewarded him with a sabbatical at Yale. His powers to hear confession were restored in his absence, and he returned to Holy Trinity as an associate pastor, to devote himself to the sick and the shut-in.

In 1982 Tom celebrated his fiftieth anniversary as a Jesuit, and the parish threw him a party. The crowd filled the gymnasium at Georgetown Visitation, the Catholic girls' school three blocks from the church. All night people came up to him, thanking him for his ministry, telling him how he'd kept them in the Church, and quoting to him from homilies he had given at the 8:00 A.M. mass decades earlier.

"You don't know how bowled over I was," he told his friend Melanne Verveer. "I had no idea I had that kind of impact."

But as he listened to his mentor reminisce, Jim Maier found Tom's impact easy to comprehend. At a time when American Catholics were just beginning to develop a new appreciation of their faith, Father Gavigan had given them permission to ask questions and permission to disagree. He helped them differentiate between what was central to their faith—such as the propositions in the Nicene Creed—and what was not. He persuaded them that sometimes the people were right and the hierarchy was wrong, and he had been willing to suffer for that tiny piece of truth.

Jim also held to tiny pieces of dissident truth, and sometimes, walking home across the Georgetown campus, he asked himself why he was not willing to face censure the way Tom had been. Times had changed.

The Church had become more conservative; that was part of it. But why did he always seek the conciliatory path?

Jim had just begun his studies in philosophy at Spring Hill College in Alabama when the first session of the Second Vatican Council convened in 1962. At first the momentous events unfolding in Rome seemed barely relevant. By 1965, final examinations were no longer conducted exclusively in Latin; he and his classmates could call each other something other than "Brother." By 1966, they were allowed to grow beards. All of this was fine with Jim, though it hardly seemed of major import.

But when the Council ended, the upheavals began, and they hit the Maryland province particularly hard. In the early summer of 1968 Father Edward Sponga, the provincial, or superior, of the province suddenly disappeared. Several weeks later he resurfaced on the front page of *The New York Times* in an article explaining that he had married.

That same year Daniel Berrigan, a Jesuit of the New York province, his younger brother Phillip, then a Josephite priest, and seven other antiwar protestors walked into the Selective Service office in Catonsville, Maryland, and set fire to files containing the names of young men about to be drafted. The older Berrigan lived at a Jesuit parish in Baltimore during his trial and the church became a meeting place for antiwar activists and a staging ground for further protests.

Jim Maier kept his balance throughout this tumultuous era, devoting himself to completing a doctorate in biology at Georgetown University in 1969, and finishing his theological studies at Woodstock College in New York in 1972. Though he went with other seminarians to stand in the rain outside the federal penitentiary in Danbury, Connecticut on the day that Dan Berrigan was released, and served on a seminary council that condemned the Nixon administration for widening the Vietnam War into Laos, he was never seized by the desire to emulate the Berrigans, nor to preach fiery homilies that would send people into the streets to protest injustice.

In his eyes, the New Left was repeating the mistake of the Old Right, for it valued its own orthodoxies more than service to the people of God.

"If you see religion as a series of truths and practicing your religion as defending certain truths, then you put your energy in that," he said. "My emphasis is on the person. I think you can have it all right in your head and be all wrong in person."

Yet as he left New York in 1973 to become ordained and assume a teaching position at Loyola College in Baltimore, it was clear to him that his religious ideology had changed. He was still a man who sought the middle, but the middle had moved left, and he had moved with it.

This was particularly true in his thinking about the nature of authority within the Church. The Council had taught that the Holy Spirit was active in the lives of all Catholics, not simply the hierarchy. Yet lay people had almost no way of making themselves heard in Rome. This was troubling, for it not only bred alienation but kept Church leaders ignorant of how God was at work among the faithful.

Jim arrived at Holy Trinity determined to make the laity full partners in governing their church, but he knew now that he had underestimated how ethically and emotionally challenging this would be. In many instances his convictions were closer to those of his dissenting parishioners than to the hierarchy he was supposed to represent, and that had forced him to devise his own answer to the question that had bedeviled Tom Gavigan twenty-five years earlier: To what did he owe his loyalty—conscience or Church?

Had he been a lay person, the choice would have been easy: conscience. But he was a pastor, a creature of the institution, and if he could not fully support the hierarchy then at least he could avoid making trouble. In addition, he realized that if he were to publicly challenge Church teaching, the archdiocese would remove him, and that would destroy the parish, which was Tom's greatest legacy.

Still, Jim found it impossible to remain entirely silent about his own convictions.

A few Sundays earlier a woman had approached him after mass and told him she was no longer certain she could remain in the parish. She had heard Jim and two other Jesuits make remarks which she believed indicated their support for homosexual relationships, and she wanted to disassociate herself from what she considered a sinful point of view.

In his own case, Jim knew, the woman had listened well. He believed that an individual's sexual orientation, like the rest of his or her nature, was a gift from God, and that homosexual activity was not wrong in and of itself. In his eyes, a monogamous homosexual relationship was as moral as a monogamous heterosexual relationship. Promiscuity of either kind was equally sinful.

"Fidelity," he liked to say, "is of God."

Though his position was not without support among Christian theologians, Jim had been careful never to explicitly challenge the teaching of the Church. In 1986, Cardinal Joseph Ratzinger, prefect of the Congregation for the Doctrine of the Faith and the pope's most trusted theological advisor, had released a letter entitled "On the Pastoral Care of Homosexual Persons," in which he asserted that a homosexual orientation could not be regarded as "good" or even "neutral." Rather, the cardinal wrote, it was a "tendency ordered toward an intrinsic moral evil" which had to be regarded as "an objective disorder." Jim had never said otherwise, but parishioners who extrapolated from his carefully modulated homilies were probably aware that he held a differing view.

The woman's complaint, however, had caused him to reconsider whether he could even hint at that view from the pulpit.

"Part of me says she is right," he said. "I have no right to be saying anything that goes against Church teaching. On the other hand, I think of Tom Gavigan, who I really see as a hero. He said, 'The Church's teaching in the area of contraception is wrong and I can't go along with it. Period.' "

But as much as he revered Father Gavigan, Jim tended not to punctuate his own sentences quite so definitely.

CHAPTER SIX

One late-spring evening, a group of parishioners gathered in the squat two-room edifice that sits atop Holy Trinity's ancient oil-burning furnace. The Horace B. McKenna Center had been named for a local Jesuit who had devoted his life to the poor, and the building manifested the homey simplicity of the man himself. A few brightly colored stuffed birds from Holy Trinity's Salvadoran "sister parish" hung from the ceiling. The remnant of the previous Sunday's canned food collection sat in a corner near the door.

A few months earlier, Margaret Costello and Kathy Hartley had convened a retreat for women who worked in parish ministries, and at the end of the evening participants had parted, promising to meet again. When the Standing began, several felt that reconvening was urgent. In early May, Margaret and Kathy had organized another gathering, and what became known as the Working Groups on Sexism were born.

The initial purpose of the groups was to provide a friendly forum for discussing sexism and the Standing. But their meetings were open and no one arrived without an agenda. To Ray McGovern and his allies the gatherings offered an opportunity to recruit new protestors; to the Quinns and the Halls, a chance to argue at close range with the people convulsing their community; and to Margaret Costello, the hope of bridging the chasm between her fractious friends.

That night, a stocky, glad-handing former Marine named Ron Farrell had come to the McKenna Center to tell the groups how painful he found their protest.

Ron and his wife, Carole, were minor celebrities in the 9:15 community. For twenty years they had baked a small loaf of bread for each child in the parish as a First Communion gift. Though Holy Trinity had long ago become a commuter's church, the Farrells bravely persisted in acting as though it were an old-fashioned neighborhood parish in which everyone knew everyone else, and in doing so they endowed it with some of the same warmth.

But the Standing was ruining all that, Ron told the group. Sorrow warred with anger in his voice, and he gestured briskly with his muscular hands. The protest was tearing Holy Trinity apart. It reminded him of the time fourteen years earlier when a band of homeless-rights activists staged a similar protest after the parish had refused to give them the money to rehabilitate a shelter. The media had seized on the incident, portraying Holy Trinity as heartless and hypocritical, and the pastor, a close friend of Ron and Carole's, had been driven into exile.

We see what happens when people drag their politics into the church, he said, his eyes moving over the faces of the protestors. Is that what you people want?

By the time he had finished speaking, it was all Kathy Hartley and Brian Depenbrock could do to remain in their chairs. How dare he compare their protest with the previous one. They were not outsiders; they were loyal parishioners. They did not want money; they wanted justice. And they were not interested in driving people from the parish but in giving alienated women a reason to remain in the Church.

You have no business protesting in church, Ron snapped.

Our business is to oppose injustice wherever we find it, one of the protestors replied.

The argument accelerated, each side expounding on its own righteousness, and by the end of the meeting Ron was wagging his finger in the face of fifteen-year-old Keara Depenbrock, who acidly asked him to remove it.

Jim Maier was absent from this disputatious gathering. He only occasionally attended the meetings of the Working Groups, but he had no trouble following their dispiriting course because the struggle over the Standing was embodied in the conflict between two of his closest friends.

One was Kathy Hartley, the guiding spirit of the Working Groups. A precise, energetic woman in her early forties, Kathy had cultivated an interest in the writings of Catholic feminist theologians such as Elizabeth Johnson and Rosemary Radford Ruether. Her brother Greg was a Jesuit priest, and she was drawn to the order because of its work with the poor.

Kathy had moved to Washington eight years earlier in the wake of her divorce and had immediately become a catechist in the CCD program. Later, Father Maier had appointed her chair of the parish's Social Concerns Committee, which allocated money to local charities and coordinated volunteer programs.

She and Jim shared a love of poetry, an interest in the Latin American Church and a conviction that the Gospel required their involvement in the struggles of the impoverished and the disenfranchised. Kathy counted Catholic women among that latter group. She admonished Jim to take a prophetic stand on women's ordination, and reproved him for his timidity when he refused.

Her antagonist was Shannon Jordan, a professor of moral philosophy at George Mason University who coordinated the Sunday morning lecture series and was past president of the parents' association at Holy Trinity School. Like Kathy, she had found great spiritual consolation at Holy Trinity in the wake of a broken marriage. She said that Father Maier had taught her to pray.

Both she and her soon-to-be husband, Stephen Skousgaard, were intense, rigorously intellectual and theologically more conservative than most active parishioners. Though both supported women's ordination, they believed the issues confronting the Church were best resolved through strenuous argument, not popular protest. "Feelings," Shannon once said, "are not a foundation for human activity; they are a dimension of human activity."

She peppered Jim with excerpts from Church documents stating that the personal must be subordinated to the communal, or else there can be no liturgy. She also urged him to denounce the protest from the pulpit.

Implicit in her opposition to the Standing was a critique of the Working Groups as weak-minded and self-indulgent, willing to put their agenda ahead of the survival of the parish. Kathy and her allies reciprocated, painting Shannon as domineering and jealous of women whose influence in the parish rivaled her own.

The dispute between his two friends narrowed Jim's world. There were few people with whom his relationship was unsoiled by parish politics. Even when celebrating the Mass, giving spiritual direction, or meeting with the delegation he would lead to El Salvador that summer, he knew that the Standing was waiting to consume him when those more fulfilling activities were over.

ᏻᎷᏯᎾ

The conflict between Kathy and Shannon, and the larger factions they represented, reflected in exaggerated form the tension between what might loosely be defined as the "confrontationalist" and the "accommodationist" tendencies in American Catholicism.

Confrontationalists advocate challenging Roman authority, experimenting with new liturgical forms and creating smaller new communities to replace or supplement traditional parishes. Some also favor beginning with a clean theological slate, rethinking humanity's relationship with its Creator from scratch, so as to rid Christianity of its patriarchal burden.

Accommodationists advocate a patient and discreet engagement with Church authorities on a much narrower range of issues, including birth control, divorce and remarriage, priestly celibacy and women's ordination. Despite their discomfort with particular teachings, they believe the Church needs fine-tuning, not radical restructuring, and they fear that the confrontationalists will destroy much of what is essential to the faith.

Advocates of both philosophies, and many who favor a blending of the two, are active in a growing network of organizations that have sprung up to contest teachings that many Catholics believe are theologically suspect, psychologically harmful and detrimental to the vitality of the Church. At Holy Trinity a number of parishioners belong to the Women's Ordination Conference, which is based in suburban Virginia. Several former priests in the congregation have joined CORPUS, which advocates an end to mandatory celibacy and the reinstatement of married clerics such as themselves. Others are members of Call to Action, a Chicago-based organization which is perhaps the primary American advocate of Church reform.

These liberal organizations are opposed by groups such as the secretive Opus Dei, the politically combative Catholic League, and Catholics United for the Faith. Mother Angelica, a Franciscan nun who operates the Eternal Word cable television network is also an avid opponent of Church reform.

Both camps in the Catholic culture wars recruit actively, and each has the support of a few sympathetic bishops, but not even the most prominent of these organizations boast the membership necessary to consistently shape Church policy. Whatever their opinion about the issues dividing the Church, Catholics tend to think of themselves as members of a parish rather than of a movement, and they concentrate their activities close to home. Holy Trinity was distinctive because for three decades it combined characteristics of both. And the Standing was dangerous not simply because it irritated the archdiocese but because it threatened to splinter the parish permanently along ideological lines.

⊙∭⊙

By late May the 9:15 community was seething. Each Sunday a new voice would call for the suppression of the Standing. But Jim, who had now written to most of the protestors urging that they sit down, was reluctant to move beyond this low-key approach.

And to his own surprise it began to work.

On the Sunday after Pentecost, seven weeks after the protest began, Kathy Hartley sat down. She had begun the Standing as an Easter observance, and with the paschal season over she had decided to quit.

A few other protestors followed her lead. By mid-June the standers, who had once numbered twelve, were only five strong. And since Brian Depenbrock was in the choir, which stood most of the time anyway, his protest was not particularly noticeable.

For several heady weeks, Father Maier allowed himself to imagine that the Standing might peter out before the archdiocese began its search for his successor. But then in mid-June the protestors received an unexpected gift. One Sunday, at the 9:15 liturgy, Father Ned Hogan, a popular assistant pastor, invited Ray McGovern to the pulpit to explain himself to the parish.

Ray had little time to prepare, and he was confronted with a problem that faces everyone who preaches at the family mass—how to speak simultaneously to children and adults. But by the time he stepped behind the white wooden lectern, he was ready.

When he was a little boy, Ray began, mommies weren't allowed to be doctors. He spoke in a chipper tone, trying to let the children know he was talking to them. Mommies weren't allowed to be lawyers and they weren't allowed to do a lot of the jobs that they do today.

Now, how many of you think it is wrong for mommies to be doctors? he asked, his eyes scanning the church. No hands went up.

How many of you think it is wrong for mommies to be lawyers? Again, no hands.

Mommies are not allowed to be priests, Ray continued. And the people who don't want mommies to be priests use the same worn-out reasons that people used when I was a boy to keep mommies from being doctors and lawyers and all kinds of other things.

Now, how many of you think it would be wrong if mommies and sisters could become priests?

A few hands went up, and a few snorts of derision from some of the adults in the congregation, but looking down from the pulpit Ray could read on the faces before him that the congregation at large supported his position if not his protest.

Father Maier was preparing to say a later mass when he learned what Father Hogan had done, and he felt himself swallowing his exasperation. Father Hogan was just about to leave for an assignment in Nigeria, otherwise Jim would have called him in for a long, stern talk. As it was, Ned, like Ray, was beyond his influence.

That was the essence of the problem, Jim thought. Ray didn't seem to *want* anything—beyond the ordination of women. There was no way to negotiate with him.

What if mommies could be priests?

He had to admit it was an ingenious way to phrase the question to a young audience. For in the eyes of a child, who better represented a loving God?

⌘

The Working Groups on Sexism continued to meet throughout the spring and into the scorching Washington summer. But opponents of the Standing largely abandoned efforts at dialogue after Ron Farrell waved his finger at Keara Depenbrock, and by fall the groups were composed almost entirely of activists.

Kathy Hartley shared the leadership with her friend Rea Howarth, a writer and editor who had been active in the labor movement. They agreed that the groups needed to broaden their base, and so they decided to create a symbol that would allow parishioners to demonstrate support for women's ordination without having to stand during the mass.

All summer they collected ideas. One woman suggested a garment such as the black sash that had been worn in South Africa by white women who opposed apartheid. Another proposed a Roman numeral II, connoting women's second-class citizenship in the Church. But Kathy wanted something more overtly ecclesial, and the brainstorming continued.

Jim Maier was also busy that summer. In July, Mary Rita Wieners, the parish's director of liturgy, informed him that she would soon be resigning. Her successor would be selected after a nationwide search, and a thorough vetting by the appropriate parish committees. But in the meantime, Jim would need someone to perform her duties on an interim basis, and that appointment he would make himself.

To his mind, there was a well-qualified candidate close at hand. Having served on the CCD board and the Parish Council, Margaret Costello knew the parish well. In her work training catechists she had evinced a talent for drawing volunteers more deeply into Church ministries. Her professors at the Washington Theological Union said she was progressing rapidly, and had a firm understanding of the liturgy. More important, Jim liked her. She was easy to work with, and her liberal views and conciliatory style were similar to his own.

He offered her the job in late August, and Margaret, feeling that her future had suddenly revealed itself, quickly accepted. Since beginning her theological studies, she had aspired to be the director of liturgy in a progressive parish. Suddenly, the opportunity had been handed to her. And if she performed well on an interim basis, she would be a strong candidate for permanent appointment when the search for Mary Rita's successor began.

But in accepting her pastor's offer, Margaret also assumed a share of his burden. Like Jim, she was sympathetic to the protestors at the 9:15 liturgy, yet now her principal responsibility was to the integrity of Holy Trinity's liturgical celebrations. She too hoped to bring about a reconciliation between the standers and their opponents. But like Jim, she soon found herself at the mercy of events.

On the last Sunday of October, the Working Groups on Sexism unveiled their newly-minted symbols of protest. Shortly after arriving for the 9:15 liturgy, Ray McGovern, Kathy Hartley, Rea Howarth and six or seven others donned light blue stoles, much like the green stoles worn by the priests who presided at the liturgy that day. Perhaps a dozen additional parishioners wore light blue ribbons pinned to their jackets, as a discreet show of solidarity with the protestors.

The stoles were symbols of membership as well as exclusion. The Church taught that all Catholics, by virtue of their baptism, were members of the priesthood of Christ. Yet, it admitted only men to the ordained ministry. In the memorable phrase of Pope John Paul II, the protestors considered their stoles and ribbons "signs of contradiction," a witness of faith against the evils of the prevailing culture—though the pope, no doubt, would have objected to having his words used in this way.

Like the rest of the parish, Jim Maier was caught off guard by the Working Groups' initiative. In the Catholic faith only priests and deacons wear stoles, and he was uneasy about the implications of his parishioners "ordaining" themselves. But he had no trouble with the light blue ribbons. If these caught on, perhaps the protestors would decide that standing was unnecessary.

Jim even began toying with the idea of wearing one of the ribbons himself.

But opponents of the Standing were outraged by the groups' new initiative. Ellen Crowley, Paul Quinn and Shannon Jordan found "self-stoling" an act of appalling arrogance. The protestors were denigrating the primary symbol of the ordained ministry, they claimed, and thumbing their noses at the Church.

That fall less temperate opponents of the Standing began talking about taking matters into their own hands. One Sunday Jim heard rumors that an angry group of men was gathering to carry Ray McGovern from the church. On another someone told him that an irate parishioner had threatened to punch Ray in the nose. No confrontation ever materialized, but the Standing dragged on into October, and in that highly charged atmosphere, the archdiocese began its search for the next pastor of Holy Trinity Church.

CHAPTER SEVEN
෴

On the afternoon of October 31, 1992, the telephone rang in Father Maier's office. The caller was Alvaro Corrada del Rio, auxiliary bishop of Washington, D.C.—a brother Jesuit and Jim's immediate archdiocesan superior.

Father Maier assumed that the bishop was calling to make plans for the open forum he would be attending at Holy Trinity five days hence. That meeting would be the parishioners' only opportunity to speak with archdiocesan officials about the future of their church, and it marked the beginning of the search for Jim's successor.

But Bishop Corrada had something else on his mind. Somehow he had learned that Jim, Margaret and Anna were planning to attend a mass on All Saints' Day sponsored by Dignity, a gay Catholic organization that had some 3,500 members in roughly ninety chapters in the United States. They had been invited by a seminarian from the Washington Theological Union.

Did Jim know, the bishop asked, that any priest who attended one of Dignity's liturgies would be suspended from his priestly faculties?

No, Jim said. He knew that Cardinal Hickey did not allow his priests to preside at Dignity's masses. He knew that Hickey had forced the group out of a chapel at Georgetown University, but he had not known that he could be suspended simply for attending one of its liturgies.

If that were the case, Jim assured the bishop, then he would not attend.

That was the case, the bishop said.

As he hung up the phone, Jim's head was reeling. He had spoken of the Dignity mass to only a few close friends. Had one of them betrayed him? Or did the bishop have a mole in the parish center who had overheard him making plans?

Jim knew that Corrada objected to the way he ran his parish, but he did not want to believe that the bishop was surreptitiously collecting information against him. Perhaps Corrada simply wanted to create the impression that Holy Trinity was under surveillance, and that any missteps would be counted against it when the selection process began. If so, he had succeeded.

A Catholic parish awaiting a new pastor is at the mercy of the local bishop just as a diocese awaiting a new bishop is at the mercy of Rome. In many jurisdictions the laity have no input in pastoral assignments. In others, parishioners are allowed to express their views at "listening sessions"—a telling locution, for it emphasizes the clergy's silence rather than the laity's speech. When these sessions are over, parishioners' involvement is at an end.

The potential for abuse in such a system is immense. Bishops enjoy almost absolute power, and the laity have no means of rejecting a candidate, no matter how unsuitable. Nor can the laity reject an unsuitable bishop.

During the papacy of Paul VI, from 1963 to 1978, the key figure in American episcopal appointments was Archbishop Jean Jadot, who was the nuncio, or papal representative, to the United States. He favored moderate men with strong pastoral instincts and well-nuanced doctrinal views. The "Jadot bishops" were distinguished by a progressive political outlook, an openness to liturgical innovation and a conciliatory approach toward alienated Catholics.

But John Paul II recalled Jadot to Rome and began remaking the American episcopacy. He instituted a stringent litmus test on doctrinal matters. Reservations about *Humanae Vitae* were enough to disqualify even the most gifted candidate.

Within a few years, some of the most prominent American bishops were outspoken ecclesial conservatives, men such as Cardinals John O'Connor in New York, Bernard Law in Boston and Francis Stafford in Denver. These bishops insisted on fidelity to the Church's most contested teachings and struggled to silence would-be reformers. They also thrust themselves into the national debate on sexual mores, campaigning against abortion rights, opposing the distribution of condoms in public schools and urging the rejection of sex education curriculums that did not insist on abstinence and condemn homosexual activity.

Their highly publicized forays energized and emboldened the Catholic Right. They may also have helped weaken the Democratic party's traditional hold over Catholic voters. But public opinion polls indicate that these conservative crusaders did little to alter the attitudes of American Catholics toward the sexual teachings of the Church.

Their efforts might have been more successful if more of the pope's appointees had been blessed with O'Connor's intellect, his personal charm, and his occasional willingness to criticize his Republican allies. But the conservative talent pool was shallow, and as John Paul's papacy wore on, his appointments became less impressive. In the National Conference of Catholic Bishops, men like Cardinal Joseph Bernardin of Chicago, Archbishop John Quinn of San Francisco, and Archbishop Rembert Weakland of Milwaukee frequently outmaneuvered the papal contingent and retained a modicum of autonomy and flexibility for the American Church.

On the parish level, however, progressive Catholics under a conservative bishop were almost powerless, a fact not lost on parishioners at Holy Trinity.

Cardinal James Hickey had come to Washington from Cleveland in 1980 with a reputation as an ecclesial conservative, a political liberal, and a critic of American policies in Central America. But during his tenure the first of these attributes had gradually eclipsed the other two. By the fall of 1992 he was seventy-two, just three years short of the standard age for episcopal retirement, and increasingly preoccupied with leaving a diocese that was doctrinally pure. To the people of Holy Trinity, no one better symbolized the devolution of the cardinal's concerns than Alvaro Corrada.

The first time that the auxiliary bishop visited the parish was not long after his consecration in August 1985. He had had dinner in the rectory with his brother Jesuits. The community at that time was a fairly distinguished one, and included a well-known liturgist, two former novice masters and the past presidents of Georgetown University and the U.S. Jesuit Conference. They were, for all their ecclesial distinction, decidedly informal men and had dressed casually for the bishop's visit, hoping to create a collegial air.

Bishop Corrada arrived wearing a black suit and his Roman collar, a sign to the others that while they might consider themselves off duty, he was still on. He comported himself so stiffly during cocktails that Jim Maier suspected the bishop might be feeling intimidated. Unlike his hosts, Corrada had not been a prominent figure within the Society of Jesus. He knew that some of his Jesuit brethren believed that he had been elevated to the episcopacy largely because he was Puerto Rican, and perhaps he felt burdened by the need to prove them wrong.

During his seminary years, Corrada's colleagues had considered him erratic, even a trifle bizarre. He was remembered for cutting a few weeks' classes to hitchhike across country. Classmates found him impish and approachable one day, icy in his dignity the next.

It was the colder of these two characters who showed up for dinner that night. The bishop never took off his suit jacket or removed the glittering cuff links engraved with his episcopal shield. Nor did he enter the spirit of the evening, presiding over the dinner table conversation as though it were a meeting one moment, and receding from it almost entirely the next. His hosts began to wonder whether the bishop was sending them a message, letting them know that he would regard their parish with an especially critical eye.

The years following this unsteady inaugural were marked by a deepening mutual disdain. The bishop believed that Holy Trinity went out of its way to flout Church rubrics. Parishioners believed the bishop went out of his way to alienate them.

But Bishop Corrada came to Holy Trinity on the night of November 4, 1992, seemingly determined to show his consoling, pastoral side. He entered the almost empty theater of the upper-school building through the rear doors and worked his way up the center aisle, clasping each person's hand in both of his, peering into each face with a narrow-eyed intensity and thanking all sotto voce for coming out on that rainy evening to offer him the benefit of their opinions. He seemed very much the man who had playfully hooked a boy in the crook of his crosier at a Confirmation ceremony five years earlier. As parishioners trickled into the theater, setting down briefcases and unbelting raincoats, the more conciliatory among them could have been forgiven for imagining that the pastoral search process might not be so painful after all.

There were perhaps ninety people in the creaking old theater-style seats when Father Maier climbed to the stage. He was dressed in a short-sleeved clerical shirt and looked distracted and drawn. It was his job to introduce the four-priest panel and then leave the room so people could speak freely about his pastorate. As he picked up the microphone, Jim spotted a few blue stoles in the audience and wondered if a confrontation was in the offing.

He began his introductions with Bishop Corrada. The bishop had assumed a decidedly more formal aspect having reached the stage. He sat bolt upright and kept his eyes on the table in front of him. A tasteful inch of white cuff protruded from beneath his black suit coat.

To his left sat Father Jim Stormes, a representative of the Jesuit provincial. That Stormes was a Jesuit did not need articulating. He was distinguished on the panel by his gray slacks—a violation of the all-black clerical dress code that no diocesan priest would have risked in front of Corrada—his relaxed posture and his willingness to smile at a well-told joke. All of this made him seem vaguely anarchic beside the bishop.

Stormes was a representative of the Jesuit provincial, Father Edward Glynn. It was Glynn's responsibility to submit the name of a prospective pastoral candidate to Cardinal Hickey, and Hickey's privilege to accept or reject Glynn's choice. No archbishop had ever rejected a provincial's recommendation for the pastorate of Holy Trinity, and the Jesuits were hoping the cardinal would continue this tradition.

To Stormes' left sat Monsignor William Ehwalt, pastor of the neighboring parish of St. Ann's. Ehwalt, white-haired and heavyset, had been at St. Ann's for nearly three decades, and in that time hundreds of his parishioners had defected to Holy Trinity. His presence on the panel was due in part to a reputation for loyalty and dependability, and in part to the archdiocese's inability to perceive a conflict of interest when one presented itself.

The man who took the microphone from Father Maier was Monsignor William English, chairman of the archdiocesan priests' personnel board which advised Cardinal Hickey on priestly appointments. In a different suit of clothes the monsignor might have passed for a young politician. He had the same bland good looks, the same friendly if formal manner and the same knack for courteous evasion.

Though he had moderated dozens of forums like this one, English probably realized that the gathering at Holy Trinity would be a bit different. He knew the laity had a reputation for being independent and outspoken, and he knew what was signified by those blue stoles in the audience. Seeking, perhaps, to avoid any unpleasantness, he suggested that parishioners speak not about Church doctrine or parish policy but about their own spiritual and pastoral needs.

This ploy did not succeed. Brian Depenbrock, balding and bearded, a blue stole draped over his shoulders, was the first parishioner at the microphone, and he asked whether the people of Holy Trinity would have the chance to meet with candidates for the pastor's job.

"That's not the aim of the process at this point," Monsignor English told him.

Depenbrock suggested that imposing someone on the community against its wishes was perhaps not the most Christian model of governance. Then, noting that there were no women on the stage, he asked Bishop Corrada whether the archdiocese was prepared to appoint a pastor who would work with parishioners to lift the Church's ban on the ordination of women.

The bishop had not been looking at Brian, and when Depenbrock finished speaking the bishop did not raise his eyes. "The teaching is clear," he said after a moment. "I do not have to answer that."

His response drew a quiet chorus of boos from the audience, while in Brian it triggered memories of a previous humiliation at the bishop's hands.

Several years earlier, he, his daughter Keara and wife Martha had belonged to a small "intentional" Catholic community that celebrated Mass each Sunday in a chapel on the campus of Georgetown University. When Keara and another child in the group were ready to receive their First Communions, the bishop had come to celebrate Mass with them.

It was a festive occasion and the group had baked its own Communion bread. But when Brian carried the bread to the altar, the bishop refused to receive it, perceiving correctly that it contained ingredients other than flour and water. While the congregation sat waiting, Brian rummaged through the sacristy until he found some stale hosts. Only then did the Mass resume.

On that occasion, Brian had contained his anger. On this one, he did not. "That's a cop-out, Bishop," he shouted, taking a seat between Keara and Ray McGovern. His voice was louder than he had intended and even his daughter drew away from him with a start.

The bishop appeared unruffled. Stormes looked uncomfortable if amused, and Ehwalt looked much as he did before the meeting began. English called the next speaker, a woman who was perhaps under the illusion that she could do Jim Maier and the parish some good by telling her story.

One of Father Maier's strengths, she said, was his willingness to work with people who had disagreements with the Church. Because of Jim's rather flexible interpretation of Catholic dogma, her husband had allowed their children to be baptized in the Church. He was even considering becoming a Catholic himself.

But, she added, the parish had a problem, and she proceeded to explain this problem in a way that made it seem as though it flowed from the very "openness" she had just praised. The community at Trinity was in conflict with itself. Some people wanted to act on their differences of opinion with the Church while others wanted simply to bear up beneath them.

"How do we have dissent within the community without it tearing the community apart?" she asked. "How can we make it so people don't have to take increasingly radical action to get a hearing?"

No one on the panel attempted a reply to the questions that had been tormenting Father Maier for more than six months. Monsignor English called the next questioner. Appropriately enough, it was Ray McGovern.

Ray was dressed, as always, in a business suit. A blue stole was draped around his shoulders. He began by telling the story of what people at Trinity referred to as "the Good Confirmation," which had taken place five years earlier. Ray's son Joseph had received the sacrament that year and Bishop Corrada had gently corrected him for standing in a slouch. As a parent, Ray said, he had appreciated the firm but tactful way Corrada had spoken to Joseph.

But at the Confirmation two years ago, Ray had not been so appreciative of the bishop's behavior. As he spoke, a few of the people who had been facing the front of the auditorium turned to face Ray, who was standing at a microphone in the rear. He was about to offer his rendition of a parish classic—a story that elucidated Bishop Corrada's chilly relationship with the people of Holy Trinity—and they wanted to take in every nuance.

It was, as Ray said, a Confirmation that brought the bishop to Holy Trinity two years earlier. Shortly before the liturgy was to begin, Father Ned Hogan had asked the bishop if he could publicly thank the volunteers who had served as instructors in the Confirmation preparation program. The bishop said there was no place in the ritual for such an announcement. Father Hogan, who felt otherwise, strode indignantly away. His anger ignited the bishop's and what parishioners came to know as "the Bad Confirmation" was begun.

A few minutes later the bishop's master of ceremonies, a dark-haired diocesan priest, gathered the altar servers to review their duties in the upcoming liturgy. Megan Tschudy, a seventh-grade student in the CCD program, had been chosen to hold the book from which Corrada would read several prayers, and when the priest found this out, he exchanged long glances with the bishop. Corrada was not altogether comfortable with altar girls. The Vatican, at that time, did not permit them, and Bishop Corrada was reluctant to have one perform so prominent a task.

"No, that won't do," the priest said, and he assigned Megan's duties, which she had performed numerous times, to a boy who was unfamiliar with the job. The transaction was conducted in full view of perhaps fifteen parishioners who were making last-minute preparations in the sacristy, and word of what had happened was circulating through the Church before Mass began.

The incident offended many in the congregation, especially those who knew Megan and her parents, Ted and Mary, who were among the most active people in the parish. During the liturgy, parishioners' indignation deepened into anger as Bishop Corrada sat pinch-faced behind the altar, and his master of ceremonies jostled several children who were not standing in proper spot when the time came for their anointing with chrism.

The bishop added to the bitterness of the evening when he turned away from the last member of the offertory party—a girl carrying a book inscribed with the intentions for which the confirmation candidates were offering their Mass. She was left standing at the foot of the altar for a few embarrassing moments until Rick Levy, the parish deacon, descended the stairs to her rescue.

Parishioners seated beneath the choir loft received a final taste of Corrada's displeasure. The mass concluded with a hymn that was apparently a bit long for his taste, and as he neared the rear of the church he said loudly: "If I wanted this much music, I would have gone to the Kennedy Center."

In his retelling of the story, Ray left out many of the more embarrassing details, concentrating instead on the incident with Megan Tschudy. He thought of her recently, he said, when Holy Trinity hosted a gathering of black Catholics whose families had broken away from the parish almost seventy years earlier to build their own church.

At that reception, Dorothy Wharton Thomas, a woman in her eighties, told of the spring morning when she and her grade school classmates were informed that for the first time they would be allowed to walk in Trinity's May procession. The girls hurried home to tell their skeptical parents, who reluctantly provided the necessary dresses, gloves and veils. Then, on the appointed evening, they arrived at the school only to be told that there had been some mistake.

"Dorothy was excluded because she was black," Ray said. "Megan was excluded because she was a woman. Whether it is a matter of gender or race, it is the same injustice. We at Holy Trinity are a justice people. We insist our young women be treated with the same respect as our young men. We must treat our Megans as we treat our Josephs. Or else we give scandal."

He finished, but remained at the microphone to ask the bishop why he had not allowed Megan to hold the lectionary. The bishop denied he had done this. "We love all our children," he said.

McGovern offered to produce witnesses. Corrada reiterated his denial, but McGovern did not immediately acquiesce. This stalemate lasted an excruciating minute until Ray sat down.

Bishop Corrada must have been feeling a bit beleaguered by this point, and people in the audience who were not caught up in the drama must have feared for the future of their church. Both got a breather when the next speaker stepped to the microphone. Carroll Carter was a descendant of the Carroll family, a large brood of Revolution-era patriots that included Charles Carroll, the only Catholic to sign the Declaration of Independence, and John Carroll, the first Roman Catholic bishop in the United States.

Carter had served for many years as the archdiocese's director of development, and he was staunchly loyal to the Church of his childhood. He wanted everyone to know, he said, that his were the comments of a caring parishioner and that he meant the people of Holy Trinity neither harm nor disrespect. He then proceeded to accuse the parish of a long list of sins, some of which were simply questions of taste—a priest saying Mass in light-colored shoes—and others which were merely departures from the practices of his boyhood.

Trinity was not a reverent parish, he said. People spoke with their neighbors in the church before the liturgies. The "Cross of Glory" had no corpus and hence was not technically a crucifix. "The rubrics require a crucifix," he said.

And finally, Holy Trinity was badly managed. The parish allowed anyone who registered to stay on its rolls. A minimum annual fee should be established, he said, and those who did not pay it should be expelled from the parish.

The crowd, which had been murmuring throughout Carter's presentation, burst into laughter at this last suggestion. "How Christian!" Brian Depenbrock shouted. But when the laughter died, foreboding set in. The priests on the panel had remained sober during Carter's talk, and a few people in the auditorium began to wonder if the archdiocese would use his testimony as evidence that Holy Trinity was out of control.

From that point, the forum became an impromptu tribute to Jim Maier. Parishioners lined up behind the two microphones in the center aisle to praise him, and to ask for a pastor who would continue his work. Some spoke plaintively. Others issued what sounded like warnings.

"I think there would be few greater sins in this world than to do something to inhibit the growth of this parish, this great movement to God," one man said.

"I am an exile from my own diocese," put in a gentleman from Arlington. "I come here because they treat the laity as though they were intelligent adults."

Another fellow with a blue stole said, "I came to Trinity because I was alienated by other parishes. This is a place of compassion, a place of forgiveness. This is a place of Christian refuge from the letter of the law. If you appoint a person who feels compelled to uphold the letter of the law rather than the forgiveness of the Spirit, you will destroy this community."

"This is the only church I have ever been to where the fire marshal comes to check out the crowd," said Julianne Aaron, chair of the parish's Social Concerns Committee. Then, looking at the men on the stage, she said what was on many people's minds. "I know you are not the enemy, but I don't know what to do with you. I hope you don't think of us as the enemy."

The meeting was almost over when Shannon Jordan's son Matthew, an eighth-grade student at Holy Trinity School, stood up. He began benignly enough. "I love Father Maier," he said. "He is a man I can connect with."

And then to Bishop Corrada he added: "One thing I learned at Holy Trinity School is that you should always tell the truth. Because that way nothing can come back to haunt you." Matthew had witnessed what had happened to Megan Tschudy, and there was no mistaking the purpose of his remarks. "I'm not saying you didn't," he concluded, "but it's just a good guideline."

The bishop's expression remained unchanged. When the meeting came to a close about ten minutes later he offered a few summary remarks. "I sense some fear," he said, an understatement which drew muted laughter from the audience. But, he continued, there was no reason for anxiety, because "certain things look much better than a few years ago," though he did not say what.

As the crowd dispersed, Shannon Jordan made her way to the stage. She wanted to explain to the bishop why her son had said what he had said, and why she had not tried to dissuade him from saying it. In her mind, she had a choice between embarrassing the bishop publicly or teaching Matthew that discomfiting truths should not be spoken to people in power, and she had chosen what she thought was the lesser evil.

"You do not have to apologize," the bishop said gently. But she had not come to apologize, Shannon replied, she had come to explain. The bishop did not acknowledge this distinction, however, and he continued to reassure her until he was called away.

CHAPTER EIGHT

In the days following the open forum, Ray McGovern and Brian Depenbrock were roundly criticized for their confrontations with Bishop Corrada. Even some of their supporters believed that they had hurt the parish's cause. Among those who had attended the forum the mood was glum; it was as though the demise of Holy Trinity as they had known it had already begun.

Only Father Maier seemed to have taken the evening in stride. "I heard that Matthew *invited the bishop to honesty*," he said as he tapped fish food into his office aquarium on the gray autumn morning after the forum.

Jim understood that Bishop Corrada's impression of the parish was so negative before the meeting that it could hardly have gotten much worse. Two years earlier, on the day following the Bad Confirmation, he had made an appointment with the bishop assuming that they would discuss what had happened the night before. Instead, when he arrived at Corrada's office the bishop produced a thick sheaf of letters and set them on his desk. The file contained complaints about Holy Trinity and its Jesuit clergy, including the priests' failure to preach against abortion, their "softness" on homosexuality and birth control and their tolerance of a feminist cabal that was taking over the parish.

Jim was hearing many of these accusations for the first time, and he had no way of knowing which were legitimate and which were not. Nor, for that matter, did the bishop, though he seemed to take all of them as gospel. Before the meeting was over, Jim understood that if Corrada had his way, Holy Trinity would soon be a very different parish, one in which the priests were unswervingly loyal, and lay people, especially women, were kept in their place.

Fortunately, the auxiliary bishop did not have the power to appoint Trinity's new pastor. That choice would be made by Cardinal Hickey, whom Jim regarded as a more moderate and reasonable man.

It was not a view that most of his parish shared. The cardinal had visited Holy Trinity only once in more than six years, even though it was the largest church in his archdiocese. Many parishioners saw that as a sign of his disapproval. More disturbing was what they considered Hickey's overzealous loyalty to the pope.

In 1986 the cardinal had been the Vatican's point man in its campaign to purge Father Charles Curran from the faculty of the Catholic University of America. Curran, one of the most respected Catholic moral theologians in the country, was ostensibly being disciplined for delineating a sexual ethic that differed from the church's teaching on contraception, and which justified premarital sexual intercourse, abortion, and homosexual activity, in rare and strictly qualified instances. But many reform-minded Catholics believed that he was being punished belatedly for organizing American theologians to protest *Humanae Vitae* in 1968.

Most of the country's leading Catholic intellectuals rallied to Curran's cause, but this did not impress Cardinal Hickey, who was chancellor of the university. Nor was he swayed by arguments that sacking a distinguished professor would seriously damage the school's academic reputation and its intellectual integrity. The pope had given him a job to do, and he did it. Father Curran was removed.

Later that same year, the Vatican assigned Hickey to investigate the ministry of Archbishop Raymond Hunthaussen, of Seattle, whose high-profile opposition to nuclear weaponry had angered conservatives in his archdiocese. The contents of Hickey's report were never fully disclosed, but after he filed it, the Vatican stripped Hunthaussen of much of his ecclesial power, and assigned a "co-adjudicator" to help him run the archdiocese.

The move aroused opposition among the usually docile American episcopate, and the Vatican, realizing it had a problem on its hands, deputized three American cardinals—Hickey, Joseph Bernardin of Chicago and John O'Connor of New York—to defuse the situation. The ensuing investigation was, in many ways, a repudiation of the first. The violations of which Hunthaussen was guilty—such as allowing non-Catholics to receive Communion, and permitting Dignity, the gay Catholic group, to hold a Mass in his cathedral—were common in the United States, so common, Hunthaussen's defenders argued, that there had to be another reason for the archbishop's humiliation, such as the Vatican's desire to please its conservative political allies in the United States.

Hunthaussen's powers were eventually restored, and he has since retired. In the aftermath of the incident Hickey was viewed as a meddler and an opportunist by many on the progressive wing of the American Church, but he continued to enjoy the confidence of Rome.

More recently the cardinal had clashed with the Jesuits at Georgetown after the university allowed Dignity to worship on its campus, and again when school administrators decided that they could not legally deny funding to a student group that supported abortion rights. In that instance Hickey had pressured Father Ed Glynn, as superior of the Maryland province, to demand the group's expulsion. But Glynn believed it was essential to respect the independence of the university, and he declined to intervene.

Parishioners' anxieties were intensified by rumors that the cardinal was interested in a position in Rome after his retirement. By making an example of Holy Trinity he could punish his Jesuit adversaries and demonstrate his orthodoxy in a single swoop.

But Jim did not believe this would happen. Though Hickey demanded doctrinal conformity from official representatives of the Church, he seemed to realize that he could not expect such obedience from the laity. As long as the Standing remained a small and isolated phenomenon, Holy Trinity would be safe, Jim thought, because the cardinal understood that on issues of gender and sexuality, a certain leeway was essential to the health of the American Church.

The libidinal urge is at the root of almost every issue that sets the

American laity against the hierarchy. Whether the subject is artificial contraception, homosexuality, premarital intercourse, divorce and remarriage or the dominion of a celibate male hierarchy, the Church's position is based on its ancient understanding of human sexuality. Pluck any strand and the entire net quivers.

This understanding is rooted in the conviction of early theological giants such as Saint Paul, Saint Augustine and Saint Jerome that lust was perhaps the most fearful and chronic of human sins. They believed that all sexual activity was suspect. Yet a loving God would not require a man and woman to risk their souls in order to perpetuate the species, so some limited lovemaking had to be moral.

In the codification of celibate churchmen, such lovemaking was limited indeed. For centuries the Church taught that intercourse between a husband and wife for the purpose of procreation was legitimate, but that the arousal or gratification of sexual passion in any other way was a perversion of the divine design. Today, spouses need not *intend* to conceive an offspring each time they make love, but they can employ no artificial means to prevent this from happening.

Though Church teaching has changed little over the centuries, a tension remains at the core of Catholic sexual thought. Through two millennia, the Church has branded as heretical the teachings of Gnostics, Jansenists and others who argued that the body was evil. Catholic liturgies, particularly before the Second Vatican Council, were sensual feasts, complete with incense, candles and bells. Catholic cathedrals were architectural wonders and sanctuaries for the greatest works of Western art. Against the austerity of the Reformation, the Roman Catholic Church claimed a place for the senses in the calculus of salvation. Human sexuality, to this way of thinking, was among God's most exalted gifts; lovemaking was sacramental, a channel of divine grace.

At the same time, however, the Church also honored an ascetic ideal. It encouraged fasting, physical mortification, even self-flagellation, and this strain of piety has had the dominant influence on its sexual thought. Through its embrace of celibacy as a religious ideal, the Church taught—first explicitly, later implicitly—that those who do not have sexual intercourse are holier than those who do.

Marriage, in this view, was the sacramental sanctioning of a fallen state. As the apostle Paul put it in his first letter to the Corinthians: "Now to the unmarried and to widows I say: it is a good thing for them to remain as they are, as I do, but if they cannot exercise self-control they should marry, for it is better to marry than to be on fire."

This viewpoint did not survive the Second Vatican Council, at least not in its official form. The council refuted the notion that personal sanctity was inversely related to sexual activity. It affirmed that intercourse existed not simply for procreative purposes but for the "mutual consolation" of the spouses. The Church, it seemed, was prepared to recognize the holiness of humanity's desire for intimacy, the sacramental nature of what transpired between loving spouses and the centrality of a healthy sex life to the endurance of a marriage.

That one bloodless phrase, "mutual consolation," gave many hope that a change in Catholic teaching on birth control was in the offing. Indeed, such a change was recommended by an overwhelming majority on the advisory committee that Pope John XXIII convened to study the issue. This compounded the disappointment—one might even say the shock—when John's successor, Pope Paul VI released *Humanae Vitae*.

The pope had been persuaded by his most conservative curial advisor that accepting the committee's recommendation would irrevocably damage the teaching authority of the Church. But the reverse was true. In restating a mechanistic and discredited teaching, Paul VI created a crisis of credibility.

In the United States, weekly mass attendance dropped from 65 percent to 52 percent in the next decade. The great majority of those who still practiced their faith disregarded the encyclical. More significantly, because Rome had displayed a willingness to place the dignity of the institution over the interests of the faithful, many American Catholics decided that they could no longer trust the moral guidance offered by representatives of the Church.

Since the release of *Humanae Vitae*, lay Catholics have undertaken a comprehensive reevaluation of the Church's sexual teachings. Questions about the nature and value of physical intimacy inspired questions about the legitimacy of a celibate male hierarchy, and led many to challenge the morality of its monopoly on ecclesial power.

Pope John Paul II has responded by disciplining dissenting theologians and appointing bishops who view seeking the opinion of the laity as a form of disloyalty to Rome. Power remains in clerical hands. Yet most young Catholics still believe that if they are to develop a moral sexual ethic, they will have to do it on their own.

On the day after he got married, Gary Cosgrove★ walked into a church in downtown Washington a few minutes before mass was to begin. He genuflected, slipped into a pew in the middle of the nave and knelt to pray. It was Gary's practice to prepare for Mass by examining his conscience and repenting for his sins. But on that spring morning, before he could remember a single transgression, he was engulfed by a tide of relief.

He felt lightheaded, and then lighthearted. Unaccustomed to experiencing these sensations in church, he pushed himself up from the kneeler and sank back in his seat, wondering what was happening.

Gary was fiddling with his wedding band when his illumination came. For the first time in more than ten years he had not marched into church feeling defensive. He had not knelt with the intention of justifying himself to the nagging voice inside his head. He was married now, and the Church no longer counted his sex life as a sin.

For a fleeting moment he savored the strange and marvelous feeling of being entirely in accord with the moral teachings of his Church. Then he remembered that he and his wife were using artificial contraceptives. The realization diminished but did not destroy his sense of well-being. Gary assumed that if they carted everyone who practiced birth control out of the church that morning there wouldn't have been enough people left for a game of volleyball.

In a moment, however, the spring of ambivalence that regularly flooded his soul was gurgling once again.

Gary's monogamous ideals had been shaped almost entirely by the teaching of the Church and the example of his parents. His dream, as a younger man, had been to give himself to only one woman, and though he had failed to realize that ideal, he had never abandoned it. He still believed that lovemaking was a sign and a strengthening of the sacramental bond between two people. Yet he knew from bitter experience that forging such a bond in the late twentieth century entailed experimentation and error. And of this, the Church seemed almost willfully ignorant.

Catholic sexual teaching forbids premarital sexual activity beyond the most tepid kiss. To Gary's mind it turned the years between puberty and matrimony into one extended occasion for sin. Many of his friends had abandoned their faith because they felt that the Church was forcing them to choose between remaining Catholic and taking the first steps toward sexual intimacy.

Yet as he sat in the pew that morning, Gary realized that his allegiance to what he considered the core of Catholic sexual teaching had saved him from the excesses and disillusionments of his peers, nurtured his belief in the dignity of women and enhanced the intensity of his sexual experiences. Would it be possible, he wondered, to free this sustaining essence from its mechanistic armor? Or thus liberated, would the values of generosity, fidelity and mutual respect evaporate into the kind of banality he remembered reading once on a dorm room wall: *I am me, and you are you, and if by chance we meet each other, it is beautiful?*

For most of his adult life, Gary had endeavored to reconcile his religious convictions with the sexual realities of the late 1970s and 1980s. But in the end, all he was certain of was his own moral ambivalence. From what he could tell, such ambivalence was widespread.

Several years earlier, Gary had begun attending the 5:30 mass on Sunday evenings at Holy Trinity. Some parishioners referred to this liturgy as the yuppie mass. The congregation was mostly young, unmarried, well-educated and upwardly mobile. It was said, only half in jest, that the seeds of future marriages were sown during the kiss of peace.

For members of this community, the Church's sexual prohibitions might be relevant on almost any weekend night. Yet the questions to which these teachings gave rise, such as the spiritual significance of sexual intimacy, were hardly ever articulated—not in homilies, not in adult education lectures and not on the popular retreats of the Young Adult Community.

Gary found this puzzling. The Church of his childhood had been obsessed with sexuality. A priest in Gary's high school used to pull boys into private conferences and ask whether they had committed the sin of masturbation; the boys all lied and said no.

Gary was grateful to be spared similar intimidation at Holy Trinity, yet he was eager for a better understanding of the Church's sexual reasoning. He began reading Catholic magazines like *Commonweal* and Catholic journals like *Theological Studies*, and soon came to view the debate over sexual ethics as a contest between theologians whom he thought of as "absolutists" on the Right, and those he called "situationalists" on the Left.

Absolutists believed that the laws of God were written into the laws of nature, and that the Roman hierarchy could determine right from wrong by examining the physical structure of an act and discerning whether it was faithful to the divine design. They supported the teaching that only genital intercourse between spouses in a Church-sanctioned marriage was moral, and then only when no artificial contraception was employed. Some held that even extensive foreplay and overly vigorous lovemaking were sinful.

Situationalists challenged this reasoning on two counts. They believed that the hierarchy did not *identify* natural law, but rather interpreted it, and that its understandings were imperfect and subject to revision. They also denied that the morality of an act could always be determined by its physical structure. The intent of the actors and the effect of the action were important as well.

Many situationalists openly disputed *Humanae Vitae*, but were more circumspect in their challenge to the remainder of Church teaching. It seemed to Gary that they were trying to provide a basis for greater sexual freedom within committed, monogamous relationships. But they seldom advanced specific claims.

Gary had much greater sympathy with the second camp than with the first. In his eyes absolutism was an awkward attempt to sanctify the hierarchy's lust for control. It resulted in a pastoral style that was rigid and suspicious and alienated Catholics precisely when they needed their Church most: in times of moral confusion.

But he had questions about the situational approach as well. Surely there were some actions, rape for instance, which were always wrong. But situationalism, open to almost endless nuance and qualification, gave him meager intellectual grounds for saying so. And in unscrupulous hands, it became little more than a sophisticated sort of self-justification.

His parents, he knew, had followed a simpler moral code. They had married right after high school, and raised a large family on a meager budget. In grade school Gary had served as an altar boy. In high school he made weekend retreats. A few of the priests he knew urged him to consider entering the seminary. But Gary was mesmerized by the intensity of the bond between his parents and wanted nothing more than to marry and raise children.

He had had a steady girlfriend during his junior and senior years in high school, but when he left his home in central Massachusetts for college near Philadelphia in 1977 he was still a virgin, and he assumed that most of his new schoolmates would be, too. It took him only a few days in a coed dormitory to understand that he'd been wrong.

The students on his floor came from backgrounds more affluent and permissive than his own. To Gary's mind they leapt into bed with astonishing alacrity. He was stunned by the number of young women who emerged from young men's rooms each morning, and by how blasé everyone else in the building seemed to feel about this. Once he told a few floormates that if a man loved a woman enough to sleep with her, he should love her enough to marry her. They informed him that he was a prig.

Gradually, he began to question his sexual ethics. It was not the dorm lounge discussions about sexual liberation that swayed him—though he now kept his opposition to recreational sex to himself. Nor did he find the Church teaching too exacting; he still assumed he would be a virgin when he got married. But he had come to know and admire many young men and women who were involved in long-term sexual relationships and who seemed none the worse for it. Indeed, they were among the most caring people he knew. God was present to him in these people, he told himself. Could what they were doing be so wrong?

Gary's questioning was motivated in part by loneliness and fear. During his freshman year he had broken up with his high school girlfriend, and in the next three years he had had only a few dates. Though he was just twenty-one, he believed that his dream of marrying and raising a large family was receding. All his friends were involved in relationships, and he couldn't help feeling that his conservative sexual attitudes were holding him back.

He might have sought the counsel of the campus's lone Catholic cleric, but he had a pretty fair idea of what the man would say. Almost every Saturday evening, regardless of the scriptural theme, this priest railed against premarital sex. His specialty was stories involving crab lice.

One weekend in the midst of his confusion, Gary remembered something another priest had said to him on a high school retreat. Making love was a form of communication, the man had said, and one should not say with one's body what one did not mean in one's heart. Gary knew that the priest had not intended this as a dispensation, but from three 'years' distance, that was how he chose to interpret it. He would *make* love when he was *in* love. And he hoped that that would be soon.

The following fall he met a young woman with green eyes, coppery hair and a contemplative manner. Like Gary she loved Eastern European literature and folk rock. Within a few weeks they had become close friends and were spending most of their free time together. One afternoon, as they sat in a campus sandwich shop, he looked at her in a way that made his feelings unmistakable, and she returned the gaze. A few nights later, they became lovers.

Gary knew that the Church regarded their lovemaking as sinful, but he believed that he had never understood Catholic teaching so well. Now he knew from personal experience that the sex act was sacramental; he felt sanctified.

But he also felt guilty. The Church taught that a man should sleep only with his wife. "She is my wife," Gary told himself. "We just aren't married yet." Once that technicality was taken care of, he would be back in the fold.

But Gary and his lover did not marry. The relationship failed after several years, as did another that Gary began a few months later. In his late twenties, beset by loneliness, he commenced a series of affairs that were less about commitment than consolation.

For the first time in his life he felt almost entirely cut off from the Church. He stopped attending mass, except on certain holy days, and when people asked him his religion he told them that he used to be Catholic. One friend suggested that he could return to the Church simply by confessing his sins. But Gary remembered his grade school catechism; absolution required "a firm purpose of amendment," and this he lacked.

As Gary was drifting away from the Church, millions of young Americans were experiencing a similar conflict. The challenge for the Church was how to respond. One approach was to read these young people the riot act and let them repent or retreat. This assured a doctrinally pure, though numerically diminished, Church.

The Jesuits at Holy Trinity were part of a countermovement. They realized that they were charged with upholding the precepts of the faith, but they were also charged with ministering to the faithful. And the faithful were in revolt, particularly on sexual issues. To complicate matters further, many of these shepherds were in agreement with their flocks. While they could scarcely challenge Rome outright, neither could they defend what they did not believe.

How to proceed? Progressive priests and theologians eventually developed a three-pronged response. The first step was to remind the laity—and the hierarchy—of a central but ambiguous tenet of the faith: that Catholics in moral conflict are bound to obey their own consciences. This did not guarantee that one would act morally, nor was it license to do as one chose—conscience had to be "formed" by prayer, study and an honest attempt to accept the teaching of the magisterium—but it did mean that Catholics at odds with Rome could sinlessly follow their own course.

The second prong in the progressive response was the continued development of what was known as "pastoral theology," a school of thought that gave the clergy a certain leeway in ministering to those whom it knew to be traducing Church teaching. The assumption that elevated this field beyond mere permissiveness was that people were more likely to change their opinions and behaviors—to repent, some might say—if they were within a supportive faith community than if they were without. If life was a pilgrimage toward God, pastoral theologians suggested, then the pilgrims deserved the support of their Church, whether they seemed to be walking the right path at that moment or not. In practice, this allowed pastors around the country to welcome couples they knew to be practicing birth control, those living together without the benefit of marriage, those remarried without annulments and sexually active gays and lesbians.

The third prong was at once the simplest and the most sweeping. The fathers of the Second Vatican Council had emphasized that the Eucharist was the fullest expression of the Catholic faith, the rite through which Christ, in the words of one eucharistic prayer, "reconciled all things to Himself." If that was the case, the Church could scarcely exclude from this sacrament the people whom it felt needed it most. This meant, at least in some churches, that any person who could receive Communion with a clear conscience was welcome to do so.

Critics of the pastoral approach argued that it conferred forgiveness on those who had never repented, and contributed to a disastrous loosening of sexual ethics among the laity. There may be some truth in this second assertion, but the evidence from Holy Trinity suggests that young Catholics did not so much abandon the Church's ethic as adapt it to their own situations.

During the early 1980s the parish used to put on a yearly variety show. One year a comic sketch featured a young couple who wanted to get married, and were trying to hide the fact that they were living together. This state of affairs was so common by that point that in the sketch it was the seen-it-all-before parish receptionist who seemed at ease, and the couple who seemed flustered.

The skit demonstrated that baby boom Catholics were no longer abiding by the letter of Church law, but that they still sought to marry sacramentally when they found themselves in a relationship they hoped would last. It also illustrated that Holy Trinity was willing to accept these young people on their own terms.

By the mid-1980s, when Gary began attending the 5:30 mass, something momentous had happened in the American Church. When it became clear to young Catholics that Rome was neither going to change its sexual teaching nor throw them out, a great accommodation took place. The once-hot topic of sexual relations was simply removed from the ecclesial table. Sexual issues continued to create a climate of mistrust between Pope John Paul II and the American laity, and to dominate the American media's coverage of Catholicism, but on the parish level these issues went underground.

Jim Maier, who had arrived at Holy Trinity just shortly before Gary did, was surprised by their absence. Issues such as women's ordination, which required the Church to change its practices, were becoming increasingly divisive, but most parishioners seemed at ease with more private dissent. Even in confession, few admitted using artificial birth control, having sex with a longtime lover, or living in a nonsacramental marriage.

This was a relief in some ways, for it saved Jim from absolving people of what he did not believe to be sinful. But it saddened him to think that many Catholics were so alienated from their Church that they could no longer discuss sexual matters with a priest. A glance at the newspapers was enough to confirm that the sexual revolution was still taking casualties, and that the counsel of fidelity and restraint might serve as a useful corrective.

After his return to the Church, Gary Cosgrove began taking this counsel to heart. He had been celibate for one mind-clearing year when he met the woman who later became his wife. Though they began talking about marriage almost immediately, they let their physical relationship unfold at an unhurried pace. The principle that guided him was the same one that had guided his first relationship: he did not *make* love until he was *in* love. The difference, this time, was that the woman he loved did not leave him.

Gary's fiancée was not Catholic, but she had agreed to marry within the Church. That meant taking Pre-Cana classes, a course of instruction for all couples who wanted to marry within the Church. Neither of them was enthused about this prospect. Gary had friends in the Arlington diocese who warned him that their courses had consisted of little beyond an endless repetition of the ban on artificial birth control.

But to his relief, the program at Holy Trinity was different. The classes were taught by a team of five lay people and one priest, and focused on helping couples understand the commitment they were about to make. No one spoke of sexual matters until the sixth and final session and there was a palpable unease in the room as one of the lay people outlined the Church's teaching and asked if there were any questions.

There were not, and Gary took this to mean that no one in his group was seriously considering observing the ban on birth control.

Like Holy Trinity, many Catholic parishes have a "Tell, But Don't Ask" policy when it comes to the Church's sexual teachings. They are willing to explain but not to enforce. And while this keeps the ecclesial peace, it also prevents American Catholics from seriously engaging sexual issues in an open way.

On the ride home Gary's fiancée said that she was glad to have a better understanding of *Humanae Vitae*, and that she had revised her opinion of Pope Paul VI. Much of what he had written about lovemaking was beautiful. It was essential, as the pope suggested, that partners be entirely open to one another. It was essential that they not be blinded by their own desires. It was essential to understand that intercourse was an inherently meaningful transaction. But when the pope insisted that the "unitive" and "procreative" aspects of lovemaking could not be separated, she could not agree. For she knew, from her and Gary's own unitive experiences, that he was wrong.

After his marriage, Gary began to become more comfortable with the prevailing silence in the Church. He was happily married, felt no qualms about using birth control, and believed that the Church's sexual teachings were no longer relevant to his life. But his equanimity was upset one Sunday when he attended the 9:15 mass and found Ray McGovern and a few others standing.

When Gary learned the reason for the protest, he felt a familiar tumult commencing within. It was about time someone challenged the Church on its misguided teachings, he thought to himself. It was about time someone broke the accommodating silence. Driving home that morning, he began to consider standing himself.

One chilly evening not long afterward, Gary attended a reconciliation service at Holy Trinity and heard Linda Arnold, a fellow parishioner, give a reflection titled "Sexual Beings/Moral Beings: What is Safe Sex in God's Eyes?"

Linda, then the associate director of campus ministry at the Catholic University of America, was a short, forceful woman in her early fifties, who effected a quiet intensity in the pulpit. She took her text from the fourth chapter of the First Letter of John: "Love is of God . . . and those who abide in love abide in God and God abides in them." Her theme was the holiness of human sexuality and its place in the Catholic tradition, and Gary was eager to hear what she had to say.

"Sexuality in general and the genital expression of love between two people in particular have an ambiguous history in our tradition and in our life as the People of God," Linda began. "As late as 1963 Church documents were still saying that marriage was, at best, a remedy for concupiscence.

"Our thinking about conjugal sexuality was shaped in patriarchy and understood primarily as a legal contract in which two persons obtained rights over each other's bodies for the purpose of reproduction . . . Any act of pleasuring which did not lead to intercourse open to conception was wrong."

She was dressed in a white hooded alb, but from the pews only her face was visible above the pulpit as she lifted her gaze from the text to survey the congregation. "Because there is profound unity and bonding in God, so must there be in us and in our relationships," she said. "The bond of unity expressed sexually, to whatever degree, in play, in mutual pleasuring, in shared ecstasy, strengthens each one to go out creatively to the other. We share a process of sanctification, coming to 'holy wholeness' as we grow together in our acceptance of our bodies and in our capacity to enjoy our own and our partner's body.

". . . Mature integrated sexual expression, in whatever form, communicates forgiveness, trust, joy, fidelity—all aspects of God's abiding in us."

Linda paused. There was a deep silence in the church. "God made all flesh," she continued. "God loves all human flesh. Do you love your own body as God does? Do we ever reflect on or experience sexual intercourse as the sacred image of how intensely God desires to be with us?"

"I don't," Gary thought to himself. He kept waiting for the steel fist that he assumed was hidden in this velvet glove, but it never came.

"In all the Gospel stories touching on sexuality and sexual sin—encounters with prostitutes, the woman taken in adultery, and so on—Jesus is amazingly uninterested in punishment. Nor is he interested in punishing us, but rather in renewing and deepening relationship, in forgiveness and in love," Linda said.

But, she added, "the Incarnate One tells us that complete intimacy, abiding in love and in God, is inseparable from total, permanent commitment—the kind of commitment that Christ makes to us. . . . Genital intimacy between human beings, like Christ's intimacy with us, is most authentic when it is the expression of a total gift of self in a context of permanent, abiding commitment.

"It is God's desire to live in intimate union, to abide with us," she said. "Our intimacy with one another is a sacred image, an icon of that divine desire. And so we must order it properly and honor it greatly. For you who abide in love abide in God, and God abides in you."

It was a wonderful reflection, Gary thought as the service continued. Without wavering from Catholic orthodoxy, without challenging the ban on artificial birth control or suggesting the legitimacy of premarital sex, Linda had taken a small step toward giving Catholics a new way to think about themselves as sexual beings.

He confessed his sins to one of the priests stationed around the church, then walked to the altar where Linda was quietly greeting penitents. "I liked what you said," he told her.

A few minutes later as he hurried toward his car, Gary began contemplating his responsibility in creating the more humane and understanding church that Linda had evoked. He realized that he and other quiescent Catholics were counting on the hierarchy to one day strip itself of power, and that this was unlikely, to say the least. Yet, when he imagined taking a concrete step, such as joining Ray McGovern's protest, he was filled with fear.

Perhaps if he spoke out on one issue, he would feel compelled to speak out on others. Then his relationship with the Church would become a source of anguish rather than a source of sustenance. He would lose the light and luminous feeling that he had carried from the reconciliation service, a feeling that was his only after sex and after church.

Slipping into his car, Gary realized that he had come to regard silence on sexual issues as the price he paid for being a Catholic. And though he regretted the expenditure, he did not consider it too high.

CHAPTER NINE

⟨≈≈≈⟩

The people of Holy Trinity did not see much of the men from the archdiocese in the weeks after the open forum. Bishop Corrada and the others were supposedly researching a report which would be used in matching the community with its new pastor, but aside from Monsignor English, who interviewed a few staff members and committee leaders, none of them ever returned to the parish.

The casual quality of the investigation led a few hopeful souls to suggest that perhaps Cardinal Hickey and his advisors were not so concerned about Holy Trinity after all. Others were aware that Bishop Corrada maintained a file of complaints about the parish, and they began to wonder if the archdiocese was cultivating independent sources of information. There would be no way of knowing until the committee released its report.

In the interim, Father Maier hoped that his parishioners' anxieties would abate sufficiently for the community to come to terms with the Standing. Drawing on his background as a spiritual director, Jim had decided that Holy Trinity would *discern* its way out of trouble. By mid-November, his plan had just begun to take shape.

First, Shannon Jordan, who arranged the Sunday morning lectures, would put together a series on the nature of the priesthood, the nature of the liturgy and the issue of women's ordination. This would be followed by a "town meeting" at which parishioners could discuss their feelings about sexism and the protest. By spring, Jim hoped that the standers and their opponents—freshly educated and steeped in parish sentiment—would be meeting once again to forge a compromise.

In the meantime, he occasionally wore the light blue ribbon on his lapel, though not when he was meeting with people whom he knew it would upset.

A number of parishioners were not keen on this new plan. One was Mike Hall, a tall, bespectacled man in his early fifties who bore himself with the rectitude of the Navy pilot he had once been. Mike was a member of the Parish Council and the 9:15 liturgy planning team. He was just finishing a term as chairman of the parish's Administrative Committee, and had definite opinions about the nature of the problems at Holy Trinity.

As much as he respected Father Maier as a priest, Mike found him lacking as an executive. Jim was so reticent about making his own opinion known, Mike thought, that he had created a vacuum of leadership which various Jesuits, staff members and parishioners competed to fill. In an effort to govern by consensus, he listened to a great many voices, but seemed incapable of rejecting even the most extreme. As a result, every decision at Holy Trinity felt tentative; little was ever settled.

In Mike's eyes Jim's handling of the Standing was no different, but this time more was at stake. Mike feared that the lectures and town meeting would further divide the parish and provoke the archdiocese, but he had failed to persuade Father Maier of this; the necessity for dialogue was one issue on which Jim would not yield.

Mike's apprehension was shared by a number of parishioners who had begun to suspect that Holy Trinity's willingness to address its divisions and confront the issues vexing the American church were being used against it by its ecclesial adversaries. This suspicion was especially strong among Anna Thompson and some of her friends, who had recently weathered a series of controversies over the sexual content of the CCD curriculum.

On a Sunday morning the previous October, the parents of seventh- and eighth-grade CCD students had assembled at Holy Trinity School to hear Anna, Father Ed Dougherty and Susan Keys, a counselor at the school, outline a program called "Good Choices: Making Moral Decisions in Today's World." The program had been designed by Susan, who in two years as a seventh-grade catechist had been struck by her students' need for a healthy understanding of their awakening sexuality.

The kids had never come right out and admitted their curiosity. They were too embarrassed for that. But Susan could tell from the tenor of their awkwardly worded questions about "honesty," "relationships" and "independence" that they were frightened and fascinated by their changing bodies.

The students were thirteen years old. The boys' voices had cracked and deepened. The girls wore bras. Most had already tasted their first kiss. Of course they wanted to talk about sex.

But Susan was not sure what she could tell them in the context of a CCD class. Should she explain Church doctrine? Roman authority? And if so, should she mention that this doctrine was disputed?

Many of the children were no doubt aware that their parents practiced birth control. A perusal of the medicine cabinet could have told them that much. Perhaps they had a relative who remarried without obtaining an annulment. Maybe an older sibling was living with a lover. Susan did not want to misrepresent Church teaching, but neither did she want her students marching home to tell their loved ones that they were lousy Catholics.

Instead, she answered their questions as obliquely as the children had asked them, hoping that a few reassuring words like "respect," "judgment" and "integrity" would pacify the class until she had a chance to give the matter more thought.

Susan, a sunny, seemingly imperturbable woman with curly brown hair and dark eyes, had a personality almost perfectly suited for her work as a counselor. Her zest made children feel she was one of them, yet her even temperament conveyed authority and good judgment. There was, perhaps, no one more knowledgeable about the emotional lives of the parish's children.

She began work on what became the Good Choices Program by reflecting on the sexual and moral education that she had received as a junior high school student some thirty years earlier. "What there was in my school was the pastor coming in and telling us what not to do," she said one rainy autumn afternoon in her basement office in the upper school. "And that's all I remember. That and the focus on what was bad."

But focusing on what was bad no longer did the trick. For one thing, the Church taught that human sexuality was a gift from God. For another, intimidation is not what it used to be.

Circumstance and society have conspired to reduce the influence of priests and even parents on the sexual behavior of recent generations. Today many young Catholics leave home after high school, but may not marry for more than a decade. In the intervening years they are bombarded with erotic imagery by the sex-saturated media, have easy access to reliable birth control and live in a culture which assumes that virginity beyond, say, eighteen years of age, is symptomatic of some psychic deficiency. Susan hoped to blend her insights into adolescent psychology with the Church's insights into the sacred nature of human sexuality, and give these young men and women a capacity for making sound moral decisions that would endure long after curiosity and opportunity had gotten the better of fear.

The issues she was dealing with could hardly have been more delicate. How does one explain to children that sex is the gift of a benevolent God while simultaneously persuading them not to fully unwrap the package until after they are married? What, if anything, should she say about condoms, which were forbidden by the Church but which might, one day, save a student's life? How should she treat homosexuality, a subject on which she found Church teaching not merely intellectually impoverished but potentially harmful to teenagers struggling with their sexual identities?

The traditional approach to this material was simply to explain what the Church taught and to brook no disagreement: anything beyond chaste kissing was sinful before marriage; anything besides potentially procreative intercourse was sinful afterward; homosexual activity was always wrong.

But this approach, to Susan's mind, required an especially docile class and a particularly authoritarian teacher. It gave kids no forum in which to talk through their feelings with an understanding adult, and left those with questions at the mercy of less sensitive and reliable informants.

Her own approach, as she explained it that night, was devised in collaboration with Father Ed, who provided the theological expertise, and

Anna, who worked on the implementation. Standing near a blackboard at the front of the room, Susan led the intent and somewhat uneasy parents through a long course of questions which she had devised to lead their children to make a moral choice.

"The first thing we ask children to ask themselves is, 'Who am I called to be as a Christian?' " she told them. Answering that question required answering a series of others: Who was Jesus? How did they relate to him? What did he ask of them?

None of these could be answered without knowledge of the New Testament, Susan said. The challenge for teachers and parents alike was to help young people integrate the example of Jesus into their daily lives. This required an additional three-step process.

"We ask them to examine their motives, their values and the potential consequences," she said. "Then we ask them to seek advice. That especially includes their parents and the teachings of the Church. Thirdly, they should pray."

The parents had few questions, none of them hostile, and as she sat down, Susan couldn't help feeling that her presentation had gone off without a hitch. The Good Choices Program was a long way from the old Baltimore Catechism, but she was sure that the people of Holy Trinity, many of whom had participated in similar choice-making exercises on their jobs, would have little trouble accepting it.

Susan was followed on the program by Father Dougherty, who began his presentation by sketching a continuum on the blackboard. Few people were 100 percent heterosexual or 100 percent homosexual, he told the group, and the nature and intensity of one's attractions sometimes shifted during one's lifetime. The core of Trinity's teaching on the subject, he said, would be that children should value their sexual orientation as a gift from God, no matter what they believed it to be. He did not suggest they were free to act on this orientation, but that was how a number of parents perceived his remarks.

One well-dressed gentleman thrust up his hand and asked with some agitation what role "On the Pastoral Care of Homosexual Persons," Cardinal Ratzinger's 1986 letter on the issue of homosexuality, would play in Trinity's presentation. This letter said, among other things, that in an effort to extend pastoral care to homosexual persons, many in the Church had become unduly tolerant of homosexual activity, and that such tolerance fostered sinful conduct.

Ed gave his typical response to a loaded moral question. Respected theologians held divergent points of view on the matter, he said. What was important was teaching the children to "form their consciences" and come to a proper understanding of their own sexuality.

But this emphasis on conscience did not satisfy a number of parents who wanted a clearer condemnation of homosexuality. "Ed was telling them, 'Don't worry about what you are. Whatever you are is a gift from God,' " said one concerned father. "He was encouraging them to stay at a point in their life where they *may be* bisexual."

A series of tense exchanges ensued, and Susan watched helplessly from her seat at the front of the room. The problem, she felt, was not Ed's explanation but in the nature of Church teaching. "When you teach that sexuality is a gift, and that homosexual orientation is not sinful, but the activity is, there is an inconsistency there," she said later. "I don't know how to bridge that for kids. All you can do is say, 'Yes, there is an inconsistency there.' "

But a small clutch of parents had definite ideas about dealing with this contradiction. They wanted teachers to tell their classes that a homosexual orientation was sinful (though this was explicitly not what the Church taught) and that those who felt so inclined were obligated to change.

"We thought that was extreme," Susan said dryly.

The meeting ended civilly enough. Everyone agreed that further conversations might help clarify the matter. But Susan, Ed and Anna left the meeting wondering whether a second group of conservative parents might be planning to challenge the curriculum of the CCD program.

⌒⌒⌒

The man who had led the first campaign against the Good Choices program was Peter Schaumber, a dark-haired, blue-eyed Washington lawyer. He had been an active parishioner for more than twenty years, and was a former member of the Parish Council, and an admirer of Father Maier and his pastorial predecessor Father Jim Connor.

Peter's concern about the CCD program had been piqued a few years earlier when he learned that his eldest daughter, then a junior high school student, did not know what a sacrament was. Or that there were seven of them. It intensified on the evening of his son's Confirmation when the boy was unable to tell him the meaning of the word "grace."

To his mind, the CCD program had substituted liberal platitudes for Catholic truth and was turning out children who were "religiously illiterate." He was tired of hearing priests, catechists and program directors extol the virtues of "love" and "service," and eager to hear someone spell out the teachings of the magisterium. He had had his fill of what Father Dougherty referred to as "conscience formation," and wanted his children to learn some rules. He looked to the Church as moral bulwark, and to its teachings as a sort of armor his children could wear into a vice-ridden world. But Holy Trinity had ceased forging that armor and was sending Catholic kids off fortified with nothing more than compassionate impulses. It was not enough.

"There are a lot of sixties' hippies at Trinity," he said one evening on the patio of his home in northwest D.C. "They say, 'Isn't is just best that the kids love each other?' But look around. We are beginning to see what happens when Church teaching is ignored: illegitimate births, suicide, depression, divorce. Everybody says our society is in crisis. You have to ask yourself why."

Concerned for the moral development of their children, the Schaumbers and a few like-minded parents had banded together and contacted Jim Maier in the fall of 1990, requesting a review of the CCD program.

Jim wasn't sure what to make of their request. He trusted Anna's abilities, and he understood that the Schaumbers' views were well to the right of his own. Yet if he was serious about seeking the wisdom of the laity, he had to include the conservative laity, and so he turned the matter over to the CCD board, the committee of parents who had been elected by other parents to oversee the program.

On one level the debate that ensued was over whether the CCD program should be guided by the neo-scholastic philosophy which is popular in the papally-charted theology schools in Rome, or the more inductive contemporary theology dominant in many American graduate schools. The former system, which builds an intricate prescriptive edifice on the assumptions at the core of the Catholic faith, was championed by the Schaumbers and their ally Diane Irving, a professor of philosophy at the DeSales School of Theology in Washington, who had children in the CCD program. The latter, which emphasizes a personal response to the prompting of the Holy Spirit and emulation of the biblical Christ, was defended by Anna Thompson and the CCD Board.

Anna had grown up in New Zealand among Catholics who never questioned their faith, and in her opinion, never practiced it either. They were well-schooled in the kind of Catholic apologetics Peter Schaumber wanted her to teach her students, but their lives, to Anna, suggested that they were barely Christian.

"They beat up their wives and their children," she said. "They steal and they cheat and they lie. They exploit their employees. Where is the evidence we have heard the good news of Jesus Christ? If you talk Kingdom language, the Kingdom isn't becoming real."

One of the reasons, she believed, was that the Church remained a repressive institution. "The authority question is at the heart of most of our dilemmas," she said one day over lunch in a basement restaurant a block from the parish center. "Leadership style, authority, power is central to what most people's experience of this church is."

Under John Paul II, that experience, she said, was of a clerical class more interested in preserving its own power than in leading people to a deeper relationship with Christ. Her critics charged that Anna was trying to foment dissent, but she replied that questioning Church doctrine was an act of fidelity to the Gospel.

As the Council fathers had proclaimed in *Gaudium et Spes*: "Let it be recognized that all of the faithful, clerical and lay, possess a lawful freedom of inquiry and of thought, and the freedom to express their minds humbly and courageously about those matters in which they enjoy competence."

At Holy Trinity adult believers had always enjoyed a certain latitude. But that didn't clear up the question of what the parish should teach its children. For there is a clear distinction between tolerating dissent and propagating it. And the Schaumbers felt Holy Trinity was doing the latter.

"The 'go inside your heart stuff'—all that is wonderful at our age," Kathy Schaumber said. "But I was alarmed that our children were becoming seventh-grade liberals."

But if the Schaumbers and their allies were alarmed that catechists might allow discussion of a sexual ethic at odds with Church teaching, a much larger contingent feared that the parish might discourage children from taking steps to prevent a pregnancy or reduce their exposure to HIV.

Initially, Peter won the sympathy of a few board members with his critique of the program's academic standards. He pointed out that children never had homework and weren't actually expected to learn anything on which they could be tested. He argued that the parish's reliance on volunteer teachers made the quality of instruction uneven, and he charged that the program did little more than foster good feelings among the children.

Anna countered that almost all CCD programs relied on volunteers and that her teachers were excellent role models who did as much as was possible in the twenty-five, forty-five minute sessions that made up the CCD school year. It was unrealistic to speak of giving tests and homework to children who were already under great academic pressure. Besides, she said, the connection between academic achievement and living a Christian life seemed fairly tenuous to her.

The debate over prayer was perhaps the best illustration of what was at issue. The archdiocesan guidelines, which Peter and his supporters largely endorsed, specified that children were to be taught the Lord's Prayer, the Hail Mary, even the Memorare, a now fairly obscure prayer of petition to the Blessed Virgin. Anna and her teachers believed such prayers should be taught in the home. In the classroom, conversations about prayer tended to focus on helping children express their feelings to God.

"We probably have a lot of kids who don't know those prayers," Susan Keys admitted. "But is their objective that they learn the prayers or that they learn how to pray? I don't think we have any kids who don't know how to pray."

Still, others felt that a few memorized pieties could be a great help in times of trouble, and there were parents who were open to forging some sort of compromise between the two sides. An effort to focus children's attention on the touchstones of Catholic tradition might have been successful. But as his engagement with the CCD board deepened, and his frustration with Anna Thompson increased, Peter began to speak of bringing a more conservative tone to the entire parish enterprise. He also talked of driving out staff members whose views differed from his own.

"There are a couple of people with real axes to grind who are in positions of staff who shouldn't be there," he said. "When I hear those people attacking that which is part of me in a self-righteous way, and not a very knowledgeable way, I get upset.

"It's still a hierarchical church. We are all obligated to follow the teaching of the magisterium."

The longer the board met with the Schaumbers, the more uncomfortable its members became with their views. Father Joe Sobierajski, an assistant pastor who took quiet issue with elements of Anna's curriculum, said that Peter and his allies were being unrealistic, that they wanted "a first-through-twelfth-grade Catholic school education of the 1950s."

In the end, no satisfactory compromise was possible. The CCD program went into schism, and in the fall of 1991, the Schaumbers, the Irvings and a few other families began holding class for their high school-aged children in the Schaumbers' living room.

Peter's two younger children remained in the CCD program at Holy Trinity, however, and he was in the audience when Susan and Ed explained the Good Choices curriculum. His presence may have intensified the staff's concerns about a second parent uprising, but Peter was too busy administering his newly-founded religious education program to take on another cause.

A few weeks after the presentation a small group of parents meet with Susan Keys and a few other staff members to discuss their reservations about the Good Choices curriculum. A review of Church teaching on homosexuality helped persuade most of the group that the Vatican did not consider the homosexual condition sinful in itself, and that the Church did not obligate homosexual Catholics to somehow alter their orientation. The parents also received assurances that abstinence would be the cornerstone of Holy Trinity's sexual teachings.

The tension engendered by the Good Choices program quietly dissipated, but the ensuing peace was short-lived. Later that year, the CCD board approved Ed and Susan's recommendation to sponsor a performance of "Secrets," a play that had been developed by Kaiser-Permanente, the giant health management organization, to educate teens about the danger of AIDS. And because the second-best way to prevent the spread of AIDS is by using a condom—a violation of the Church's ban on artificial birth control—the staff at Trinity had to devise a way to deal with this dilemma.

Ed, Susan and several board members had attended a performance and were impressed by the frankness and sensitivity of what they saw. They read the instructional material prepared by the company and developed a presentation to put the performance in what Susan calls "a Catholic context." Then, as they always did before sessions on sexuality, the teachers called a meeting of parents to discuss what they were about to present in class.

It was a lively but friendly session. Parents wanted some assurance that abstinence was the principal thrust of the parish's message, and they received it. The performance which followed was so successful that parishioners with children in a suburban Virginia school district persuaded officials to present *Secrets* in several schools.

At last, Susan thought, a balance had been struck. But Cardinal Hickey disagreed. After his religious education advisors had reviewed the program, he banned it from archdiocesan schools. Hickey also made it clear that he wanted no discussion of artificial birth control in the schools' "family life" curriculums. His decision created an excruciating dilemma for Catholic school principals throughout the archdiocese, one of whom was Ann Marie Santora of Holy Trinity.

Ann Marie is a tall, silver-haired woman with large, light eyes. In twenty-five years as principal she has built Holy Trinity School into one of the better elementary schools in the city, Catholic or otherwise. But resolving the moral issue at the core of the sex education controversy nearly exhausted her considerable diplomatic skills.

"I told Cardinal Hickey, you are tying our hands behind our backs," she said one day in her office on the first floor of the upper school. "I think Catholic schools should promote Church teaching. On the other hand, we have to be realistic enough to know that all kids are not going to buy what we are saying.

"I have on the one hand Church teachings, and on the other hand the moral responsibility for the life and safety of the child. Right now we are in the middle of a huge dilemma. I don't know if Cardinal Hickey just doesn't understand where kids are."

To wrestle with the problem, she had appointed parents and teachers to a Sexuality Committee. "We had a wide range of views," she said. "We had conservative Catholics and we had liberal Jews."

Father Dougherty gave a workshop on the Church's sexual teaching and spoke, as he often did, about conscience formation. But Ann Marie didn't think this approach was useful. "These are children," she said. "Dissent in conscience is okay for adults, but these kids aren't at that point yet."

As part of its deliberations the committee had considered the hypothetical case of a thirteen-year-old girl who told her teacher that she was sexually active. Suppose the teacher knew her attempts to dissuade the girl from this conduct had failed: Could the teacher tell the girl to make sure her lover used a condom?

No, the group had decided, but the teacher could suggest that the girl speak to someone at Planned Parenthood.

The committee's solution to teaching about contraception was also—fittingly—jesuitical. In science class students could be taught that ways exist to inhibit conception. In religion they would be taught that almost all of these methods were forbidden to them. When the school was preparing to teach these subjects, it would alert parents so they could give their children information about condoms and other methods of birth control if they so chose.

"Some of the parents are uncomfortable with it," Ann Marie said. "You can't mandate they talk to their kids. But if every parent who has a problem will talk to me or Susan Keys I think we will do okay."

Jim Maier liked to believe that the passionate debates that sometimes erupted in his parish over the Church's sexual doctrine were evidence of how seriously Holy Trinity took its responsibility to apply the teachings of Jesus, and the insights of his people, to the exigencies of the modern world. But archidiocesan officials, who received occasional reports on the controversies at Holy Trinity from disgruntled parishioners, thought otherwise. In their view, lay Catholics were not supposed to shape Church teaching, they were supposed to obey it. And they interpreted Trinity's efforts to devise its own religious education programs as an unwillingness to support Catholic orthodoxy.

Among those who articulated this conservative critique of the parish most forcefully was an archdiocesan priest named Peter Vaghi. Father Vaghi, a lawyer and former Senate staff member, was one of the brightest of the archdiocesan clergy. He had entered the seminary in his early thirties, studied in Rome and returned to a series of prominent assignments. With his dark good looks and meticulous personal style, he made a lasting, if rather forbidding impression on lay people. His clerical peers respected his intellect and his zeal, and they feared his abilities as an infighter. He was almost certainly episcopal material.

Though he had been raised in the parish and had graduated from a Jesuit high school, Father Vaghi was troubled by the freedom which lay people enjoyed at Holy Trinity. He complained so vigorously about the parish within clerical circles that several Jesuits suspected that he wanted the pastorate for himself. Though this was merely conjecture, one thing was certain: as a member of the priests' personnel board, he would play an influential role in choosing Jim Maier's successor.

Father Vaghi was moderator of the John Carroll Society, and Peter Schaumber was among its members. The two sometimes talked theology, and Peter found these conversations most rewarding, for he found in Father Vaghi a rigor he thought missing from his home parish.

"There isn't a great deal of deep theological, philosophical thinking at Holy Trinity," Peter liked to say. "People are thirsting for that. There is a lot of fuzzy thinking."

But what Peter saw as fuzzy thinking, others saw as a frank difference in theological points of view. Peter's own theological education had been recent and informal, absorbed from Diane Irving and books by the conservative theologian Peter Kreeft. It differed significantly from what Margaret Costello, Anna Thompson and others were being taught at the Washington Theological Union; from what a few dozen parishioners had learned in the certificate program at Georgetown University, and what members of the Working Groups were reading in Sister Elizabeth Johnson's *She Who Is*.

Holy Trinity was certainly not immune from "fuzzy thinking." Many parishioners knew just enough theology to be dangerous. Yet compared with other parishes, the level of theological literacy at Holy Trinity was extremely high.

"The question is, does one feel that by going to Holy Trinity one is freeing one's self of limits?" Peter said.

Perhaps one did. Perhaps that was why so many fled their own parishes for the Jesuit church. Perhaps that was why parents drove such distances on Sunday morning to bring their children to its CCD program. The broader question was whether that attitude was legitimate.

Is being faithful the same thing as being obedient? And can a parish that says no to this question survive?

CHAPTER TEN

On most evenings that fall, Jim and his Jesuit colleagues gathered in the tranquillity of their community room on the second floor of the stately brick rectory. Lined with bookshelves and furnished with deep couches, the room opened on to a simply furnished sun porch, where they could share a few drinks and enjoy the dwindling daylight before descending to the dining room a story below.

The company was small but distinguished. Besides Jim, it included Fathers Jerry Campbell, former president of Georgetown University; William Byron, former president of the Catholic University of America; Larry Madden, founder of a liturgical think tank; Joe Sobierajski, an accomplished sculptor and Joe Lacey, who had spent two decades teaching and working with orphans and lepers in India. Like most priestly communities, the group was rather old. Only the newly ordained Father Brendan Horan was under fifty.

Each evening the men waited to begin dinner until the celebrant of the 5:30 mass had returned from the church. In the meantime they talked of sports and politics, of Jesuit friends and parish personalities. By an unwritten rule, they avoided controversy for the sake of good fellowship. The Standing was not something they spoke often of, yet each of them realized that Holy Trinity was under critical scrutiny, and that this meant they were under scrutiny, too.

The Society of Jesus had become accustomed to suspicion during the papacy of John Paul II. The pope believed that under Pedro Arrupe, the Jesuits' superior general from 1965 to 1983, the order had become dangerously independent. Its seminaries, in the pope's eyes, were places of theological speculation; its priests had been seduced by secular ideologies; its parishes were havens for reformers and malcontents.

When Arrupe was incapacitated by illness in 1983, John Paul took the extraordinary step of refusing to authorize a temporary transfer of power to the Jesuit's vicar general Father Vincent O'Keefe. Nor would the pope accept Arrupe's resignation, which would have allowed the Society to choose a new general. Instead, he imposed his own interim vicar who served for a year, until the chastened Jesuits were allowed to select a new leader.

The Society's liberalism and the pope's displeasure with its views have earned the order enemies in the American Church. "In seminary culture there is this hatred for the Jesuits," said a Washington pastor who admires the Society. "We learned to hate what they did and what they stood for, except for the few ultraconservative ones out at the University of San Francisco."

Antipathy, in many cases, was exacerbated by envy. The Society operates twenty-eight colleges and universities in the United States, and its priests enjoy a reputation as the Church's intellectual elite. As a result, Jesuit parishes are frequently magnets for well-educated and affluent Catholics who might otherwise worship in diocesan churches.

This is particularly true of Holy Trinity, where roughly one of every three adults holds a graduate degree, one in ten is a lawyer, and scores are influential in politics, commerce, academia, law or the media. Though 70 percent reside within the boundaries of other parishes, each Sunday they flock to the Jesuit church.

"Holy Trinity has sucked the marrow of progressive Catholicism," the Washington pastor said. "They've gotten the crème de la crème of the Catholic intelligentsia on the Left, and maybe even some folks on the Right. That combination of money and brains, they've got most of it."

The parish's popularity is particularly vexing to archdiocesan clergy who had studied in Rome and returned wearing their contempt for the Jesuits as a sign of fealty to the pope. In the late 1980s these men developed a critique of Holy Trinity that took hold in conservative circles and was soon being voiced by priests who had seldom set foot in the church.

"They are people who are extremely educated, but they do not know the teachings of the Church," said one Roman-educated cleric. He described the parish's liturgies as "avant-garde"; its religious education programs as "all social work and no Jesus"; its groups for single and divorced Catholics as "more like pickup places than the bars."

Contributing to these problems was Father Maier's desire to "be everybody's buddy." Jim did not realize that having friends among the laity was a luxury that priests could not afford. "When people pull that with me," the cleric said, "I tell them, I am not here to be your friend; I am here to be your priest."

The Jesuits at Holy Trinity scoffed at most of the conservative critique. They found the comments about the liturgy and the meetings of single and divorced parishioners particularly absurd. Yet a few of the men wished that Jim had done more to cool the passion of the parish's ideological foes.

Father Madden had privately advocated strong measures against the Standing, and Father Sobierajski had urged Jim to devote more time to his relationship with the cardinal. It was dangerous, they told him, for the parish to be perceived as a community of provocateurs.

For most of his pastorate, Jim could count on Father Ed Dougherty to articulate the opposing view. Ed believed that the Jesuits at Holy Trinity should be less deferential to ecclesial authority and more responsive to the needs of the community. By late November, however, Ed was gone, and his ministry was being used by the parish's adversaries as evidence that Holy Trinity was out of control.

But when Jim reflected on his young friend's departure, he saw it less as a judgment on himself and the Society than as an illustration of the forces pulling apart the American priesthood.

Ed had entered the Jesuit novitiate in the summer of 1975, just one month after his high school graduation. For the next twelve years he studied at Jesuit universities, taught at Jesuit schools and lived in Jesuit communities. His assignment to Holy Trinity, after his ordination in 1987, offered him his first sustained exposure to the life of the laity.

To Ed, the parish seemed a perfect fit. He knew from previous visits that it was a dynamic community. There would always be something to do, somewhere to go, some way of escaping the creeping sense of isolation he had begun to feel as a Jesuit.

Upon his arrival, he thrust himself into parish life, taking on a steady succession of responsibilities and spending few of his waking hours in the rectory. Jim Maier admired his colleague's energy and his generosity, but he wondered whether Ed was seeking a sort of sustenance that the priesthood could not provide.

In the days before the Second Vatican Council, Catholics tended to regard their priests as emotionally self sufficient, existing beyond the need for more companionship than could be found with their fellow priests. The clergy, to a lesser extent, regarded themselves in the same way. Their social lives consisted of visiting their relatives and catching up with seminary classmates. Beyond that, there was work, prayer and the few parish families who would invite Father for dinner now and again.

This isolation took a tremendous toll in bitterness, depression and alcoholism, but it diminished the clergy's exposure to sexual temptation. The boundary between priest and people was clearly drawn in those days, and both sides took pains to observe it. Then came the Second Vatican Council, and though it did not tear down this wall, it did build a few gates.

After the Council, seminary professors began urging their charges to move among the people as Jesus had, to experience the joy and suffering of human relationships, to live more fully so that they might minister more fully. This teaching, enlightened in many ways, was short-sighted in others. For the more young priests learned of intimacy, the more they questioned why they could not experience it in its physical form.

For centuries Catholics had assumed that their priests could not marry because sexual intercourse was inherently corrupting, a surrender to base desires that left a man unfit to celebrate the Eucharist. But the Second Vatican Council had taken pains to correct this notion. Making love, under the approved circumstances, was a sacred experience, one that exalted rather than degraded.

This teaching was a boon to the married laity, but it sowed confusion among priests. If sexual activity was not corrupting in and of itself, then why did they have to abstain from it?

The hierarchy's responses were multiple and not wholly satisfying.

Some church leaders argued that priests had to be at their bishop's disposal and therefore could have no dependents, but this ignored that in other denominations husband-and-wife teams frequently took on missionary work, and that in the corporate world married executives were frequently transferred. Others contended that a wife and children would divert a man from the needs of his flock, but it can as easily be argued that family life would bind a priest, through common experience, to the families in his care. Other defenders of celibacy maintained that it was necessary to symbolize the totality of a priest's commitment to God. But for most Catholics it was in giving, not abstaining, that a priest demonstrated his devotion to Christ.

Jesus had called married Apostles, the opponents of mandatory celibacy pointed out. And priests had been allowed to marry until roughly the eleventh century. If a married clergy was permissible then, why was it not permissible in the contemporary Church?

Many Catholics perceived the Vatican's refusal to reconsider this teaching as evidence that the hierarchy had never truly abandoned its belief that sexual intercourse was inherently corrupting. Perhaps more troubling was the fact that it signaled Rome's intention to maintain a monopoly on ecclesial authority. For by forbidding priests to marry, the hierarchy ensured its preeminence in their emotional lives, and prolonged the survival of a ruling caste.

Energized by the reforms of the Council, however, the American laity began demanding the right to participate more fully in the life of their parishes, and initially many priests were eager to assist. But as time wore on priests found themselves facilitating their own diminution. If Father was no longer the authority on all things spiritual, then what exactly was he? A social worker? A parish administrator? A sacramental functionary?

The release of *Humanae Vitae* in 1968 exacerbated clerical alienation. Many priests regarded it as Tom Gavigan had, as a theological mistake, a pastoral nightmare and a betrayal of the ideals of Vatican II. They could neither defend it nor, most felt, resist it. The encyclical introduced an element of hypocrisy into their ministries, making it impossible for them to speak frankly on issues of sexual conduct or papal authority.

The combination of fallout from the Council and disillusionment with the encyclical was more than many priests could bear. According to figures reported by the late Richard A. Schoenherr in his book, *Full*

Pews, Empty Altars, more than 4,600 American Catholic priests resigned from the priesthood between 1966 and 1974, a loss of almost eight percent of the Church's clerical workforce in the United States.

At this moment of historic confusion, the American Church was also beginning to realize the price of its people's prosperity. Before World War II, entering the seminary was the only way for many Catholic boys to escape a life circumscribed by the necessities of industry. But by the late 1940s, the percentage of priests and seminarians in the Catholic population had begun to fall, thanks in part to the passage of the G.I. bill, which opened higher education to unprecedented millions. Between 1965 and 1975, the number of seminarians in the United States dropped almost 64 percent, from nearly forty-nine thousand to fewer than eighteen thousand.

Ed Dougherty knew he was choosing a vocation in a state of incipient crisis. Yet he, like many young men who entered seminaries in the 1970s, believed he understood the role of the clergy in the new Church. Its task was to call the faithful more deeply into discipleship, to advance the democratization of the Church, and to discern with the community how the Holy Spirit was shaping its life.

But John Paul II, who assumed the papacy while Ed was still an undergraduate, had radically different notions. He was intent on maintaining sharp distinctions between priests and lay people and protecting the functions of the former from encroachment by the latter. Essential to his effort was the restoration of a vigorous and self-conscious clerical caste.

In Washington, the priests who rallied to this cause became known by their critics as the "take back the Church guys." To Father Dougherty their ascendancy in the late 1980s signaled the decline of the communal ideals which had led him into the priesthood, and he was determined to resist.

During graduate school Ed had heard female classmates speak of their thwarted priestly ambitions, and he had embraced their cause as his own. At Holy Trinity he collaborated with Mary Rita Weiners to render prayers and readings in inclusive language. He spoke during the Mass of a "Mother-Father God," and at one liturgy on a CCD retreat he allowed a woman to raise the chalice at the end of the eucharistic prayer—a function the rubrics restricted to the ordained.

Some parishioners suggested that Father Dougherty was playing a bit fast and loose with the rules, but he did not see it that way. "The Roman Catholic Church today is a church of many voices," he liked to tell people. "On some issues respected theologians and bishops would teach one thing, and other bishops would teach a different kind of thing. It sort of depends on how you interpret the documents."

Ed's interpretations were always rather liberal, and Jim occasionally found himself explaining the young priest's behavior to indignant parishioners or suspicious archdiocesan officials. But aside from the battle over the Good Choices Program, none of Ed's activities had prompted extended archdiocesan scrutiny, and Jim was happy to protect him, for few priests had Father Dougherty's ability to draw the alienated back into the Church.

Ed's leniency, his compassion and his gentle intensity made him a popular confessor and spiritual director, especially among female parishioners. By the end of his third year at Holy Trinity, he was spending almost half his time giving counsel and hearing confessions. For several hours each day he listened as parishioners complained of their obligations, lamented their obsessions with success and wept over their adulteries, broken marriages and ruined relationships.

At times he found himself overwhelmed by his penitents' sense of guilt, and by his own desire to free them from their torment. Some of what he heard was sinful by even the loosest definition. But much of the anguish, Ed thought, resulted from the scrupulousness of people still frightened by their childhood images of a harsh, judgmental God.

"My general observation would be that people are very good," he said. "They have a strong moral sense and they find themselves worn out by it. One of the things I could do for them was show them that a good choice can sometimes be made when you are doing something different than what the public teaching of the Church is. It kind of gives them permission to be adults."

By the summer of 1991, Ed was beginning to realize that his reservations about Church teaching had implications for his own life.

In the months before his ordination he and his spiritual director had focused primarily on a single question: could he commit himself, irrevocably, to the celibate life? It seemed a rash promise to make. Who could say at the age of 30, or for that matter at 60, that he was prepared to foresake the ecstasies and consolations of romantic intimacy?

Yet, at that time, Ed believed that the companionship of his Jesuit brothers would be enough to bear him along. Now he was beginning to have doubts.

"I often imagined what it would be like to have an intimate relationship, to be married, to have children," he said one day after he had left the parish. "I was very happy in a professional sense, and I found community life as sustaining as community life can be. But I wanted to step beyond that and explore what an intimate relationship would be. I had intimacy needs that weren't being met."

When Ed informed his Jesuit superiors of his turmoil, they arranged for him to undertake a lengthy period of prayerful discernment under the direction of Father Joe Sobierajski. For the next eight months, he tried to determine whether his desire for sexual intimacy and his interest in having a family constituted a new kind of calling, or whether he was simply weathering a rough period in his priesthood.

Occasionally he tried to pursue the matter with Jim Maier, and though Jim was always attentive, he seldom articulated his thoughts about Ed's situation, for fear of unduly influencing the young priest. Privately, however, Jim was increasingly certain that Ed would leave the Jesuits. He knew that Father Dougherty had been born with an experiencing nature, that he craved newness, discovery and rebirth. Sustaining a priestly vocation required that these qualities be balanced by patience, a respect for routine and an enthusiasm for compromise. In Ed's case, they were not.

Unless Father Dougherty quailed at the practical difficulties of leaving the priesthood—such as making a living—he would leave. And Jim knew him well enough to believe that the younger man would not remain a priest out of fear.

In February of 1992, Ed officially requested a leave of absence from the Society of Jesus, and began informing his spiritual directees of his decision. He asked them to keep the news to themselves, so that he could continue to preach and preside until he and Jim had worked out the details of his departure. The rest of the parish did not learn that he was leaving until spring, shortly before Ned Hogan gave Ray McGovern his moment in the pulpit.

By that time Ed had some fairly definite plans for his immediate future. A few years earlier, he had met a woman named Ellen Kerley, a legal recruiter, who volunteered in one of the parish's religious education programs. After a few months of working together, they began to meet occasionally for lunch and dinner, and in time developed what Ed described as a close, but entirely platonic friendship. Ellen's firm had transferred her to Chicago in December of 1991, and Ed, seeking some distance from his ministry on the East Coast, but not wanting to be entirely alone, thought it might be nice to join her there. When he received an offer that spring at a small institute that trained spiritual directors in the Windy City, he jumped at it.

The timing of Ed's and Ellen's departures caused some consternation among a handful of parishioners who believed it was proof that they were romantically involved. A few even boycotted the joint going-away party the parish threw in May for Ed and Ned Hogan, who was leaving for his assignment in Nigeria. It was wrong, they told Jim, to celebrate Father Dougherty's decision to forsake his vows. But Jim disagreed. Ed had requested his leave after intensive prayer and soul-searching. He was doing what he believed God required of him, and there was not shame in that.

Most of the crowd that thronged the gymnasium at Visitation school that night shared this sentiment. Parishioners were effusive in their support of Ed's decision. One Jesuit observed sardonically that they seemed to regard leaving the priesthood as the zenith of a priestly career.

In the slow summer days after Ed's departure, Jim found himself contemplating the calling they had once shared. "God is doing something mysterious with the priesthood," he said one warm afternoon in his office. "We are drying up."

The statistics bore him out. In 1975 there had been one priest for every 1,100 American Catholics. If current trends continue, by the year 2005 there will be one for every 2,200, and the average active American priest will be 52 years old.

Jim was familiar with the most obvious reasons for this decline. Priests were overworked. The emotional demands of their jobs were tremendous and the sources of human support were few. He and his colleagues labored in a Church that was increasingly suspicious of them, and perhaps for good reason, for many dissented from its teachings on sexual issues and emphasized the primacy of conscience in making a moral choice.

Since the Second Vatican Council, the Church had urged them to strike a difficult balance. They were to be compassionate, yet unyielding on doctrine; loving, yet beyond the need for physical intimacy; collegial, yet entirely in command. It was little wonder that so many chose to collapse these tensions—retreating, like some of Holy Trinity's critics, into a remote and authoritarian precouncillar style; or escaping, like Ed, into a world where emotion and impulse had freer rein.

Like most American Catholics, Jim believed that the Church should allow priests to marry and allow women to become priests. But unlike his progressive lay friends, he was not certain that these would be enough to reverse the decline of the American priesthood, for there were factors at work that were beyond the Church's control.

During his lifetime, the distinctive characteristics of his vocation had begun to dwindle. The faithful heard sermons from pundits and talk-show hosts. The troubled sought counseling from therapists, and the needy found succor from social workers. Priests were unique only in their ability to administer the sacraments, and though Jim took great joy in this ministry, he knew that Catholics' allegiance to their rituals was ebbing.

Only 40 percent of the American laity attended mass each Sunday. He doubted whether half as many went to confession more than once or twice a year. And fewer than half still believed that Jesus was truly present in the bread and wine consecrated at the Mass.

Priests were becoming increasingly insignificant to many Catholics, and the priesthood was withering as a result.

To compound the problem, the number of American nuns had also plummeted. There were more than 180,000 women in religious orders in the United States in the mid 1960s, but fewer than 95,000 by 1993. While this precipitous decline did not threaten the viability of Catholic sacramental life, it raised serious questions about who would staff the Church's vast network of schools, hospitals and social service centers. In Jim's view, it was further evidence of the crisis that would envelop American Catholicism if the Vatican did not recognize the importance of granting lay people a greater decision-making role in the Church.

In the face of mounting statistical evidence, however, Rome clung to its belief that the decline in vocations was temporary, and that change in the Church's governing structures was neither necessary nor desirable. Meanwhile, some of Jim's friends on the Catholic left were flirting with what he thought was an equally dangerous delusion, that the Church could somehow survive, united and intact, without a corps of men and women whose mission in life was to make it work.

Both sides, he thought, underestimated the gravity of the situation.

Some time in the first half of the next century the priest shortage would reach a critical point. And what happened next would be anyone's guess.

Perhaps Rome would respond with an avalanche of foreign-born clergy. Or perhaps American congregations would begin ordaining their own priests. Perhaps the American Reformation would come when there were simply too few priests to man the pulpits.

The Standing had been inspired, in part, by parishioners' concerns about the integrity of an all-male priesthood, so perhaps it was a sign that reformation was closer than Jim supposed.

Sometimes that fall, as he contemplated the quality of his own priesthood, Jim wished for the protestors' clarity and their zeal. Without it, he muddled along, trying to reconcile the survival of the parish with his own desire to advance the reform of the Church.

CHAPTER ELEVEN

On the Sunday morning after Thanksgiving, Father Maier donned the deep purple vestments of Advent and slipped out the side door of the sacristy. Though leaves still clung to the young trees that rose from small dirt squares along the sidewalks in Georgetown, the chilly wind presaged the encroaching winter. Perfect, Jim thought. The Christ child had been born as a light into darkness. It would have seemed incongruous to begin preparations for His feast on a bright and balmy morning.

Inside the church the lights burned softly. The processional party was already waiting for him. In the sanctuary, the earthy hues of autumn had given way to the soft green of pines. Beside the altar, four small wreaths rested on brass stands. A white candle jutted from each, three backed by thin purple banners and one by a banner of rose. In a few moments Jim would touch flame to the first candle. On successive Sundays he would repeat this ritual until every wick was alight.

Advent was a time of hope and forbearance, a time for believing, as the ancients had, in the return of a sun now unseen. In that way, Jim thought, the season was a perfect metaphor for the Christian condition. And, at that moment, for the condition of his parish as well.

Three weeks after the open forum, the clerical committee investigating Holy Trinity had yet to release its report, and parishioners believed that no news was bad news. Jim, who understood the geologic pace at which ecclesial bureaucracies often moved, was less worried. But he, too, threw himself into the busyness of the season. It helped take the edge off his doubt.

Advent was a tumultuous time at Holy Trinity. There were extra liturgies to be planned—ten on Christmas Eve and Christmas Day alone—music to be rehearsed and a welter of charitable activities to be coordinated.

At Holy Trinity, the third Sunday of Advent was known as Toy Sunday. Each year on that date, the children of the 9:15 community came to church with presents for the children of the Sursum Corda housing project in Trinity's local sister parish, St. Aloysius Gonzaga. Ideally, these gifts were well-loved toys, toys that it was a sacrifice for the children to part with. The notion was that the kids should learn to share from their substance rather than from their surplus. Often, however, the items donated were either newly bought or no longer wanted.

For Jim, Toy Sunday captured all the ambiguities of his affluent parish's relationship with the poor. Materially speaking, the collection was an undeniable success, and the parents at Sursum Corda were always profoundly grateful. Yet Jim worried that the children of his parish were learning that they could buy their way out of sacrifice. Or worse, that what the rich owed the poor was what they planned to discard.

Each year he surrendered these concerns, however, to the joy of the season, the effectiveness of the enterprise, and the cheerful chaos of Toy Sunday itself, when a caravan laden with toys, games, dolls and stuffed animals would depart from the Holy Trinity campus for the project on the other side of town. It was not such a bad thing to allow people to feel that they were being generous, he realized, even if he had questions about whether his parish was generous enough.

To his mind, the people of Holy Trinity, like the people of most Catholic parishes, lacked what St. Ignatius of Loyola, the founder of the Jesuits, had called "spiritual freedom." They were bound by their devotion to an ethic of success, Jim thought, shackled by the assumption that professional fulfillment and economic prosperity were the necessary and sufficient conditions for spiritual growth. Sharing some small portion of their wealth came naturally; contemplating how their success estranged them from the great mass of humanity did not.

His parishioners' unwillingness to examine the moral significance of their privilege frustrated him. It was, perhaps, the parish's great failing. Yet he did not judge the community too harshly, for in his six years at Holy Trinity he had come to realize that he was bound himself—unable to speak his beliefs about women's ordination, homosexuality or the nature of authority within the Church, because of his concerns for the future of the parish and for his priesthood.

If he was to free his parishioners, he realized, he would first have to free himself, and that would require taking risks.

A few weeks earlier Margaret Costello had given him a series of homilies written by Natalie Ganley, who worked on the parish's retreat team. These brief, moving sermons were based on the readings for the first week of Advent. One was derived from Natalie's observation that in calling his first disciples, Jesus had chosen two sets of brothers, as if to emphasize the importance of intimate friendship in revealing the Kingdom of God, and sustaining authentic faith. Another, based on Christ's observation that the Kingdom had been hidden from the learned, but disclosed to the unlettered, suggested that God valued attentiveness more than achievement. And a third told of how Saint Francis Xavier was sustained on his missionary journeys by letters from his Jesuit friends which he sewed into his cassock so they would be close to his heart.

Jim loved Natalie's homilies. He thought the congregation at the eight o'clock weekday masses would love them too, and he was determined that Natalie should deliver them herself. The only question was whether she should speak after the gospel, when priests delivered their homilies, or after the Communion when lay people were sometimes allowed to offer "reflections."

The second would have been the safer choice, but Jim thought that separating the homily from the Scriptures did more violence to the liturgy than allowing a woman to preach. The problem was that giving a woman his pulpit might be interpreted as taunting the archdiocese. But since these were weekday masses and the congregations would be small, Jim believed the archdiocese's reaction would be relatively mild.

And so, on the first Monday in Advent, he read the Gospel, closed the lectionary and introduced the three dozen people in the pews before him to a woman they already knew. Natalie Ganley was short and gray-haired, with blue eyes and gold-rimmed glasses. Her dress was simple and her manner matter-of-fact. She had been baptized at Holy Trinity fifty-five years earlier and educated in the parish school. She and her husband, Fred, were married at the altar beside which she now stood, and Holy Trinity was where her three children had learned their faith.

No one else could have given the eight o'clock community such a keen sense of being addressed by one of their own. That was one of the reasons Jim had decided to take this risk. If parishioners could accept that a person like themselves was capable of interpreting and expounding on the Scriptures, they might feel more comfortable exploring the Bible for themselves.

Natalie's own life was testament to the power of such an exploration. One morning in the late 1960s, she had heard Father Tom Gavigan tell the people who had crowded into his building that *they* were the Church, and she remembers thinking, "Geez, if we are the Church, we better get off our asses."

At Tom's urging she began to read contemporary theologians and found, to her surprise, that they were immediately relevant to her life. "When you have three babies at home and you pick up Teilhard de Chardin and you read, 'Nothing is profane to him who knows how to see,' it gives you a different way of looking at things," she said one morning at her home in Arlington.

A levelheaded woman with a capacious curiosity and a fondness for the fiction of Flannery O'Connor, Natalie soon immersed herself in a study of the Christian spiritual tradition and its parallels in American literature. In 1989 she completed a master's degree in liberal studies with a concentration in literature at Georgetown University. She also wrote articles for Catholic periodicals. One day one of her professors asked if she would like to contribute to a homily service, and Natalie quickly accepted.

Homily services provide priests with anecdotes, insights and other material for their Sunday sermons. In some instances the services supply completed texts which the preacher can tailor to suit his own needs. Within a year of her initial effort, Natalie was contributing both brief reflections and fully-formed homilies to two different services. Her success and that of other female contributors raised an interesting question: If women can write the words that a priest reads from the pulpit, why can't they preach the words themselves?

Preaching is supposed to be a "charism," or power, conferred at ordination. But the power of Natalie's work was evident to anyone who heard it. She had a gift for explaining how the mundane transactions of everyday living were infused with the sacred. She had a style that was literate yet accessible, and she had an implicit understanding for the concerns of the two to four dozen people who drifted into Holy Trinity just before 8:00 A.M. on those wintery weekday mornings.

As he sat listening to her preach and scrutinizing the faces of the men and women in the pews, Jim indulged the small satisfaction of knowing he had done the right thing, and this quiet success sustained him through the holy riot of Advent at Holy Trinity.

On Christmas Eve the church was awash in white light. The altar gleamed like an alabaster clearing in an evergreen forest, and the old Nativity set, with its two-foot-tall figurines, sat on a bed of straw before the tabernacle. The pews were filled with smiling parishioners, their cheeks still bright from the scourging of the wind, cold wafting from their overcoats. When the choir commenced the first carol, even the most self-conscious among them burst into song.

Ray McGovern was not in the church that night, but from the altar Jim could see other parishioners who had been quarreling since the Standing began; all were brimming with the spirit of the season. They had no need for the blazing Advent wreath on that festive night; their darkness had been dispelled; they were celebrating the birth of their Savior. Yet Jim knew that in the fortnight before the feast of the Epiphany their thoughts would return to the future of their parish, and they would look to him for a new reason to be hopeful.

He had resolved to begin the communal discernment that he hoped would end the Standing on the Sunday after the Epiphany. In a lecture after the 9:15 liturgy he would outline exactly what he hoped to accomplish. The text was not yet completed, but he knew its outline by heart.

He would begin with an appreciation of St. Ignatius and his genius for "discerning spirits," or determining the will of God. Ignatius' masterpiece, *The Spiritual Exercises*, had been conceived, at least in part, as a tool for helping individuals make decisions and choose vocations. Its principles could be employed by communities, too. If the people of Holy Trinity would commit themselves to study, prayer, and a true openness to the Holy Spirit, they could solve their problems in a way that would make their parish a light to the fractious American church.

That, at least, is what he was going to say. But as Jim prepared for the parish to begin its discernment, Holy Trinity was about to embark on another project whose outcome would demonstrate the difficulty of fostering conversation on the emotionally charged issues convulsing American Catholicism.

For several years, Holy Trinity had been one of the only parishes in the Archdiocese of Washington that had no coordinator of pro-life activities. Its occasional diocesan-mandated collections for antiabortion activities were always quite low, and in one instance, the archdiocese had simply assessed the parish a higher fee. But after taking a patient approach with the parish for several years, Cardinal Hickey had a representative of the archdiocesan pro-life office call Father Maier in the fall of 1992 and urge him to establish a pro-life presence at Holy Trinity.

The task was perhaps more complicated than the cardinal understood. Holy Trinity is the spiritual home of an unusually large number of single, highly educated, professional women—the demographic group most committed to abortion rights. The parish is also solidly Democratic, and many parishioners have resented the American bishops' none-too-subtle embrace of pro-life Republican presidential candidates. Jim knew that if he did not move carefully, he might start the sort of skirmish that would deepen the divide between Holy Trinity and the archdiocese, and this he was eager to avoid.

As a biologist he believed that human life began the moment that sperm fertilized egg. When else could it begin? But his acceptance of the teaching against abortion was rooted more deeply. Jim believed in a personal God, a God who called each human being into existence and endowed each person's life with dignity and with meaning. Abortion was saying no to the God who had already said yes, and this refusal was permissible in only the rarest of circumstances.

Despite his own convictions, Jim understood the pastoral necessity of speaking gently on abortion. "I know there are people in the congregation who have experienced abortion," he said one afternoon in his office. "Or who know someone who has." And the last person they want to hear discoursing on the issue is a celibate man with no sense of what they went through, he said.

Women who have had abortions are not a visible presence at Holy Trinity—more of a "secret sisterhood," as one of them put it. But some came to Jim for counseling, and he knew that years after their abortions many remained conflicted about the choice they had made and resentful of the Church's condemnation.

One of those women was Theresa Marino*, a slight, olive-skinned pharmaceutical saleswoman who had been in her late thirties on the night several years earlier when she and her husband Paul*, had come to meet with Jim.

Theresa was halfway through the Christian initiation (RCIA) program. After almost ten years of marriage to a Catholic man, and the baptisms of two Catholic sons, she was ready to join the Church herself. Or so she had thought until a few nights earlier when one of the men in her class said: "Abortion is murder, plain and simple, and that's all there is to it."

No one had disputed him, and Theresa sat there thinking, "Well, that makes me a murderer."

She drove home that night feeling condemned, no longer certain she wanted to join the Church and no longer certain the Church would have her. Paul tried to reassure her, to tell her that Catholics held divergent opinions on abortion, but his usually soothing words could not penetrate her pain. She wanted to talk with Father Maier, she told him. She wanted to hear it from an authoritative source.

A few nights later, the Marinos sat in the cluttered intimacy of Father Maier's office. Theresa had always felt comfortable around Jim, but that night she could not stop fidgeting. Paul sat beside her, utterly still, a small, sad smile on his face.

They exchanged only the briefest of pleasantries before Theresa, clasping and unclasping her hands in her lap, made it clear that she was impatient to begin. Jim sat back in his chair, and for a few moments the only sound in the room was the quiet humming of the filter in his fish tank.

Almost twenty years earlier, Theresa began, she had married a doctor named Walter Carr*. They bought a home in suburban Maryland, and a year later she gave birth to their daughter, Patricia*.

Walter drank. Theresa had known that when she married him. She had not known that he continued to sleep with other women, but after their daughter was born he became less concerned about hiding his adultery. Nor had she known that Walter had an amphetamine habit, acquired pulling all-nighters during medical school. The combination of booze and drugs made him violent.

The first time he beat her, Theresa resolved that she would force him to see a psychiatrist. The second, third and fourth times, she reiterated her vow. But Walter was beyond her influence.

If her own life had been the only one at stake, she might have stayed with him indefinitely. But after months of abuse, Theresa realized that she was raising her daughter to believe that domestic violence was normal, and perhaps preparing the child to become a victim of such violence herself.

Her husband seemed to sense that she was planning to leave him. In a drunken rage, he threatened to kill her. Later, cold sober, he bought a gun.

One night, waving his loaded weapon, Walter forced Theresa and Patty into a bedroom, stepped into the hallway, and barricaded the door. Fortunately, the room had a telephone. As Walter screamed threats, Theresa whispered her address to the police. She and Patty were hostages in their own home until squad cars came screaming through their leafy neighborhood and the negotiators persuaded her husband to surrender.

Walter was released from police custody several days later and served with a restraining order to keep him away from the house. That night he swallowed a bottle of prescription sleeping pills, washed them down with whiskey, and died.

"It is horrible to say this," Theresa said, "but it was a great relief when he committed suicide."

She was suddenly a single mother, and one with no immediate prospect of employment. Yet she was free of the fear that had marked her life for four years. "I felt like I was dating for the first time," she said. "Like I was coming out of a cocoon. I had a lot of boyfriends." But none offered her the stability she craved.

Theresa's first job was selling office supplies, and she traveled frequently while friends looked after Patty. On one trip she got stuck for several days in a small town, met a man in a bar, had too much to drink and went to bed with him. She had just recently begun using a diaphragm, and remembers thinking that it did not fit quite properly.

Theresa awoke the next morning in a haze of self-loathing. She was furious with herself for having gone to bed with a stranger, and frightened that she might be pregnant. "It was repulsive to me realizing that this asinine mistake might have such devastating consequences for me personally. And for my child," she says.

Two weeks later, her period had not come. Her first pregnancy test was inconclusive. A second test confirmed her fears.

She was taking an ethics course at the time, working piecemeal toward her bachelor's degree. The class was debating abortion, and as she sat listening to her classmates spout abstract certainties, she agonized over the intractable particulars of her own situation.

Having this child would cost her her job. Which meant that it would cost her her home. Which meant that they would all have to go on welfare until the child was old enough for day care and Theresa could find a job that would allow her to pay for it.

"I suppose if I were an adolescent my parents could have sent me away to a home somewhere until I had the baby," she said. "But I had no one to help me and no place to hide."

Several years earlier, while Walter was still alive, Theresa had had a miscarriage, and the experience came back to her in her crisis. She remembered her sadness the morning that the damaged ovum had swirled down her toilet, but she also remembered thinking that what had passed from her body was not yet a person, that a miscarriage was not the same thing as a death.

The life inside her was at just that stage, about five weeks old, when she decided to have the abortion.

"I went by myself. I paid for it myself. I cried by myself," she said. "I wondered what the baby would have been—what sex? What would it have looked like?

"It was terribly painful to go through. Just physically painful. And I remember being kind of glad it was painful. There was an element of punishment in it."

A few years after her abortion Theresa met Paul Marino and they began dating. He was a Catholic, and she feared that telling him about her abortion might change his feelings toward her. But Paul listened quietly to her story and told her that he still wanted to marry her.

On the night they met with Father Maier, Theresa described her abortion as a sin. "But from my own experience," she said, "I can understand women being desperate enough to want abortions. I can understand being trapped in a relationship that was a bad idea to begin with and would be a disaster if it went forward."

What she wanted to know was whether the Church would accept her in her ambivalence.

Yes, Jim said. The Church would accept her because it had to accept anyone who had repented her sins and embraced its teachings.

But she had not entirely embraced its teachings, Theresa said. Not on abortion, and not on a number of other sexual matters.

But the core teachings, Father Maier responded, the nature of God, the identity of Jesus, the centrality of the Eucharist . . .

Those were what had drawn her to the Church in the first place, Theresa said.

And as for the sanctity of life?

She believed in that, too, though she also believed that there were circumstances in which it was unwise, and perhaps even immoral, to bring a child into the world.

Then the Church would receive her, Jim said, as it had received thousands of others who shared her reservations, and as it continues to nurture its own questioning and contentious children.

Many Catholic pastors would have been alarmed by Jim's position. The Church teaches that abortion is sinful unless the mother's life is at stake. It makes no exception for rape, incest, or cases in which the child would be born with an imminently fatal disease.

Pope John Paul II has lectured world leaders on the evils of abortion, calling it part of the "culture of death" that plagues Western democracies. He has urged Catholics to make banning abortion their chief political priority, and he has questioned the fidelity of Catholic politicians who support abortion rights.

But despite his fervor, the pope has never attempted to drive those who disagree with him out of the Church. And if Rome was not going to excommunicate Catholics who believed in abortion rights, Jim reasoned, then he was not going to exclude Theresa for holding similar views.

The Marinos seemed at peace when they left that night, and Jim was at peace, too. Counseling women *after* their abortions was not so difficult from a priestly point of view. The Church forgave more egregious sins. Indeed the American Church supported a nationwide ministry—Project Rachel—aimed at helping women who had had abortions repair their lives and resume the practice of their faith. What Jim feared was a situation like the one that had confronted a Jesuit colleague several years earlier.

A young woman had come to this priest pregnant, frantic, penniless and seemingly on the verge of suicide. The priest had to decide whether to counsel abortion, in which case one life would certainly be lost, or counsel perseverance, in which case *mother and* fetus might perish.

In the end, he had decided that the woman's suicide threats were serious, and he not only advised her to have an abortion but helped to pay for it as well. Regarding the issue from an analytic distance, Jim could only be thankful that the choice had not been his.

As he contemplated how to foster a pro-life spirit in his own parish, Jim kept that young woman's story in mind. He thought of Theresa Marino, too. Was it possible to articulate the wisdom of the Church without driving away women who were in crisis?

It was his good fortune that two of the more respected women in the parish were active in the antiabortion movement. Maureen Dowling, the principal of a Catholic elementary school in nearby Alexandria, Virginia, had spent two and a half years as field coordinator of the National Committee for a Human Life Amendment, and Christine Flanagan*, a lawyer studying bioethics at Georgetown University, was a member of Feminists for Life.

Maureen was a slender woman in her mid-thirties, with dark hair and mournful blue eyes, who spoke with great feeling about how the liturgies at Holy Trinity had changed her life. Yet she was frustrated by the parish's silence on the issue of abortion.

"We are very proud of our church when she speaks out on El Salvador or Bosnia or the pastoral letter on the economy," she said one January night in the living room of the parish center. "But on this issue some people are adamantly opposed to the Church speaking out. With most other social issues you can disagree on *how* you want to do something. When it comes to abortion there is a disagreement about *whether* we should do something."

Christine, in her late forties, still wore the open, inquisitive expression of the Midwestern girl she had once been. In just a few years at Holy Trinity she had established herself as one of the parish's most original thinkers. Her membership in Feminists for Life identified her, in some minds, as a woman of the Right, while her membership in PFLAG, Parents and Friends of Lesbians and Gays, marked her, for others, as a woman of the Left. On most Sunday mornings she and her friend Tim McLaren* had brunch after the 9:15 liturgy with a group that included the Quinns, the Halls and the Farrells. And in that rather partisan atmosphere they sometimes spoke about the issues behind the Standing in what their friends found an irritatingly evenhanded way.

Not long after receiving his orders from the archdiocese, Jim invited the two women to his office, and when he asked if they would share the newly created position of pro-life coordinator, both, after some hesitation, agreed.

Maureen and Christine understood that theirs was a quixotic task. Despite more than two decades of effort the Catholic hierarchy has not succeeded in persuading a clear majority of the laity that abortion, in most instances, should be illegal. According to most public opinion polls, a thin majority of American Catholics believe abortion should be legal in many or all instances. And this opposition to Church teaching had arisen without a visible Catholic leader seeking to galvanize it.

Nor had the bishops been particularly effective in persuading the female faithful to give birth to unwanted children. According to statistics reported by the Alan Guttmacher Institute, the rate of abortion among Catholic women is almost precisely the same as the national average, and higher than that of Protestants and Jews.

Yet Christine and Maureen were determined that the people of Holy Trinity should have the opportunity to reflect upon what they believed were the compassionate principles behind a position that was often portrayed as purely punitive.

Both women were skillful exponents of what has come to be known as the "seamless garment" approach to the abortion issue. This argument was first advanced in the late 1980s by Cardinal Joseph Bernardin of Chicago. It rolls opposition to abortion, euthanasia and capital punishment, as well as support for a broad range of education and welfare initiatives, into what the cardinal called "a consistent ethic of human life."

"The question is, how do we emphasize that our Church has a very human, logical, beautiful vision of God's creation?" Maureen says. "In that vision we respect all life no matter how intelligent, how physically appealing. What we'd like is for people to say, 'Maybe respect for the life of the unborn is part of this beautiful vision. Maybe it is linked to our opposition to the death penalty, our care for those with terminal illnesses.'

"What Jesus is about is inclusivity—how do we include all of life, even those on the fringes."

The seamless-garment argument removes many of the obstacles that retard liberals with pro-life sympathies from joining the movement. By challenging conservatives to reject capital punishment and to embrace some variant of the welfare state, it demonstrates that the Church is not hostage to its right wing. By placing other social issues on or near a moral par with abortion, it allows voters who want to choose a prochoice candidate to do so in good conscience.

Seamless-garment advocates have also helped move the Church into constructive methods of combating abortion such as offering material support and counseling to women with problem pregnancies, facilitating private adoptions, establishing homes for unwanted children and lobbying against cuts in day care programs and government aid to single mothers. If any sort of pro-life argument had a chance to receive a favorable hearing at Holy Trinity, this was the one.

By early January, Maureen and Christine had arranged a pro-life lecture series that they thought might induce thoughtful supporters of abortion rights to consider a different point of view. Their hope was that the series might foster conversation in the parish, and that conversation might gradually lead to conversions.

"Abortion is not going to be won in the political arena," Maureen liked to say. "It is going to be resolved in one-on-one situations."

Perhaps, but many Catholics are not ready to trust their Church or their coreligionists with their feelings about the issue. On a clear and moonlit January evening twenty people assembled in the lower-school cafeteria to hear Father Maier present a "biologist's perspective" on human life. They listened in respectful silence as Jim explained that life had intrinsic integrity and intrinsic worth, that human beings were essences not instruments, and that each individual, no matter how damaged, no matter how seemingly forsaken, was loved by God.

It was the only lecture in the series attended by more than eight or ten people.

Theresa Marino thought she understood parishioners' reservations about engaging the abortion issue. In her women's group a number of her friends said that they were frightened by the virulence of their fellow Catholics' pro-life passion. Others suggested that because of its rigid opposition to birth control, the Church had forfeited its credibility in the reproductive debate.

Theresa's own reservations about the Church's position were political as well as personal. In its zeal to ban abortion, the American bishops had allied themselves with politicians such as Senator Jesse Helms and Representative Robert Dornan, men whose punitive approach to public policy was entirely at odds with her sense of what it meant to be a Christian. In doing so, she believed, the hierarchy had effectively abandoned the poor.

Despite her feelings of betrayal, Theresa sympathized with the bishops on one point. For she had learned how difficult it was to uphold the sanctity of human life without alienating women in trouble.

A year earlier, she and Paul had befriended one of Patty's classmates, a young woman whose erratic behavior had sundered her family. Patty's friend was pregnant, a fact Theresa did not learn until the woman was in her twentieth week.

Since she had entered the Church, Theresa had come to believe that abortion so near the point of fetal viability was usually wrong. She could see how deeply conflicted her daughter's friend was about terminating the pregnancy. For your own peace of mind, she told the young woman, you should think seriously about having this baby.

But one day soon afterward, Patty's friend called to say that at her parents' insistence she had had an abortion.

Theresa lost track of the young woman after that, but the incident had a lingering influence on the Marino family. Several months later, Patty became pregnant. The man she was involved with was physically abusive, just as her father had been, and rather than risk her mothers' ordeal, she broke off the relationship and had an abortion. Only a few weeks afterward did she explain to Theresa what had occurred.

"With as open a relationship as we had had, I was surprised she couldn't tell me," Theresa said. "When I asked her why, she kept coming back to what I had said to her friend."

Theresa tried to explain the difference she saw between an abortion at six or eight weeks and an abortion at twenty weeks, but she wasn't sure that Patty accepted this distinction.

It was then she came to realize how difficult it was to speak with both conviction and sensitivity on the issue of abortion. For if pro-life sentiments as mild as her own could distance a mother from her daughter, how could any church or government hope to speak with sufficient compassion? And how could the Catholic hierarchy, after a quarter century of thunderous condemnation, win back the trust of women carrying children they could not raise?

Thinking back on her meeting with Father Maier, she remembered how Jim had put her at ease and how he had made it possible for her to come into the Church. His acceptance had made it easier for her to reconsider Catholic teaching, and to move, though partially, toward its view. Perhaps she and Maureen Dowling, who would always differ on the legality of abortion, could agree on one thing: the issue was being resolved one woman at a time.

CHAPTER TWELVE

Father Maier gave two or three lectures each year as part of Holy Trinity's adult education program, and his presentations always drew the largest crowds. Jim had a knack for tossing out questions and making his speeches feel like conversations, even though he did all the talking. Parishioners were comfortable with him, and that helped take the edge off their apprehension as they gathered on the third Sunday in January to hear him outline his plan to resolve the Standing.

There were perhaps one hundred people seated on folding chairs in the lower-school cafeteria that morning. Though some had come simply to learn more about "communal discernment," many were partisans in the battle over the protest. Scanning the crowd clustered in the L-shaped white-walled basement, Jim spotted Kathy Hartley and Rea Howarth, Shannon Jordan and Ellen Crowley. He wanted to believe that he could find some ground on which these women could meet.

Jim wore a blue ribbon on his black lapel. Placing his notes on an unsteady lectern, he welcomed his parishioners to what he hoped would be the beginning of a rewarding, if difficult, process.

St. Ignatius of Loyola taught that God actively guides each of us, he told them. The essence of Christian discipleship is to discern the nature of this guidance. But since Catholics do not seek their salvation individually, but in communion with the larger Church, it is imperative to discern where God is leading us as a community, too.

As he explained how Ignatian techniques, such as scriptural contemplation, could be used to resolve conflict, Jim searched the faces before him. Usually his parishioners listened to his lectures with a slight smile, an engaged expression. They let their eyes meet his. But that morning he could feel the uncertainty wafting toward him. People were coughing, shifting in their seats and studying their hands.

Where had he lost them? Did they doubt that spiritual methods could be effective in addressing political problems? Were they reluctant to open themselves, as the process required, to people they disliked and disagreed with? Or did they simply doubt his willingness to drive two strong-willed factions toward a resolution?

Sometimes he doubted that himself. The Standing was in its ninth month, and there seemed little hope of compromise. Ray McGovern's opponents regarded any idea generated by the Working Groups as suspect. The groups were planning lectures, amassing a mailing list and organizing as though for a political campaign. Neither side trusted the other, and he had begun to wonder if they still trusted him.

"I'll be happy to take some questions," Jim said, wrapping up his remarks and stepping away from the lectern. His parishioners applauded more out of charity than conviction, and the emptiness of the ovation embarrassed both speaker and audience alike.

There was a moment of uneasy silence before Ray McGovern raised his hand. When Jim acknowledged him, a barely audible groan rippled through the room. Since the onset of the Standing, Ray had become the screen onto which parishioners projected their feelings about the Church and about one another. And though there were plenty of strong opinions, much of the parish still seemed profoundly ambivalent about the protest.

People like Gary Cosgrove were privately cheered by the Standing but made no effort to support it. Others, like Anna Thompson, were afraid that the controversy was poisoning the parish atmosphere and that there would be no further progress on women's issues at Holy Trinity until Ray sat down. A third group, which included Carl Sylvester, the president of the Parish Council, wished the protestors would desist but adamantly opposed forcing them to do so.

Among those who had entertained conflicting feelings was Ray's mother, Marie. She and Ray's father, Joseph, had come down from suburban New York City one weekend, and over dinner Ray had explained to them what he was doing and why he was doing it. His mother was so impressed that she announced her intention to join the Standing, too. But on the following morning, as they drove to church, she told her son that she had changed her mind. A few weeks later Ray received a letter from her, saying that she was praying for him to sit down.

But Ray did not feel the need to answer his mother's prayer. St. Ignatius was a spiritual giant, he told the crowd in the auditorium that morning, but the founder of the Jesuits was not the man to help them create a less authoritarian church. Ray had spent a few hours that week poring over the saint's writings, and he had been troubled by what Ignatius had to say about obedience. In one instance the saint had declared that Catholics should be prepared to call black white if the Church determined it was so.

Subservient obedience is what has gotten us into this mess, Ray said. It is not what will get us out.

Jim drew a deep breath. He respected Ray and his willingness to fight for his ideals, but this was a low blow. Ignatius was a man of his time, Jim said. There was no escaping that. He said and wrote many things which today would strike us as peculiar. But his deeper insights, spiritual and psychological, were still vital. They were still leading people to God and they could still help the parish come to an agreement over the Standing.

Searching, perhaps, for someone to second that opinion, Jim called on Linda Arnold. For seven years she had been directing parishioners at Holy Trinity and students at Catholic University in the Ignatian Exercises. But what she had to say that morning did not help Jim's cause.

It was one thing, Linda said, to use Ignatian discernment in a small group in which people already knew one another and were committed to a common goal. But it was an entirely different matter to attempt a communal discernment in a large and already polarized parish. How was Jim going to induce the contending factions to sit down peacefully and share their ideas and their feelings with people whom they would rather throttle?

Father Maier mentioned the upcoming lectures which Shannon Jordan had organized, and the open forum that would follow. He alluded to the difficult work of meeting in small groups, praying together and charting an agenda to resolve the issue. But listening to his words, he realized how hollow they sounded.

People left the auditorium that morning trailing their doubts behind them like children dragging exhausted helium balloons.

They don't understand what's at stake, Jim thought. He was not thinking solely of the future of his parish. To Jim's mind, Catholics who yearned for a less authoritarian Church did not sufficiently appreciate the need for some sort of authority to keep the Church from atomizing. They did not understand that if doctrine was to be reviewed and reformulated, some version of the magisterium would always be necessary to promulgate these teachings.

The authority of this body would flow, ideally, from the *sensus fidelium*, the sense of the faithful, but determining what the faithful believed, and reconciling divergent visions, required precisely the kind of engagement that his parishioners were resisting. Faced with a conflict, they had fallen back on two familiar models, the ecclesial and the electoral. In the former, the pastor or bishop or pope dictated terms, and the faithful responded or were punished. In the latter, parishioners staked out positions and courted support as though an election loomed.

He was trying to show them a course that cut between the authoritarian tradition they were heirs to as Catholics and the interest group politics they were heirs to as Americans. But what Jim had not resolved was where power resided when agreement could not be reached. And because he had no answer for this question, the continuation of the Standing was viewed by the competing factions as evidence of their respective intellectual vindication.

Those on the Right, such as Bishop Corrada and Father Vaghi, saw in the unrest at Holy Trinity the need for a man with orthodox views and a firm hand. Those on the Left believed that their fellow parishioners' equivocal response to the protest demonstrated the need for prophetic lay people to press their challenge to the oppressive hierarchy.

Over the next few weeks, Father Maier was occupied more with the political than with the priestly. He spent much of his time mediating disputes and absorbing the free-floating rage that the Standing had un-leashed. By mid-February the archdiocese had yet to release its report on the parish, and he was beginning to worry.

In the midst of this turmoil, life on the surface at Holy Trinity went on much as it always had. Couples were married. Babies were baptized, and the parish continued to bury its dead.

People still rang the bell at the parish center at 7:30 on weekday mornings to meet with one of the spiritual directors. The masses re-mained as vibrant as ever. That February a dozen non-Catholics entered the RCIA program, their first step toward joining the Church.

The 9:15 community was still under a cloud, but that winter brought the prospect of a morning on which the querulous congregation might be united in a moment of joy.

At a meeting of the 9:15 liturgy planning team, Christine Flanagan, the co-coordinator of the pro-life lecture series, and Tim McLaren, a mainstay of Trinity's Saturday morning men's group, had announced their plans to be married in the spring. When the congratulatory hubbub subsided, Michael Gribschaw, the director of music, suggested that rather than holding a small private ceremony, the two should get married during the 9:15 Sunday mass.

Tim and Christine loved the idea. They had met at Holy Trinity, and parish activities had formed the web in which their relationship had grown. It seemed only appropriate to exchange their vows before the entire congregation.

Jim loved the idea, too. Christine had friends in the Working Groups, and Tim wore the blue ribbon. But they were also close to the Quinns and their circle—so close that Paul and Cathy had agreed to host the wedding reception at their new home. The wedding would be a symbol of the reconciliation Jim was trying to promote.

There was only one hitch. Both Tim and Christine had been mar-ried before, and Christine did not yet have her annulment. She had applied for it two and a half years earlier, but it had not come through yet. And without the annulment, there could be no wedding. At least not in the Church.

Throughout that winter, Christine waited for a decision from the diocesan marriage tribunal in Denver, where she and her former husband had been married. It was unsettling to know that a panel of celibate strangers were scrutinizing her most intimate affairs. But she remained hopeful, because she did not believe that the God who had guided her this far would let her down.

She and her former husband had been married for eighteen years when he announced, in 1986, that he needed his space and was moving out to find it. A devoted wife—"I worshiped the water he walked on"— and a devout Catholic, Christine had always believed that their marriage could withstand any test, and so she chose to view the separation less as an ending than as a sabbatical, an opportunity to improve herself and, indirectly, her marriage, while her husband exorcised his demons.

Rather than sit around their home in Denver fighting back despair, she and her thirteen-year-old daughter Karen* decamped for Washington, D.C., where Christine began work on her master's degree at the Kennedy Institute of Ethics at Georgetown University. Holy Trinity was their neighborhood parish, and they fell quickly into its embrace. Karen attended the grade school and sang in the choir. Christine made friends with other parents at the 9:15 liturgy.

But as the separation from her husband lengthened, she found herself becoming increasingly despondent. They had been living apart for eighteen months before he told her that he was having an affair with his secretary and wanted a divorce.

On top of that shock came a second. Karen, who had been pining for her friends in Colorado, decided to return to Denver and live with her father. She left Washington at the end of the 1986 school year. "Suddenly," her mother recalls, "I was Christine, single woman."

With her daughter gone, Christine became more deeply involved in the parish. She joined a prayer group that met weekly to read and reflect on the Scriptures. She went on a few outings with the Young Adult Community, though she was a bit older than most of its members. She joined the Women's Group, an informal gathering of female parishioners who met to discuss whatever came up. She acted in a variety show.

"Trinity was a place of nurturing and of solace at a very devastating time in my existence," she says. "They supported me when I was too broken to keep fighting by myself."

The Roman Catholic Church has not, traditionally, been an institution which the separated and divorced could count on for a great deal of support. The Church considers marriage an indissoluble union; remarriage without the benefit of an annulment is understood to be adultery. This teaching, based on a literal interpretation of Jesus' remarks in the

Gospels of Mark and Matthew, spawned a phobic attitude toward couples whose marriages were in trouble.

For generations, divorce was a kind of Catholic death. It signified failure not simply as a spouse, but as a member of the faith, and led to a kind of unofficial ostracism from the Church. It was dangerous, many pastors thought, to have divorced people in the parish, because contact with such people might breed sympathy, and sympathy might breed dissent.

Until recent decades divorce has been rare among American Catholics. One study in the early 1970s indicated that only 16 percent of Catholic marriages ended in divorce. But by the late 1980s, the Catholic divorce rate had climbed to almost 30 percent.

This new reality helped engender a more sensitive ecclesial approach to the plight of Catholics in broken marriages. After the Second Vatican Council, the Church began to regard the separated and divorced less as likely adulterers than as people in psychic pain. From this insight sprang a new field of specialized ministry, as a small number of priests, nuns and lay ministers reached out to the separated and the divorced, offering spiritual direction, organizing support groups and urging them not to let their sense of failure drive them from the Church.

These programs allowed thousands of Catholics to continue practicing their faith as they attempted to reassemble the pieces of their lives. But it also kept them in a kind of limbo. Divorced Catholics who cannot, or will not, obtain annulments must make a choice between sex and sacrament. If they remain single and celibate they may continue to receive Communion; if they remarry and have intercourse they cannot.

Initially, Christine had no trouble accepting this teaching. She was devastated by the breakup of her marriage and had no interest in seeking the solace of a new relationship. Secretly, she hoped her husband might still change his mind. In the meantime, she turned for comfort to her studies—and her church.

One day at the 9:15 liturgy she discovered the words that would become her sustenance, printed on a song sheet. She felt certain that she had sung them before, but that morning they resonated like a well-struck bell.

> As the deer longs for flowing streams
> So longs my soul for you O God.
> My soul does thirst for the living God.
> When shall I come to see Your face?

My tears have fed me day and night,
While some have said,
'Where is your God?'
But I recall, as my soul pours dry,
The days of praise within your house.

Why do I mourn and toil within
When it is mine, to hope in God?
I shall again sing praise to you.
You are my help. You are my God.
You are my God.

(Psalm 42)

Nothing captured her longing, her agony and her stubborn hopefulness quite so well. But in her more honest moments, Christine admitted to herself that she was no longer certain what she was hoping for.

A year earlier, she had met Tim McLaren at a Halloween party sponsored by the Separated, Divorced and Remarried Catholics (SDRC) group at Holy Trinity. He was a career diplomat who specialized in Latin American affairs. Seven years earlier, he had begun attending Holy Trinity as the newly single father of two. Drawn by the reputations of the family mass and the CCD program, he quickly discovered that the parish would nurture him as well as his children.

The SDRC program, in particular, was a revelation. "Here were people who had been through this hell, and come out the other side," he remembers. "They were leading normal lives, for God's sake."

Christine liked Tim's easy manner and his piquant Scottish sense of humor. She especially appreciated his willingness, so rare in the men she knew, to reveal and analyze his feelings. He was one of the most honest men she had ever met.

Tim, for his part, was impressed by Christine's intelligence, enamored of her simplicity of spirit and moved by the obvious grace with which she carried her grief over her marriage. He was looking for someone with whom he could spend the rest of his life; perhaps she was the one.

To his chagrin, Christine kept him at arm's length. Though they would go for bike rides, see movies, and talk, talk, talk, she had made it clear that she still regarded herself as a married woman, and him as a friend.

"It took me a long time to give up on my marriage," Christine says. "To really start the psychological work I needed to do on me."

Many people begin to do this work in the SDRC group. "It's not intended to be a social 'meet' factory," says LaSalle Caron, one of the group's earliest members. "People are not there to mate as with some other groups. It tends to be a comfortable, open reception of people we know to be the walking wounded. People are there because they realize they can't cope with the problem on their own."

The group presents lectures and workshops once each month. While these presentations often focus on practical matters—single parenting, handling the holidays, living on a budget—the meetings serve a deeper purpose. They allow separated and divorced Catholics to feel a sense of spiritual companionship as they wrestle with the issue that has driven millions of people from the Church.

The guiding spirit of the SDRC movement was a Paulist priest named Jim Young, who taught a course on marriage and the family at the Jesuit theology school in Cambridge, Massachusetts, during the mid-1970s. Young understood that by depriving separated and divorced Catholics of spiritual solace, the Church made it more likely that they would continue to hurt themselves and their families. One of his former students founded the SDRC group at Holy Trinity in 1977, and when Young was transferred to Washington a few years later, he became its chaplain.

A quietly charismatic man, he told the members of the SDRC that they should not expect their sexual appetites to disappear simply because they were single again. He told them that new relationships could help them heal. And he told them that if they found themselves in a committed sexual relationship, they should continue to receive Communion.

The Eucharist, he said, was "food for the journey, not the reward for a job well done."

Father Young helped scores of divorced Catholics find a comfortable corner in the Church, but he could not change canon law. A divorced Catholic who falls in love still faces a choice: get an annulment or give up on getting married within the Church.

When Christine and Tim began dating late in 1987, she did not consider this dilemma. For one thing, she didn't want to put the cart before the horse, but for another, she knew the issue might become painful. She couldn't imagine marrying outside of the Church, and the annulment process was fraught with the potential for delay and disappointment.

The laws governing annulments are an utter mystery to most Catholics, in part because they are complicated and in part because few people bother to study them until they become painfully relevant. The SDRC group at Holy Trinity invites a speaker to address the topic once every six months, and these presentations evoke equal parts of hope and contempt.

The hope springs from the knowledge that the overwhelming majority of those who seek annulments obtain them. More than fifty-nine thousand were granted in the United States in 1992. The contempt is inspired by the nature of the process, which is lengthy, expensive (roughly four hundred dollars), emotionally exacting and exceedingly legalistic; by the knowledge that marriage tribunals are composed almost entirely of people who have no firsthand experience of marriage; and by the Church's requirement that to receive annulments, petitioners must prove that their marriages were never *valid* in the first place.

This last condition strikes many Catholics as repugnant. What does it mean to say that a marriage which may have lasted decades was never valid? What is the Church saying to children when it declares that their families are based on a bond which never existed?

The Church's credibility is further undermined by the fact that most decisions regarding annulments are based entirely on technicalities.

A Catholic who marries outside the Church can divorce and remarry within the Church regardless of his or her culpability in the breakup of the marriage because the Church did not recognize the initial bond. A non-Catholic who is married to a non-Catholic can have that marriage annulled in order to be baptized and marry a Catholic. In this instance the petitioner must prove that he or she was not *solely* responsible for the failure of the first marriage. But when two Catholics who took their faith seriously enough to marry within the Church are involved, matters get a good deal more complicated.

The person seeking the annulment must write a four- or five-page essay stating the reason that he or she is seeking an annulment. The tribunal then contacts the former spouse and asks if that person wishes to respond. It seeks witnesses, preferably people who knew the couple at the time of the wedding. Often it consults secular experts—psychologists, social workers and counselors—to help collect and analyze information.

When this research is done the tribunal produces a narrative analysis of the marriage which must be read by both parties. The case then goes to a judge or panel of judges who have been educated in canon law and appointed by the diocese. There, the petitioner's advocate makes the case for annulment and the "defender of the bond" makes the case against.

For the marriage to be judged valid, the Church stipulates that both parties must have been able to give "meaningful consent" on their wedding day. Difficulties that develop *during* the marriage are germane only if they point to a problem that existed from the start.

Three requirements must be met: (1) *Discretion*—Was the person able to understand himself, his spouse and the nature of marriage on the day of the wedding?; (2) *Capacity*—Was the person psychologically capable of making an enduring commitment?; and (3) *Intention*—Was the person seriously dedicated to the "four goods" of marriage: permanence, fidelity, children and the creation of a "community of life and love"?

If one of these requirements is not met, then the tribunal rules that the couple was never truly married, and annuls the bond.

For some people the annulment process is cathartic. "There are a tremendous number of people who, after it is all over, write to me," Father Mark Mealy, who heads the marriage tribunal in Arlington, told the SDRC group one night. "They say two things most often. One, that it was faster than I thought, and two, it was important for me in terms of coming to terms with what happened."

Perhaps, but Christine and Tim knew several couples at Holy Trinity who had decided that the process was pointless, degrading, and involved submitting themselves to an authority they believed incompetent to judge them.

Barbara and Tom Gryzmala, who also met in the SDRC program, had investigated the annulment process after they began dating seriously in the mid-1980s.

"I saw it as a rationalizing process," Barbara said one morning in the suburban Virginia office of the financial services firm she and Tom founded. " 'Here's a way to make you okay.' "

"I see a lot of people looking at the process as very, very threatening," her husband said. "They see it as a survey of the wreckage of the past and at the same time they are under the watchful eye of the pope."

Rather than filing for annulments, the Gryzmalas were married in an Episcopal ceremony. The priest who presided was a friend of Tom's, and he told them he had performed many second marriages for Catholic couples. After the wedding, Tom and Barbara considered joining the Episcopal Church, but one stuffy Sunday at an old-line parish in Virginia convinced them that Holy Trinity was their spiritual home.

Holy Trinity quietly welcomes those who have remarried without annulments. Many are active in the parish's programs and ministries. The church's acceptance of these Catholics is based on how its Jesuit clergy interpret the ambiguous codes in canon law regarding the internal forum.

Canon 130 of the Church's *Code of Canon Law* states that the "power of governance," usually exercised in the "external forum"—meaning the forum governed by Church law—is sometimes exercised in the "internal forum," which the *Encyclopedia of American Catholicism* defines as "the realm of conscience." In other words, circumstances exist in which the Church permits Catholics to follow the dictates of conscience, rather than the letter of Church law. But large sections of cannon law are devoted to defining such circumstances narrowly and policing exceptions as closely as possible.

The Vatican does not recognize a role for the internal forum in the case of Catholics who have remarried outside the Church but want to continue receiving the sacraments. However, many American pastors do. The *Encyclopedia* notes without judgment that, "Internal forum solutions to otherwise insoluble marriage situations are very widely accepted in pastoral practice."

At Trinity the internal forum is sometimes suggested to couples like Barbara and Tom, who have decided not to seek annulments for reasons of conscience. Invoking it allows them to continue receiving the sacraments.

"God will receive you," Father Maier told one such couple. "And the Church can do no less."

The SDRC group occasionally invites a speaker to explain how Catholic teaching on divorce has come to such a convoluted pass, and whether there is any hope for change. One evening not long after Father Maier's presentation on communal discernment, some twenty parishioners gathered for such a presentation in the cheerless cafeteria of the lower school.

The speaker was Monika Hellwig, a professor of theology at Georgetown University, former nun and past president of the Catholic Theological Society of America. She was a stout woman with an Austrian accent who dressed so simply that one might have supposed she was still a nun. That night she disdained the podium and pulled up a folding chair. Without benefit of notes, visual aids, gestures or humor she spoke for ninety oddly mesmerizing minutes.

One's opinion about the teaching on divorce hinges on one's thinking about Jesus and the nature of his mission on earth, she said. One view holds "that Christian teaching is divinely determined and passed into the human realm through Jesus. It can't change. You have to keep your hand on the 'box' and don't let anything drop out."

The other view holds that "Jesus *is* the revelation." Not that he "*handed on*" the revelation but that he embodied it: "Jesus *is* the prototypical human being."

And if one holds that view, she said, then one might argue that Church teaching should be based on the totality of Christ's life rather than on isolated sayings.

It was a life, in the human sense, that was "marked by failure." Jesus came with a "sublime vision" and learned through painful experience what could and could not be accomplished on earth.

"Jesus was not a magical figure," Professor Hellwig said. "In the end He hands over to His Father a failed project. He fails in human relationships, just as marriages fail. The disciples are unable to cooperate."

And yet the redemption of humanity is predicated on this failure.

There was a quiet round of applause when she finished speaking, then a chunky young man asked whether she was optimistic about the possibility for a change in Church teaching.

"Where there is unnecessary suffering we can have a great hope of redemptive transformation," she said.

"But when has the Church ever changed its mind?"

Professor Hellwig mentioned Galileo.

"Great," said a woman in the rear of the room. "We only have 350 years to go."

Tim McLaren was not going to wait 350 years. He didn't care whether he and Christine could be married in the Church, just so long as they could be married. But Christine insisted that their marriage be sacramental, and so they had filed for annulments.

Tim had no trouble. "I've had more painful experiences trying to register a car in the District of Columbia," he said. But Christine's was a stickier situation.

She filed in the fall of 1989, and at that time, her former husband did not contest the petition. But later, when he fell behind on his alimony payments, she took him to court and he responded by trying to block the annulment.

Despite the fact that it was he who had left her, his opposition slowed the process to a crawl. Christine began to wonder if she and Tim would ever be able to get married. After a year, her husband proposed a compromise: if she would grant him concessions in the property settlement that had finalized their divorce, he would drop his opposition to the annulment.

"I said to myself, 'Do I trust the Lord on this one? Or do I rage against the Church bureaucracy?' " she remembers. Christine decided not to compromise.

By February 1993, she still had no news. The wedding was planned for early May. And like everyone else at Holy Trinity, she found herself waiting, wondering, and trying to believe that the men who ran her Church would make the right decision.

CHAPTER THIRTEEN

It was one of those years in which Lent seemed redundant. The people of Holy Trinity felt they had been doing penance since the archdiocese initiated its search for Jim Maier's successor, if not since the onset of the Standing. But the holy season began on February 24, and parishioners thronged their church to receive the ashen forehead smudge that reminded them of their mortality and marked them as Catholics at work and at school.

In the sanctuary a huge swath of burlap obscured the cross of glory. Before the coarse brown fabric hung an austere gibbet, constructed of two weathered wooden beams. Floral arrangements were at a reedy minimum.

Over the next forty days, the liturgies would become increasingly meditative. The music would slip into a minor key, and Father Maier and his fellow preachers would lead their affirmation-hungry parishioners down darker and more demanding homiletic paths.

Jim loved Lent. He rejoiced in it. At no other time was the pulse of prayer so powerful in his parish.

When he was a young man, Jim thought of Lent as a season of contrition, spiritual discipline and personal purification. It was the time when Christians contemplated the sufferings of Christ and their own culpability in nailing him to his cross. But after the Second Vatican Council, the Church's attitude toward sin had undergone what might be called a relational revision, and its thinking about Lent had been revised as well.

Many Catholics Jim's age had grown up imagining their sins—each impure thought, each instance of pique—as a lash on the back of the scourged Christ. But after the Council, the Church had opened itself increasingly to the insights of modern psychology and evolutionary biology. Much of what it once considered sinful—indecent urges, unruly desires—it now understood as native to the normally functioning human psyche. Sin lay in surrendering to temptation, not in recognizing it.

But the Church was hardly relaxing its standards of holiness. Sin had once been defined as a voluntary violation of divine law, but Jim's professors in theology school spoke of it in broader terms. It was a callousness toward suffering; an indifference about injustice; an unwillingness to struggle against the evils of the world. The question for Catholics was no longer simply whether they were wielding the whip against Christ, but whether they were wielding it, *or allowing it to be wielded*, against others.

Jim knew that conservative parishioners like Peter Schaumber considered this new ethic less rigorous and less specifically Christian than the old. They would have preferred to hear him preach his Lenten sermons on the necessity of self-discipline and the importance of fasting. But Jim viewed Lent less as a season of self-denial than as a time of transformation, an occasion for measuring every aspect of one's life—personal, professional, economic, even political—against the example of Jesus, and trying to conform one's actions to his.

Lent was also the season when the Church confronted perhaps its most vexing intellectual challenge. For millions of atheists and agnostics, "the problem of suffering," as theologians called it, was the strongest impediment to belief. They could not reconcile the existence of a loving God with the agonies they saw all around them. Lent, with its scriptural focus on the Passion of Christ, compelled the Church to address this question, to speak of suffering, of evil, of randomness, of all the forces that nurtured the darkness of doubt.

When he was a young priest, this challenge had sent Jim back to the writings of theologians whose work he had studied in the seminary. But in recent years he had come to believe that the problem was beyond resolution. God did not offer an answer; God offered himself.

Rather than manifesting the meaning of human suffering, God sent his Son to share in humanity's pain, to accompany and redeem his fallen people. We wish for enlightenment, Jim told parishioners, but God has given us greater gifts: the companionship of Jesus and the assurance that He will be with us, both in our suffering and beyond.

Sometimes, stepping down from the pulpit, he wondered how this argument played among the people who filled the dark wooden pews of his church each Sunday. His own sense was that Catholics were less interested in arguments *about* God than in experiences *of* God. And this was another reason for his devotion to Lent, for in no other season did his parishioners seek such experiences so vigorously.

Their passion for these experiences would have surprised the parish's archdiocesan adversaries, he suspected. These men advanced the same arguments against Holy Trinity that conservative theologians employed against the progressive Church. According to their thinking, in questioning traditional Catholic morality and in demanding a more active role in their Church, liberal Catholics were repeating the mistakes of the Enlightenment—elevating human reason over divine revelation and abrogating for men and women God's rightful role as the agent of human redemption.

As a result of these errors, freedom had replaced obedience as the path of progressive Catholics, and "self-fulfillment" had replaced salvation as their goal. Captives of a therapeutic ethic, they valued knowledge of themselves above knowledge of God. Hence the shallowness of their spiritual lives and the weakness of their commitment to prayer.

There were elements of truth in this critique, Jim supposed. Progressive Catholics walked a fine, faint line between narcissism and principled humility in voicing their dissent. They were not immune from identifying their own desires with the Almighty's. And it was true that many liberals shunned traditional devotions such as the rosary.

Yet he had no doubt about their hunger for God. As a novice master, Jim had immersed himself in the growing literature on Catholic spirituality, and he knew that since the Second Vatican Council, progressive Catholics' restless search for a more satisfying spiritual life had fueled a renaissance of interest in some of the Church's great spiritual guides.

In response to burgeoning lay interest, the Jesuits, Carmelites, Benedictines and others began making the writings and practices of their founders available to large lay audiences. Feminist scholars popularized the writings of medieval mystics such as Julian of Norwich and Hildegard of Bingen. Workshops on meditation, contemplation and praying with the Scriptures sprang up around the country, and Christian spirituality emerged as an academic discipline and a cottage industry.

Progressive Catholics might not be praying in the same way as their immediate forebears, but from Jim's vantage point there had been no diminution in their devotion to prayer.

On the first Sunday of Lent, he and the other members of Holy Trinity's retreat team gathered with a group of more than thirty parishioners in the basement cafeteria of the upper school. Thick, square pillars supported a low white ceiling. A wide circle of folding chairs dominated the room. For five days each week, this was where boys in blue button-downs and girls in plaid jumpers consumed their antic lunches. But for one hour that morning, it became a place of prayer and the starting point for a new band of parish pilgrims.

The group was about to begin a five-day retreat based on the techniques outlined in *The Spiritual Exercises* of St. Ignatius of Loyola, the small volume that was the fountainhead of Jesuit spirituality. But before they scattered to their own homes, Jim and the rest of the team wanted them to meet one another, to instill in them the sense that this was not a journey they were making alone, and to instruct them, if briefly, on St. Ignatius' techniques.

Father Gerry Campbell, the director of the Jesuit Center for Spirituality, which had its headquarters in a small sitting room on the second floor of the parish center, offered the opening prayer. A tall, bald, avuncular man with a halting step, a steady gaze and a fondness for cardigan sweaters, he had come to Holy Trinity twelve years earlier hoping to spend his retirement leading lay people through *The Spiritual Exercises*, but uncertain there would be sufficient interest.

Before 1950, the laity had little opportunity to make the Exercises, which were typically given during a thirty-day silent retreat. But after Vatican II the Jesuits began to make greater use of "Annotation 19," a version of Ignatius' masterwork that can be undertaken over a nine-month period in the midst of daily life.

Within a few years, Father Campbell had guided more than twenty parishioners through the long, meditative process. He had also trained a few of his most eager and insightful retreatants—including Natalie Ganley, Linda Arnold and Ellen Crowley—to direct the Exercises themselves. When Jim Maier became pastor, there was a six-member retreat team already in place, providing spiritual direction to whoever sought it.

By the winter of 1993 some 350 parishioners had participated in one of the five-day retreats, and perhaps 60 had completed Annotation 19. And though Father Campbell was as surprised as anyone else by the popularity of these programs, in retrospect it was easy for him to understand the appeal of Ignatian spirituality to contemporary Christians.

The founder of the Jesuits was a former soldier who wanted his men to be active and influential in worldly affairs. In his spiritual writings he depicted a God who was intimately involved in human endeavors, ceaselessly laboring to help men and women realize the immanence of his Kingdom. This vision had particular resonance for lay people who sought their salvation, and their livelihoods, in the workaday world, for it acknowledged no distinction between sacred and secular spheres. Ignatius' God was alive everywhere.

Perhaps more importantly, Ignatius was rare among the Catholic thinkers of his time in refusing to equate desire with temptation. For him human appetites were gifts from God, and channels of grace. Desire was not to be repressed, but to be identified, analyzed and understood. This was best done, he thought, through the techniques he outlined in the Exercises—such as projecting one's self into gospel stories and reflecting with a director on one's experience.

Though he was a loyal soldier of the Counter-Reformation, Ignatius anticipated much of modern psychology. Today, through his teachings, Catholics who abhor the rigid fundamentalism of the Christian Right and reject the flaky solipsism of the New Age movement can find a God who speaks to them in the pages of Scripture and in the silence of their own imaginings, who calls them to emulate the compassion of His Son, and who wills them to join in building the Kingdom.

As the people seated on the hard metal chairs folded their hands and lowered their eyes, Father Campbell prayed in a slow, steady voice that each of them would have the willingness to follow where the Holy Spirit led them, and the courage to move more deeply into God's bottomless love.

When he had finished, Father Campbell introduced Linda Arnold, who read from the Gospel according to Luke. It was a brief passage in which Jesus' disciples seek him out where he meditates in silence, and ask that he teach them to pray.

The room was silent as retreatants reflected on their own prayer lives: on silent bargains struck beside childhood beds; the memorized rush of Our Fathers and Hail Marys; special saints with special talents—like Saint Anthony, who helped find lost things; rosaries that glowed in the dark, and ejaculations whispered rapid-fire (thirty years ago each recitation supposedly shaved time off the petitioner's sentence in purgatory). After all these years, some of them still felt that they didn't really know how to pray.

A long minute passed before Father Joe Sobierajski began a "guided meditation."

Father Sobierajski was a tall and broad-shouldered man with dark, thinning hair and a wiry beard. The most theologically traditional of the Jesuits at Holy Trinity, he preached frequently and compellingly about the nature of sin and the need to struggle against it. A runner and a sculptor, he had a finely developed sense of what it meant to be an embodied spirit—of the glories, the limitations and the failings of the flesh.

Try to relax, he said to the group. Breathe deeply, and slowly if you can. Close your eyes.

Imagine you are walking in a desert. It is hot. You are thirsty, sweaty, tired. In the distance you see the figure of a man, but the man does not see you. He is lost in contemplation.

As you draw closer, you recognize that the man is Jesus, and that he is at prayer.

What does he look like? Can you see his expression? Can you sense his intensity? How does it feel to be so close to him as he prays to his Father? And how do you react when he raises his eyes and invites you to join him?

This week is about joining Jesus in prayer, he said. It is about understanding Jesus *through* prayer. It is about quieting the noise in your own mind long enough to hear what God might be saying to you.

Open your eyes.

When Father Sobierajski had finished, the retreatants broke into smaller groups led by their spiritual directors. Gary Cosgrove took a seat near Father Campbell. He had decided to make the retreat because his inner wrangling over the Standing and other issues had dampened his spirit and made him feel quarrelsome. He took avid notes as Father Campbell outlined the program for the week.

Each day the retreatants would be assigned three Scripture passages. They would select the one that affected them most deeply, reread it several times, close their eyes, relax into their chairs and begin to pray.

Father Campbell encouraged them to project themselves into the readings. They should imagine themselves sitting amid the crowd that partook of the loaves and the fishes. They should imagine themselves as Mary and Pilate and Judas. They should try to imagine the feelings of Jesus himself.

The retreat was organized around a series of "graces," he told them, and the readings were chosen to focus their meditation. Each day, they would pray for a specific kind of blessing, such as a deepened awareness of God's love.

After half an hour, they would break off their meditations and turn to their journals for what Saint Ignatius referred to as the Review of Prayer. They needn't write for long, Father Campbell said, but they ought to address certain important questions. How had the reading made them feel? What had cheered them? Frightened them? What had they found most difficult to accept? What were the implications of these feelings for their spiritual progress? For their daily lives?

Each day you will meet with me, Father Campbell said, and we will try to understand what God is saying to you.

Gary went home eager to begin. For the next week he arose early, prayed, and met with Father Campbell before work. And each day he felt himself crawling more deeply into the core of a contradiction. He was a sinner, a lukewarm Christian, a man given to half measures, the custodian of small resentments and lifeless good intentions.

Yet God loved him. God loved him unconditionally and immensely. Everything he had read—from the poetry of Psalm 139 to Jesus' discourse on the lilies of the field—made that magnificently clear. It was the single greatest revelation of his religious life. Yet he could not fully accept it.

How dare God love him, when he only half loved himself? How dare God rejoice in him, when he might betray God at any moment? This all-embracing love made him feel powerless and pointless. Why should he go on striving if God was going to love him whether he succeeded or not?

On Thursday, Gary took the day off from work. After he met with

Father Campbell, he went into the church. A man with tousled hair was practicing the piano and Gary settled into a pew near the rear of the nave and listened to the swelling sound as he skimmed the readings.

When the music stopped, Gary concentrated on the parable of the prodigal son. He found himself meditating first on the actions of the older son, the dutiful one who had remained home laboring under his father's orders. This son was outraged by the celebration that greeted his brother's return. "I would be, too," Gary thought.

He began to wonder if perhaps that was the reason for his spiritual dilemma. He believed that salvation was something one earned, rather than something one found. He believed that God kept meticulous moral score, like a diving judge at the Olympics. But the God of this parable seemed to love people even if they broke training and ruined their careers. Why was that?

Gary began to imagine himself as the younger son. He tried to picture himself lying in a bed in his father's home after the great feast was over. What would happen now? How should he behave? Would he get bored and run away again?

Suddenly Gary had the sense that he was being watched. Not physically, but mentally. Someone, or some presence, was inspecting his thoughts. His awareness of this presence encouraged him to keep praying.

He imagined himself waking up in his father's household on the morning after the feast, sitting at the breakfast table, accepting the chores assigned to him, taking pleasure in the feeling of the air in his lungs and the muscles in his legs. Then he broke off.

He wanted to contemplate whatever was watching him. He wanted to acknowledge its presence and open himself to it. For the next hour he imagined this presence hovering above and behind him, over his left shoulder perhaps, or just inside his left ear.

The presence had no voice. It had no form. It was not anything in particular; it simply was.

Gary had read in his Bible that Yahweh, the Old Testament name for God, meant "I am."

"You are," Gary said.

He had entered the retreat hoping for a more intellectual sort of enlightenment, something that would be easy to explain to his wife, something that might impress Father Campbell. But as he left the church that morning, still feeling accompanied by this formless force, he realized that nothing he could have summed up in a few deft phrases would have felt half so powerful.

On Saturday morning he strolled into the upper-school cafeteria for the close of the retreat, yearning to know whether any of the other retreatants had had an experience like his. He felt a peculiar bond with these men and women, though most of them he barely knew. It was as though sharing this week of prayer had made them friends, or at least acquaintances. He felt a vague goodwill toward them all.

In the weeks ahead, Holy Trinity would need as much of this goodwill as parishioners could muster, for as Gary was about to learn, its time of trials had just begun.

In the corner of the cafeteria that morning, he saw Fathers Maier and Campbell standing with Linda Arnold and Natalie Ganley. Each seemed possessed by a serene sorrow, and in a moment he learned why.

Father Tom Gavigan had died.

⌒♈

Father Gavigan was eighty-two, and his death was not unexpected. Still, when the news of his passing reached the rectory the previous evening, Jim Maier had felt suddenly alone. Tom was gone, and at just the moment when his achievement at Holy Trinity seemed most in jeopardy.

By the following morning Jim had resolved to give his old mentor a rousing sendoff. In the process, he would remind his parishioners of Holy Trinity's heritage, and of what it was that their feuding had put at risk.

Four nights later Tom's open casket stood in the center aisle of the church. He was dressed in radiant white vestments and his hands were folded on his chest.

Mourners began arriving at 5:30 P.M., two hours before the Mass of the Resurrection. By 7:30 the church was three-quarters full. The sweet, mournful strains of Bach's "Prelude" and "Fugue in A Minor" wafted through the nave as a phalanx of Jesuits, perhaps sixty strong, along with a few diocesan priests, processed up the center aisle and seated themselves to the left of the altar. On the right, behind the Gavigan family, sat the women of the Altar Society, who were Tom's special friends during the last years of his ministry.

Near the rear of the procession walked Jim and the priests who would concelebrate the mass: Father Edward Glynn, the Jesuit provincial, and Fathers Jerry Campbell and Jim Connor, two of Tom's closest Jesuit companions. Behind them all walked Bishop Corrada, who sat in the sanctuary, solemn and stone-faced, throughout the liturgy.

As he passed through the congregation, Jim picked out the faces of people who had helped Tom transform Holy Trinity. There was Dick Lucht, the retired organist who had taught the parish to sing; Melanne and Phil Verveer, the young friends with whom Tom had spent the holidays during his pastorate; Larry O'Rourke, the newspaperman whose research had helped persuade the archdiocese that Trinity should be allowed to draw parishioners from beyond its geographical boundaries; George and Linda Arnold, who between them had held most of the positions on the parish staff; and Kitty Nolan, now in her eighties, yet still as committed to the study of Scripture, theology and ecclesial gossip as she had been when she and Tom forged their friendship thirty years earlier.

When Father Maier reached the altar, the music died and a silence, broken only by soft coughing, descended upon the church. Jim greeted the congregation in the name of the Father, the Son and the Holy Spirit, then stepped forward to bless Tom's body and commend it to God. When he had finished, organ and trumpet introduced Tom's favorite hymn, "A Mighty Fortress Is Our God," and soon the church was filled with its triumphant tones.

In his homily, Jim evoked Father Gavigan's courage and his sense of humor. Leaning close to the microphone, Jim imitated the great, gravelly whisper in which Tom addressed his Jesuit novices during the hours they were supposed to be observing silence. He talked of Tom's independence and, in an oblique reference to the feud over *Humanae Vitae,* he mentioned Tom's "vindication," for most of the Church had come to view the matter of artificial contraception Father Gavigan's way. Mostly, however, Jim spoke of Tom's compassion, his humility and his willingness to trust the people of his parish in a way no priest had ever trusted them before. He had been a gift to them, Jim said, and his gift had called forth their own.

As if to illustrate that point, Natalie Ganley succeeded Father Maier in the pulpit. On this occasion she did not preach, but simply read the prayers of petition. Yet she and other parishioners, however, were active in Tom's funeral mass in a way that disturbed some of the more conservative clerics on hand.

Despite the presence of more than five dozen priests, it was the laity and the celebrants who distributed Communion. Technically speaking, this was a violation of Church rubrics, but the people of Holy Trinity had always reasoned that the parish belonged more to them than to the visiting clergy, and that these priests should be treated as guests.

Bishop Corrada, who did not endorse this line of thinking, complained about the practice afterward. So did Father Vaghi, who included it in a laundry list of criticisms about Holy Trinity which he aired in a phone call to Father Glynn the following day. What Tom Gavigan would have seen as inviting the laity to fuller participation in their Church, these men saw as an insult to the ordained and a challenge to their authority. But for one night, at least, Tom's vision prevailed.

As the mass was ending, the Jesuits sang a hymn crafted from the words of their founder. "Take and receive, O Lord my liberty. Take all my will, my mind, my memory. Do thou direct, and govern all and sway; Do what Thou wilt; command and I obey."

The nature of obedience had been at the center of Tom Gavigan's ordeal over the encyclical on birth control. He had asked himself what he owed the Church in an instance when he was convinced that the Church was tragically wrong, and decided that the answer was respectful dissent. Thirty years later most of the people of Holy Trinity still believed that he had been right, which helped explain why, despite the ever more critical scrutiny of the archdiocese, the parish had recently embarked on a public examination of women's ordination.

It was possible, the most cautious among them knew, that this examination might lead the cardinal to appoint an authoritarian pastor. It was possible, in that event, that many of them might soon find Holy Trinity an inhospitable place. But on that particular night, it was difficult to imagine that Tom Gavigan was anywhere but heaven, and easy to believe that they could get there by following him.

As Tom's casket was carried from the church, the congregation sang the chorus of "We Shall Rise Again" a rousing hymn by local composer Jeremy Young.

We shall rise again on the last day,
with the faithful, rich and poor.
Coming to the house of Lord Jesus,

we will find an open door there.

We will find an open door.

And they sounded as though they believed it.

ᠬᠠᠣᠣᠣᠣᠣ

A few days later, Jim Maier and his Jesuit superiors received a copy of the archdiocese's assessment of the parish. It was scathing.

The drafters of the report charged Jim and the other priests at Trinity with failing to proclaim and uphold Church teaching on the role of women in the Church and the immorality of homosexual relationships. They also upbraided the CCD program for lacking focus and failing to teach Catholic dogma and tradition.

These criticisms were expressed in an unusually aggressive tone. "Everything about the report said, 'Out of control! This place is out of control!' " said a former member of the cardinal's staff.

Father Maier was stunned. He expected to be criticized for his failure to suppress the Standing and for Trinity's occasional prayers on behalf of gays and lesbians. He knew some people in the archdiocese did not like the CCD program. But he had anticipated a more balanced appraisal of his work.

The document said nothing about Holy Trinity's retreat and spirituality programs, which were as successful as those at any parish in the country. It said nothing about the RCIA program, which was the second largest in the archdiocese, nothing about the liturgies, preaching or music which attracted worshipers from throughout the region, and nothing about the social concerns program, which was the most active in the archdiocese. Indeed, if the investigators found anything praiseworthy about the parish, they omitted it from the report.

"It saddens me," Jim said. "It feels like a rejection and a misunderstanding. It is a clash of ecclesiologies. It reflects the top-down decision-makers in the church, trying to reestablish control."

He was saddened not simply because the archdiocese had judged his work so harshly, but because the report reflected little understanding of the real challenges facing the Church. A recently completed survey indicated that only about 17 percent of Catholics between the ages of 18 and 29 attended Mass each week. Holy Trinity had reached out to this population with a Mass that featured lively liturgical music, outstanding preaching and a strong focus on social justice. As a result some 800 people jammed the church each Sunday evening at 5:30. The majority of these people were under the age of 35, and many had found Holy Trinity as they were on the verge of giving up on their faith. The parish had kept them in the Church, yet of this, the archdiocese took no note.

Nor did it seem to appreciate the accomplishment of Holy Trinity School. Since the mid-1960s, one of every three Catholic schools in the United States had been closed, and the ratio of Catholic children being educated in church-run institutions had dropped from roughly one half to less than one quarter. But at Holy Trinity, where Ann Marie Santora had managed to blend an emphasis on traditional moral values with peda-gogic innovation, classes were full, parents were intimately involved in shaping their children's education, and the waiting list grew longer each fall.

The parish was not without its problems; no one knew that better than Jim. But it seemed to him that in refusing to acknowledge Holy Trinity's successes, Cardinal Hickey's advisors were ignoring lessons that might have helped enliven the many stagnating communities in their jurisdiction. And ironically, in so doing, they were adding to the steady flow of worshippers who fled their geographic parishes to attend the Jesuit church.

As news about the archdiocesan report began to circulate, the pres-sure increased on Ray McGovern to abandon his protest. A conciliatory gesture, some argued, would appease the cardinal and Holy Trinity would live to fight another day.

Ray was having none of this. "What does it say about the institu-tional Church if you have to live in fear?" he asked. "This impulse of ours to accommodate whoever is in charge—particularly when it could be worse—is so palpable."

Ray knew that people were already blaming him for the misfortune they assumed was about to befall the parish, but that seemed not to bother him. "The Church has always flourished in oppressive circum-stances," he said. He recognized, however, that the Standing played heavily on the nerves of some fellow parishioners.

"There have been some tense Sundays when I thought things might be coming to a head," McGovern said. "And I've told Christin that I was going to be nonviolent about it."

While Ray was the nexus of parishioners' anxiety, the report made it clear that the archdiocese was more concerned about the activities of two other lay people: Anna Thompson and Margaret Costello. Every specific criticism leveled by the drafters reflected negatively on them.

Their early support had helped legitimize the Standing and launch the Working Groups. Margaret had been responsible for the prayers on behalf of gays, lesbians and others marginalized by the Church. Both women had attended the Dignity mass, even after Bishop Corrada warned Father Maier that he should not. And Anna, as director of the CCD program, had been instrumental in implementing the controversial Good Choices curriculum and bringing Kaiser-Permanente's *Secrets* program to Holy Trinity.

Within days a variety of rumors raged through the parish: the Jesuits were scouring the country for a candidate acceptable to the cardinal; Father Peter Vaghi was lobbying behind the scenes to have himself named pastor; Bishop Corrada would assume residence at the parish.

Jim tried to persuade parishioners that these moves were unlikely. Cardinal Hickey, in his view, was not without pastoral or political sense. If the cardinal imposed an unpopular pastor in a manner that suggested he was punishing the parish, the resultant upheaval would generate a raft of unfavorable publicity, further damage his relationship with the Jesuits, diminish the revenues reaped from an affluent congregation and consume much of the remainder of his term as archbishop. Not incidentally, it would cripple one of the most spiritually vibrant parishes on the East Coast.

"It's a real possibility, following one line of reasoning, that he would want to take over the parish," he conceded. "But if he takes it over he will destroy it. And he is a very smart man. I don't know if he wants all those people, for whom this is their last gasp as Catholics, going over the edge. My sense is that he will reassert, through the Jesuits, more of a sense of order and control."

But even as he made his case, Jim knew that if the cardinal decided that the purity of essential Catholic doctrine was in peril, he would take whatever steps he deemed necessary, just as he had in the Charles Curran case. And that might mean telling the Jesuits to leave.

Sometimes it seemed Jim was preparing himself for such an eventuality. "Even if that happened, the Lord would work with that," he said one overcast afternoon in his office. "There is a lot of trouble in the church, people scurrying around trying to find a safe place, someplace where they can be nourished. Maybe it is time to face up to our divisions."

His parishioners were trying to do precisely that. Just before Tom Gavigan's funeral they had begun the process Jim had devised to deal with the Standing. But it was not working very well.

CHAPTER FOURTEEN

꧁ᴥ꧂

It would not, in the long run, make a great deal of difference to the universal Church what was said about women's ordination in an elementary school theater in Georgetown on three Sunday mornings in March of 1993. The people who attended the 9:15 mass understood that, but as they gathered for the initial presentation many felt that they were about to embark on a significant endeavor nonetheless.

The Catholic Church offers its local communities no model for dealing with conflicts among the faithful. It does not engage, in any official way, with members who accept the fundamental tenets of the faith but cannot assent to the totality of Church teaching. There is no institutional mechanism, short of a papally convened synod or worldwide council, for dealing with the sort of debate and dissent now widespread in the American Church.

Father Jim Maier was trying to create such a mechanism at Holy Trinity. He had involved lay people at every level of parish administration, convened endless committees to solicit parishioners' opinions and tried, when possible, to govern his fractious flock by consensus. But a chasm yawns between giving people a voice in how their money is spent and what their children are taught, on the one side, and creating forums at which they can challenge Church teaching on the other.

The 9:15 community was by now so polarized, however, that only a few members spent any time mulling the wisdom of leaping this gulf. In the next month they would hear two scholarly presentations on the pros and cons of women's ordination, and then discuss the issue and its impact on their parish at an open forum. Perhaps it would help them clarify their thinking. Or perhaps it would simply be an opportunity to vent their spleen.

There were roughly 120 people in the theater on Sunday morning, March 7, when Shannon Jordan introduced Sister Mary Collins, a Benedictine nun who was then chair of the religious studies department at the Catholic University of America. Sister Mary was a tall, sturdy-looking woman whose dark hair was simply cut. Her skirt and blazer approximated the brown of a Franciscan's robe, and she spoke in earnest, measured tones. Her large-lensed glasses reflected the muted theater lighting when she glanced up from her text.

It was not her intention to argue that women should be ordained, she began, but to argue that the question of women's ordination should remain open. In this she joined many distinguished theologians including the late Karl Rahner, who held that the matter had not been explored deeply enough to warrant closure, the Vatican's arguments notwithstanding. Her position, she added, was based on a review of scholarly findings about the role of women in the early Church.

In 1976 when Vatican officials were researching *Inter Insigniores*, one of the more recent formulations of the Church's opposition to women's ordination, they asked the Pontifical Biblical Commission to provide them with scriptural support for their position, she said. The commission replied that the Biblical evidence was inconclusive.

"This matter had not been determined in the New Testament," Sister Mary told the people in the theater that morning. "While it is true that Jesus did not ordain women, it is also clear that Jesus did not ordain anyone." The word "presbyter," or priest, did not enter the Church's vocabulary until at least thirty years after his death, and the sacrament of holy orders was not instituted until A.D. 200.

During his earthly ministry (somewhere between A.D. 27 and 33), she continued, Jesus invited women as well as men to be his disciples. This was highly unusual at that time. Women had no legal rights and could not own property. Though they could be divorced by their husbands, they could not obtain a divorce themselves. That Jesus numbered so many women among his followers has long been interpreted, particularly by liberal scholars, as a sign of his willingness to transgress social norms and minister to the dispossessed.

In the four decades after Jesus' death, men and women worked together as ministers in the early Church. Saint Paul's writings make it clear that women led house churches. In Romans 16 he mentions Phoebe, who was a deacon. A woman named Junia is called "an apostle." Priscilla was an itinerant preacher, Sister Mary said, and the daughters of the Apostle Philip are referred to as "prophets."

Yet it was clear that women were struggling to maintain their status in the Church. In his account of those who saw the risen Jesus, Saint Paul mentions the Apostles but not the women who had accompanied Jesus on his ministry. Yet these women, particularly Mary Magdalene, are central figures in all four Gospel accounts of the Resurrection.

Why the omission? Perhaps because women in first-century Palestine were not permitted to testify in court, so citing them as witnesses might not have convinced skeptical audiences of the authenticity of the Resurrection.

The Church followed Saint Paul's lead on the position of women, Sister Mary said, trimming its sails to gain acceptance in the larger world. This process accelerated around A.D. 70. "The Church had to be organized so as not to be a laughingstock to men of power," she said. "It became a church ordered institutionally, according to the preferences of the society." And so, women were gradually disenfranchised.

One opponent of this trend was the author of the Gospel according to John. All three of the synoptic Gospels reach a crescendo when Simon Peter confesses his faith that Jesus is the Messiah. "John's Gospel comes to a high point with a confession of faith too," Sister Mary said. But it is the confession of Martha, the sister of Mary and Lazarus. "Scholars tell us this is not an accident. . . . The Gospel of John is very clearly designed to [argue] that the witness of women was central to the [Christian] tradition."

This viewpoint did not prevail. Women were increasingly pushed to the margins of the Church. But the argument that this repositioning

was divinely ordained is not well supported, Sister Mary said. "My reading of the tradition is that we are given a question about the role of
women in the Christian tradition." Conservatives in the Church are
hoping that "if we ignore the question it will go away, or that if we
call the protestors disloyal they will become alienated and leave," she
said. "But I made a decision a long time ago; I'm not leaving."

Women who remain in the Church, however, face a difficult question: "What do we do in the face of powerlessness?" And then, looking
down at the half-dozen people in the audience wearing stoles, she said,
"Though your numbers are small, your renown has spread throughout
the city."

Their protest reminded her of the story of Bartolomé de las Casas,
the Spanish Dominican who was the first European witness to protest
the treatment of native people in the Americas. He was reading the Book
of Wisdom when he came upon the verse that read, "To deprive workers
of their wages is to kill them," and he felt so guilty about his own
complicity in the oppression of the Indians that he stopped celebrating
the Eucharist. After a long period of self-examination las Casas committed
himself to acting as an advocate for the enslaved natives. Having made
that decision, he found he could once again say Mass.

If standing is what it takes to keep you in the Church, Sister Mary
seemed to be saying, if standing is what allows you to remain in contact
with your community and your God, then by all means, stand.

The applause in the auditorium was loud and long, and the members
of the Working Groups were particularly pleased. Rea Howarth felt so
good that she drove home, bounded down to the television room, turned
off the college basketball game her husband Tom was watching and
proceeded to recount the entire lecture.

The success of Mary Collins's presentation represented a break-
through for the Working Groups, for it bestowed on them a kind of
historical legitimacy. By implicitly comparing their situation to that of
women who ministered in the primitive Church, Sister Mary had effectively blunted the criticism of those who claimed that Christian feminism
was a come-lately offshoot of the women's movement with no precedent
in the Christian tradition. Those who continued to view members of
the Working Groups as rabble-rousers now had to admit that they were
rabble-rousers with roots, and that the issue they were addressing was an
ancient source of discontent.

The upcoming town meeting was a more contemporary source of discord. Father Maier had deputized Shannon Jordan and the members of the Dialogue Group, which he had created in the futile hope of initiating an intellectual give-and-take with the American episcopate, to compose several questions to focus the proceedings. Shannon was preparing to distribute those questions on the morning of Sister Mary's talk, so parishioners would have an opportunity to consider them in advance. But Kathy Hartley had gotten a copy of the handout and began picking it apart, objecting to each question and charging the Dialogue Group with plotting the public humiliation of Ray McGovern.

As faculty moderator of a pro-life group at George Mason University, Shannon was no stranger to controversy, but Kathy's objections were so vehement that she felt compelled to withhold the questions. When she reported her decision to Jim afterward, he told her he was disappointed. He had hoped to avoid any intercommittee wrangling, but now he felt he had no choice but to let the Working Groups help plan the forum.

Several nights later, members of the Working Groups and the Dialogue Group were seated around a table in the Upper Room. The tension between Kathy and Shannon was palpable, and a few members of the Dialogue Group, who had no partisan interest in the Standing, felt they had been dragged into a fight of which they wanted no part.

After the opening prayer, Shannon explained why the meeting had been called, and she suggested that they begin by reviewing the questions. Perhaps a few could be revised.

No, Kathy said. The questions reflected a prosecutorial bias. The Dialogue Group was simply looking for a clever way to intimidate Ray.

That was not true, Shannon said. People had strong feelings about what McGovern was doing, and they deserved the opportunity to voice them. Ray had to be ready to face the judgment of his peers.

The focus should be on sexism, Kathy returned, not on the Standing.

As the meeting progressed Kathy broadened her attack. What was the Dialogue Group but a committee the pastor had formed to do his bidding? By what right did it attempt to speak for the parish?

Shannon tried to counter her charges. Almost every exchange between the two women became contentious. By the end of the meeting, the questions had been abandoned, everyone was exhausted, and several people sat with their hands trembling on their laps. Worst of all, they realized, they would have to meet again.

Two Sundays later William E. May, the Michael McGiveny Professor of moral theology at the John Paul II Institute for Studies of Marriage and the Family in Washington, stood at the podium in the upper school theater, prepared to defend the Church's teaching on women's ordination. Professor May is among the handful of married Catholic theologians who can offer a rigorous and spirited defense of the teachings of the magisterium on sexual issues. The father of six children, he understands the consequences of adhering to the teaching on birth control. A man who assents willingly to ecclesial authority, he cannot be charged with bending his arguments to protect a system that endows him with special powers. In short, he does not arouse the same suspicions as the conservative clerics who are his principal theological allies, though he says much the same thing.

May, a portly man with receding white hair and an air of abstracted humility, is a theologian of the old school. He anchors his arguments almost exclusively in natural law. His presentation that morning was based on a hermeneutics of the human body. An engaging blend of poetic characterization and deductive reasoning, it was delivered for the most part in a weary monotone.

Some critics have charged that the Church is being discriminatory and hypocritical and perpetuating inferior status in the household of the faith by refusing to ordain women, he began. But the charge is erroneous, he asserted, because the teaching of the Church is true.

The Congregation for the Doctrine of the Faith had made this clear in 1977 with *Inter Insigniores*. At that time the Vatican acknowledged that though denying women the right to be ordained might "cause pain," such pain "does not compel the conclusion that this is an instance of injustice." The reason, he said, was that men and women "imaged Christ" in different ways and that "difference in the body reveals differences in the depth of their beings."

Professor May's defense of the teaching centered on his interpretation of the "marital act" and the different ways that men and women "image" God in the process of procreation. During intercourse the man "receives in a giving sort of way," he said, while the woman "gives in a receiving sort of way." A man releases millions of sperm and hence represents superabundance and diversity, whereas a woman, with one egg, symbolizes unity and abidingness. Man is a wellspring; woman an ocean depth. Man images God as transcendent, while woman images God as immanent.

Because the male represents the transcendence and otherness of God, and because otherness is more like the relationship of a father to his children than a mother to hers, the first person of the Trinity must be thought of as a father, he said.

The second person of the Trinity had to be a son, he continued, because only a man, during his earthly ministry, could have offered credible example against the oppression of women so prevalent in his time.

While God, as embodied in the first two persons of the Trinity, was most appropriately thought of as male, humanity and the Church were most appropriately thought of as female. Quoting the conservative Jesuit Joseph Fesio, he portrayed the Blessed Virgin as the true symbol of humanity and of the human being in an encounter with God. She did not initiate the salvation of the world, but at the Annunciation, she willingly assented to her role in God's plan. What Mary accomplished is metaphorically possible for human beings; what the Father and Son accomplished is not.

Further, Professor May added, the image of the Church as Christ's bride is central to the New Testament, lending increased support to the male-female motifs for conceiving of God and humanity.

All this is important, he said, because the Lord unifies himself with His people in the person of the priest at the Mass: "During the sacrifice of the Mass the priest is a representative of Christ precisely as the Father's Son and precisely as the head and pastor of his bride, the Church."

Quoting *Inter Insigniores*, he said, "It is for this reason, rooted in the sacramental character of God's creation and redemption, that the Church 'in fidelity to the example of the Lord, does not consider herself authorized to admit women to priestly ordination.'"

Professor May's theological method, heavy on philosophy and light on history, was unfamiliar to most of his audience. Parishioners, for the most part, did not engage it directly in their questions. The tone of the discussion that followed had more to do with knowing injustice when one saw it than with understanding the limits of a theological approach.

"What about the priesthood of the baptized?" one woman asked. Don't all Christians by virtue of their baptism become full members of the body of Christ? And if so, on what grounds are women excluded from holy orders?

There was a difference between the universal priesthood, Professor May said, which is open to all Christians, and the ordained priesthood, which for the reasons he had just explained was not. This was not a question of rights or of equality, it was simply a matter of conforming to the will of God as expressed through the order of creation.

Charlie Davis of the Working Groups told Professor May that even if he accepted his rationale for excluding women from the priesthood, he would still wonder why women had been excluded almost entirely from the ecclesial power structure.

May responded that this exclusion did not constitute discrimination, nor did it degrade the status of women in the Church. Submissiveness, he said, was not a sign of inferiority.

Among the last people in the audience to speak was Ellen Crowley, director of the RCIA program. Few people had suffered as much anguish over the Standing as Ellen, who had opposed it vehemently almost from the outset. She believed the Church would gradually move in the direction that the Working Groups wanted, but that sustaining a strong communal spirit during that transition was essential to its success. She had become alienated from women who were once her friends, and found herself in the uncomfortable position of criticizing people whose aims were ultimately similar to her own. This was her one public opportunity to speak her piece about the Church's resistance to women's ordination, and she made the most of it.

Professor May's presentation, she said, was based on the interpretation of profound images designed to "carry us further and further into the mystery of God." But rather than exploring the multiplicity of meanings implicit in any symbol, she continued, he insisted on a single correct interpretation and built an exclusionary system upon it.

"It seems to me you truncate the power of these symbols when you use them this way," she said. "It takes the male dominance in our culture and uses that to limit the power of the symbol. The truth that is there in the symbol is obscured."

Professor May's presentation had a peculiar effect on the parish. Sister Mary Collins had persuaded the community that an all-male priesthood had no basis in Scripture. Yet many parishioners assumed that the Vatican had some other justification for its position. Now that they had heard it, some were puzzled and others outraged.

How could the Church justify excluding women from the priesthood on the basis of this inventive but exceedingly fanciful argument which, pushed to its extreme, suggested not only that all priests should be men but that all worshipers should be women? How could such an important policy rest on an analysis of sexual intercourse which neglected that women have orgasms, and that at least in that regard they are more likely than men to image God in "superabundance"? How could gender be the essential characteristic in imaging the risen Christ in whom, Saint Paul wrote, there was "neither male nor female"?

As the open forum approached, Kathy Hartley and Shannon Jordan continued to battle one another, each angling for favor with Father Maier, each trying to sabotage the other in none-too-subtle ways. Shannon continued to argue that the Working Groups should be prohibited from meeting on parish property, and Kathy, at one point, requested that Jim remove Shannon from her position as coordinator of the adult education series.

But when the Working Groups and the Dialogue Group reconvened, it was as though a storm had passed. Working with Ted Tschudy, a parishioner who specialized in "organizational development," the groups fairly quickly agreed on two questions for the open forum: How do you feel about the Standing? and, What is at stake in this issue for you?

Several nights later Shannon and Rea Howarth were sitting in the Jesuit dining room at Georgetown University reviewing plans for the forum with Sister Sheila McNiff and Father Curtis Bryant, who would moderate the discussion. The table talk centered on Professor May's presentation, which Rea and Sheila dismissed as "plumbing theology."

"It makes too much of sex," one of them said.

"You can't make too much of sex!" Shannon exclaimed rather loudly.

Heads turned. Forks froze. Several elderly Jesuits looked over to the table where the only women in the dining hall were seated and then went on with their meals.

Shannon lowered her head. She had found Professor May's talk powerful in an odd way. She had been struck by his metaphors; she wanted to be the "ocean woman" he spoke of. Yet there was much about the talk that troubled her. It reminded her of the men she had grown up with who regarded women as both finer than and inferior to themselves. For several days afterward, reflecting on what he had said, she found herself close to tears.

Organizing the open forum had been emotionally taxing as well. She neither enjoyed the contentiousness of her relationship with the Working Groups nor felt inclined to step back from her opposition to the Standing. That night, as she and Rea left the dining hall, she felt herself again giving way to tears. Rea put an arm around her and they walked together toward the gates of the university—reconciled, if only for the moment.

⟨⟩

On Palm Sunday morning a parade of frond-waving children accompanied Father Maier down the aisle of the wide, windowless theater of the upper school. Because the 9:15 liturgy attracts more than fourteen hundred worshipers, it is celebrated in two places, the church and the school, and Jim was presiding at the second of those sites. He was playing the part of Jesus, who entered Jerusalem on the back of a donkey, and the kids were cast as the crowd that had laid palms in his path.

Palm Sunday is the first day of Holy Week, the most sacred time of the Christian year. It was not the moment that Jim would have chosen for his parishioners to debate the Standing, but a blizzard had played havoc with his discernment schedule and left him little choice. When the mass was over he removed his deep purple vestments and, after the temporary altar had been removed from the stage, he walked to the foot of the center aisle and picked up a microphone. There were perhaps 150 people in the creaky seats.

"Thanks be to God that most of us can hear," he said in an oddly joyous voice. "Our apparatus is working. It is very hard to hear and to listen without thinking about what we are going to say when we have the opportunity." But he asked them to concentrate at least as hard on what their adversaries were saying as on the remarks that they were planning to make themselves. Then he turned the program over to the five panelists who sat behind him on the stage.

It was only natural that Ray McGovern should speak first. He was the text, and much of what had gone on in the parish over the last eleven months was commentary.

Ray wore a suit but no tie, and the top button of his shirt was open. He began by asking everyone to take a deep breath of the warm spring air that was wafting into the auditorium through the open rear doors. His gaze moved from the audience to the floor in front of him and back.

In preparing for the forum, he had been reminded of a line spoken by Jim, the runaway slave in *Huckleberry Finn*, he said. His daughter had read it to him just a few days before: "Just because you were taught that something is right and everyone believes something is right, that don't make it right."

What brought that to mind, he said, was that several years earlier the parish had helped pay for him to get his certificate in theology at Georgetown, "to prevent me from preaching heresy to our CCD children," and he had learned something that surprised him.

"This God is a one-issue God," Ray said. "He cares passionately about justice. What does that mean for me when I see a Church that is full of the injustice of subordinating women?"

He had been exploring that question for more than a year now, but he still wasn't sure what he could do to improve the status of women in the Church.

"What I can't do is nothing," he said. "I stand not with any agenda, not with any judgment. I stand just to be faithful to this God."

When Ray finished, he passed the microphone and lowered his head. Each of the next three speakers defended a different position. Pat Gormeley of the CCD board wore the light blue stole, but refused to stand. Pauline Flynn supported what Ray was doing, but could neither stand nor wear a stole herself. Ellen Crowley, as most people knew, found both the Standing and stole-wearing abhorrent.

The last speaker was Paul Quinn. With his unruly beard and comfortable paunch he looked like a well-fed prophet. Paul had been seething about the Standing from the Sunday it began, but this was his first opportunity to address an audience of any size. Bristling with energy, he made his case with a palpable if restrained anger.

As a liturgy coordinator he had heard scores of complaints. "People say, 'It's distracting,'" he said. "Or, 'I can't see.' Or 'It disrupts my ability to concentrate.'"

It was getting to the point where certain Communion ministers didn't want to give Communion to stole wearers, and presiders found it hard to preach.

"What I think we have to understand is that as Catholics we do not have a right to stand at our liturgy," he said. "It is insulting to what we do and it may be sacrilegious. There certainly is a lot that needs to be done. The Eucharist just isn't the place to do it."

When Paul finished his remarks, Father Bryant opened the floor for discussion.

The first respondent was Father Larry Madden. Larry was best known in the 9:15 community for his success in preaching to children. For years he had appeared in the pulpit at the Family Mass accompanied by Mr. Blue, a hand puppet who bore a passing resemblance to the Cookie Monster. Mr. Blue served as Larry's interlocutor, asking all the questions about that day's readings that the kids might have wanted to ask themselves.

Larry worked half-time as an associate pastor at Trinity and half-time as director of the Georgetown Center on Liturgy, Spirituality and the Arts, which he had founded thirteen years earlier. The center devoted itself to implementing the liturgical reform begun at the Second Vatican Council. It gave workshops and seminars to help priests and lay people plan liturgies that were expressive, inclusive and theologically sound. He was a man with very definite opinions about what kind of behavior was permissible at mass.

"I am a dues-paying member of the Women's Ordination Conference," he said, standing at the aisle near the front of the theater. "But I'm just about ready to stop preaching at the 9:15. It is hard to give a sermon, because there is already somebody giving one. It is a disruption."

Then, turning his gaze from the audience to the panel, he said to Ray, "I defy you to prove that's not what standing is all about."

It was true, he added, that the Church was divided over the issue of women's ordination, but in the liturgy, Catholics celebrate the promise that they will eventually be one in Christ. "You work toward making things better," he said. "But you don't stop celebrating the promise."

This was the first public criticism of the Standing uttered by a priest at Holy Trinity, and it boosted the morale of Ray's opponents in the theater. One by one, they rose to echo Ellen and Paul and Larry's complaints. But Ray had his defenders, too, people who characterized what he was doing as a sign of hope to alienated women, an act of prophecy and a form of prayer.

Christin McGovern said that the way the parish was responding to her father's protest fit the classic pattern of denial. It was like punishing a child for mentioning an adult's alcoholism while the drinking continues unabated. "Maybe a lot of older women have given up on the idea of becoming a priest," she said. "But people my age haven't, and I ask you to keep that in mind."

When his turn came to respond, Ray directed himself to Father Madden. "Larry, you know the liturgy is already disrupted by this injustice," he said. "My crime, if there is one, is to make it more difficult for us all to remain in denial about it."

As the morning wore on the level of vitriol rose. It seemed the forum might degenerate into an exchange of accusations. But then a young woman named Margie Doyle stepped to the microphone. "What I don't understand," she said, "is how one man standing, or several people standing, can cause such disunity."

This brief statement was as perceptive as any made that morning, for it indirectly challenged parishioners to reflect on the disproportionate ruckus Ray had raised.

Why were people on both sides so angry? Why couldn't Ray's opponents simply ignore him or go next door to the theater, where Mass was being offered at the same time? Why couldn't Ray and his supporters understand that people who are powerless to resolve the issues behind a protest will eventually come to resent the protestors?

Ray's opponents seemed unwilling to admit that the injustice of the Church's teaching on women's ordination might require them to inconvenience themselves or to take certain risks. Ray and his supporters, on the other hand, seemed to have little to offer strategically beyond continued protest. If parishioners embraced Ray's logic, they would probably have to stand at every Eucharist they attended for the rest of their lives.

Both sides were stymied by the Vatican's refusal to discuss the issue in a rational and collegial fashion. The result was predictable. People who should have been united in opposition to the unjust action of an unresponsive authority were divided, instead, over whether and how such opposition should be expressed. And rather than directing their anger at the authors of that injustice, they were directing it at one another.

This became particularly clear when Father Maier rose to make one of the last interventions of the morning. Jim realized by this point that no compromise was at hand, and that his best effort to end the Standing and divert further archdiocesan attention from his beleaguered parish had failed. And so he began tossing out ideas as quickly as they came to him, in the hope that somehow he could pull out some kind of resolution.

"Sometimes I've worn the ribbon," he said, turning in his seat near the stage to face the people in the theater. "I'm very supportive of us moving toward the ordination of women in the Catholic Church." But, he added, he was concerned about the Eucharist being used as a forum for protest. "We gather not to talk to one another, but to worship God," he said, and that had been forgotten.

What shall we do next? he asked. "Should we protest outside the [Vatican embassy] Sunday after Sunday? Do we say the rosary outside the cardinal's residence? I don't know. But I think the time for protesting at Holy Trinity is past."

After Jim sat down, the audience spent barely a moment reflecting on his suggestions. The pastor of a Catholic parish had just proposed demonstrating outside the homes of his ecclesial superiors, and his proposal had gone almost entirely unremarked upon. Even the staunchest supporters of women's ordination ignored Jim's ideas and trained their fire on opponents within the parish.

"The people who say to sit down never offer concrete suggestions," Kathy Hartley said. "They are a voice for compliance. The request to take it somewhere else is rather typical of an avoidance of the problem."

After the discussion petered out, Father Curtis Bryant climbed to the stage to make a few concluding observations. "Holy Trinity is a leader in the American Church," he said. "It is one of the five or six parishes in the country which provides a witness to the American Church that is a source of envy."

Those were consoling words to hear on such a sour morning, but like all the other words spoken in the theater that morning, they made nothing happen.

CHAPTER FIFTEEN

While the 9:15 community was arguing its way to nowhere, the Jesuits at the provincial office in Baltimore were awakening to the seriousness of Holy Trinity's plight. For more than two hundred years the Maryland province of the Society of Jesus had chosen the parish's pastor, with little interference from the archdiocese of Washington, and it had taken Ed Glynn and his staff several months to appreciate how radically Cardinal Hickey's new personnel policies, which mandated an archdiocesan review of each church, had changed the nature of the game. By mid-March, however, Glynn and his staff understood that if the report on Holy Trinity was not challenged, it might easily serve as grounds for removing the Jesuits from the parish.

It was an odd document, Father Glynn thought, and he doubted whether it expressed the cardinal's personal views. The criticisms were too broad, the tone too severe. Hickey was nothing if not meticulous, and he had a flair for obscuring bad news in a fog of pieties. Furthermore, Ed knew that the cardinal did not nurse silent resentments. If James

Hickey had serious problems with Holy Trinity, he would have let the Jesuits know.

No, the report had the feel of an opening argument. It was composed by men who knew that their word might not be the last. That accounted for its stridency and its determined effort to provoke alarm.

Father Glynn surmised that the document was the work of a small circle of Hickey's advisors, Bishop Corrada and Father Peter Vaghi principal among them. Clearly these men had the cardinal's ear. Father Glynn's job was to make certain that theirs were not the only voices Hickey heard.

After rereading the report a few times, he called the chancery and arranged a meeting with the cardinal and Bishop Corrada.

Holy Trinity was unusual in having an ecclesial advocate. Most parishes are staffed by diocesan priests, men whose careers depend upon the favor of their bishops. They are in no position to stand up to hostile superiors.

But the provincial of a religious order, such as the Jesuits, is usually selected by a committee of his peers, and he serves at the pleasure of the order's "father general" in Rome. He can afford to argue with the local hierarchy when the interests of his order require it.

Father Glynn was a large man with sloping shoulders and heavy-lidded eyes. He brought a combative good humor to his dealings with the archdiocese. Like many of the Jesuits in the Maryland province, he came from the eastern Pennsylvania coal fields, and despite a career in and out of academia he still moved easily in a working-class milieu.

In the Society he was regarded as something of a jock. While president of St. Peter's College in Jersey City, Ed had enjoyed socializing with the New York reporters who covered the school's athletic teams. But Father Glynn was also a sensitive spiritual director, and while teaching at Georgetown University he had sown the seeds for a revival of Ignatian prayer on campus.

Beside the refined and attenuated presences of the cardinal and the auxiliary bishop, Father Glynn could seem particularly proletarian. Yet he was cagey and knew when to be blunt. Bluntness being rare in ecclesial circles, Father Glynn had the reputation of a forceful negotiator.

The cardinal and the bishop began the meeting that March morning by acknowledging their pleasure with Holy Trinity's vitality. They were relieved to learn that only a handful of people were involved in the

Standing, and they seemed to realize that a forceful reiteration of Church teaching would not induce the protestors to sit down. But they were upset that Father Maier had allowed the Working Groups on Sexism to meet on church grounds. It was also their opinion that the religious education program was run by "unhappy women," eager to share the reasons for their unhappiness.

Father Glynn knew that there were some real differences between the parish and the archdiocese. But these were not what disturbed him; they could be negotiated issue by issue. More nettlesome was the prosecutorial attitude the archdiocese had assumed. Bishop Corrada, in particular, seemed willing to believe false and easily refuted accusations against the priests at Holy Trinity.

The bishop had been told that on the day the gay Catholic group, Dignity, was expelled from St. Edward's Chapel on the Georgetown campus, Jim Maier had led them in a march to St. Margaret's Episcopal Church, where Dignity had found a liturgical refuge. There had been such a march, Father Glynn replied, but when it occurred Jim was involved in his usual Sunday duties at Holy Trinity.

The bishop had been told that Father Larry Madden supported the Standing. This was false, as anyone who had heard Larry threaten to walk off the altar if Ray McGovern did not sit down could have told him.

The bishop had also been told that Father Madden was a disciple of Joseph Campbell's, the mythology scholar whom Bill Moyers made famous in a series of interviews on public television. Campbell, who did not believe in God, was on the board of Larry's liturgical think tank, Corrada said. The two reportedly conversed with some frequency.

Father Glynn replied that Larry had organized a conference to study the significance of the "Campbell phenomenon" for the Catholic Church. But if the two men were conversing, then the significance of this phenomenon was greater than anyone had supposed, since Joseph Campbell was dead.

The meeting sputtered to a close, and Ed Glynn left the chancery puzzling over the bishop's state of mind. Corrada could only have hurt himself by airing such baseless accusations. Was the man simply reckless or was this part of a larger strategy to throw so much at Holy Trinity that something would have to stick?

Whatever the case, the provincial was encouraged. If his opponents were intent on overplaying their hand, it could only improve his position with the cardinal. With that in mind, the Jesuits set about turning the intemperate tone and faulty logic of the report on Holy Trinity against the men who wrote it.

The drafters of the document clearly wanted an end to the Standing, but they offered no ideas on how to achieve this. It was true that Jim Maier was unwilling to have Ray McGovern carried from the church, but so, apparently, was Cardinal Hickey, who owned the building and could have ordered this himself. One reason for the cardinal's restraint may have been the questionable legality of such an order. What statute supports the eviction of a man who has assumed the wrong posture for prayer?

The drafters' desire to force the Working Groups off Trinity's property was equally clear, but this was a matter of preference, not Church policy. In November of 1992, after the American bishops had rejected a draft of the controversial pastoral letter on the role of women in the Church, Cardinal Joseph Bernardin of Chicago had introduced a resolution urging that the matter be the subject of further discussion. The resolution passed. It seemed peculiar to site the Working Groups' compliance with this directive as evidence of unorthodoxy.

The criticism of the parish's relationship with the gay community was not much more firmly founded. The prayers on behalf of lesbians and gays had been quietly halted a few months earlier. The Jesuits no longer made the unobjectionable claim that fidelity was the bedrock Christian value in any relationship. Beyond these, the parish's only transgression was that Margaret Costello, with Jim's approval, had told several members of Dignity (including several seminarians) that they, as individuals, were always welcome at Holy Trinity.

In the neighboring archdiocese of Baltimore and in a few other jurisdictions around the country, Dignity was allowed to worship as a group in Catholic facilities. Telling individual members of the group that they were welcome at Trinity hardly seemed a seditious step. Nor was it clear what effect the invitation had had.

The most visible gay men at Holy Trinity were of the older bachelor-gentleman variety. They had been attending the parish for years and were, the cardinal would have been cheered to know, sticklers about the liturgical rubrics. If there was a substantial homosexual contingent at any one mass, it was composed of fairly discrete people. How the archdiocese proposed to rid the community of gays, short of stopping people at the door to inquire whether they were sexually active homosexuals, was not clear.

The critique of the CCD program was the most revealing of the criticisms against the parish. Several previous archdiocesan directors of religious education had given the program excellent evaluations. Now suddenly it was insufficiently orthodox. But the program itself had barely changed. What was different was the ideology of the cardinal's advisors.

This was not to say that Anna Thompson's approach was above criticism; Peter Schaumber was not the only parent who thought the content of the program a bit thin. Still, it seemed odd that the archdiocese should come down so hard on a program that by most objective measures—training of catechists, support of parents, enrollment—was among the most successful in the area. Hundreds of families had left their own parishes to have their children educated at Holy Trinity. Few voiced substantive complaints. The archdiocese seemed to be saying that these people had been duped.

It may have been consoling for the parish's critics to suppose that a few headstrong staff members had caused Holy Trinity to run off the rails of orthodoxy. But the notion that Anna Thompson and Margaret Costello had imposed their wills on the cowering laity could not have been propounded in the parish with a straight face.

Ed Glynn planned to make some of these points in his conversations with the archdiocese. He also planned to recommend not one, but three solid pastoral candidates of whom the cardinal could take his pick. He would do everything he could to accommodate Hickey, short of radically altering the ethos of Holy Trinity.

In the meantime, Father Glynn hoped that Jim Maier could keep a lid on the place.

☙

On Holy Thursday morning Jim Maier sat in his office, examining his aquarium and enjoying perhaps the last restful moment he would have for several days. He had three cichlids or convict fish, two male and one female. The female was ready to spawn, and the larger male was hounding the smaller one away from the corner where the female had cleared a circle in the granite. Though Jim knew the smaller fish might be in danger from the larger fish, his biologist's curiosity was stronger than his pastoral compassion, and he chose, uncharacteristically, not to intervene.

On his desk lay scripts for the Easter Triduum, the three most profound and extravagant liturgical celebrations of the year. That evening the church would be filled to overflowing for the Mass of the Lord's Supper, at which Catholics commemorate the Last Supper, when Jesus instituted the Eucharist. This liturgy was among Jim's favorites, for after the Gospel he would summon a few parishioners to chairs in front of the altar, wash their feet as Jesus had washed the feet of his disciples, and send them, with basins, pitchers and towels, to wash the feet of other parishioners seated around the church. For him, this ritual captured the essence of Christian discipleship nearly as well as the Eucharist itself.

On Good Friday evening, the church would be jammed once again for the Church's most somber celebration. The Liturgy of the Lord's Passion is an invitation for Catholics to reflect on their own sins and their own suffering as they contemplate the suffering and sacrifice of Christ. Near the end of the liturgy, several parishioners would bear a massive cross through the congregation to the foot of the altar, where others would file forward to kiss, touch, embrace or caress it.

On Saturday evening came the Easter Vigil, a night of lilies, fire and flowing water. For much of the week, Jim had been working on the homily he would deliver that night. The words were coming slowly. This would be his last Easter at Holy Trinity, and he wanted the homily to be among his best. But speaking from the heart did not seem wise. The parish was divided. Parishioners were afraid, and he was growing more certain that the future of his priesthood was in jeopardy.

The turmoil over the Standing and the struggle with the archdiocese had made him increasingly aware of how isolated he was, how rigid and unforgiving the Church was becoming, and how little room remained in the priesthood for a man of his convictions. In attempting to lead his parishioners toward "spiritual freedom," he, like Ed Dougherty, had come to realize that his deepest and seemingly truest desires were at odds with the discipline of celibacy and the teachings of the Church.

Father Maier had been in his mid-thirties when he acknowledged to himself that he was gay. This understanding had come to him slowly and in much the way he would later hear others describe their own unfolding realizations.

"Whenever I would ask somebody when they first knew they were gay, they would say, 'Well, in my twenties,' " he said that morning in his office. "But then they would look back to certain things in their lives and say, 'Click!' "

In high school Jim had had a steady girlfriend who loved him enough to follow him to college in Pittsburgh. He had entertained thoughts of marrying her and raising a family, but he entered the Society instead. By the time he began his tertianship—the period of service and reflection a Jesuit undergoes after he is ordained, but before he has made his "final" vows to the Society—Jim had been attracted to enough other men to understand that he was gay.

He could not be certain, at first, whether this jeopardized his future in the Society. The Church regarded a homosexual orientation as an "inclination" to evil, and homosexual activity as a grave sin. But Jim had been living a celibate life for nearly eighteen years and planned to continue doing so. Did his sexual orientation alone disqualify him from becoming a priest?

He did not think so. There were many homosexuals in the priesthood and in the Society. The ordained ministry was attractive to gay men who accepted the Church's teaching on homosexuality, for it offered male companionship and a socially acceptable alternative to marriage; it also consecrated the celibacy that Catholic doctrine demanded of them to the higher purpose of serving the Church.

Jim knew all this when he decided to discuss the matter with his tertianship director, but he was still not sure how the man would respond. His director was an Irish priest with traditional views, and Jim had visions of the man sagging with disappointment, rising in fury, or recoiling in disgust. Instead, the priest received the news with equanimity, counseled him to remain in the order, and told him to be judicious in sharing his secret.

It was nearly three years before Father Maier had occasion to raise the issue with his superiors. By that time, he was being considered for the post of novice master in the Maryland province. The job involved working intimately with each of the young men entering the Society. "I thought for that reason I needed to be up front about it with the provincial," he said.

But Father Maier's disclosure did nothing to affect his superior's decision. The provincial simply asked for Jim's assurance that he would be candid if his homosexuality began to compromise his effectiveness.

Father Maier served seven years as novice master and earned a reputation as one of the best spiritual directors in the Maryland province. In that time, he said, his sexual preference never presented a problem in his work with the novices.

During his years as master of novices, however, Jim met a brother Jesuit not stationed at the novitiate who seemed interested in him as more than a clerical colleague. "We decided to explore that," he said cryptically on Holy Thursday morning. He would not elaborate on whether they became intimate. Neither man, at that point, imagined a future outside the priesthood, and that, in some ways, made the brief relationship possible.

"There was kind of a safety net," Jim said. "You assume you have the same basic commitments and you can work this out." Father Maier's friend died during Jim's early years at Holy Trinity.

Life in the parish exacerbated Jim's sexual dilemma. No longer could he fall back on the comforting routines of the novitiate to give structure to his life. No longer could he count on his novices to provide him with the intense but one-sided intimacy that made him an expert on their inner lives but kept them basically ignorant of his. The new work was varied, stressful and all-consuming. It made him feel needy in ways he had not experieced before. He shared his anguish with a few Jesuit friends, and to his surprise and regret, these conversations became public during his second year as pastor.

In January of 1989, Jim turned fifty, and the Costellos, Halls, Quinns, and a few other families had organized a parish-wide party in his honor. There were more than 200 people in the auditorium of the Knights of Columbus Hall in Arlington when a Jesuit from Georgetown University, made bold by the evening's libations, rose to offer a toast.

In the course of his passionate disquisition the man revealed that Jim was yearning for physical intimacy and contemplating leaving the priesthood. "Stay with us, Jim!" he concluded, near tears. "Stay with us!"

Father Maier was mortified. He had never felt so exposed. To complicate matters, the emotional nature of the other priest's remarks suggested to some guests that he had a crush on Jim, and that set them to wondering whether Father Maier might be gay. Others simply assumed that Jim was involved with one of several high-profile women in the parish.

At first, the speculation about his sexual conduct amused Jim, particularly since the rumors of his affairs were so fundamentally misguided. Part of the talk was to be expected, he realized. People often engaged in such gossip about their priests. But part of his problem, he came to understand, was of his own making.

"I'm not consciously trying to flirt with people," Jim said. "But I see that I am a seducer, in some ways, because I do find it fairly easy to talk about myself, and to tell people intimate details about myself. And that's seductive."

One person who felt drawn to Father Maier was a man in his late twenties whom Jim encountered regularly at the parish. They often spoke privately and, Jim thought, casually. Then one day, in the winter of 1989, the man suddenly confessed his feelings in a letter. Father Maier was disarmed by his friend's willingness to risk rebuke and lay himself bare. They quickly became close companions.

Their relationship was both a solace and a torment. For obvious reasons Jim could not conduct a public courtship, and so he learned to make a secret of his movements. He could not anticipate the demands on his time, so he could seldom commit to any meeting in advance. And he felt extremely conflicted about what he was doing, so he insisted on setting the parameters of the relationship unilaterally.

"One day he asked me, 'Are you always going to be the priest and holding all the cards?' " Jim remembers. That question made clear to him the fundamental unfairness of their relationship. Jim could not be true to his friend while remaining a priest, and he could not be true to his priesthood while remaining with his friend.

"What was clear was that I really needed to break off this relationship," he said. His friend wasn't "pushing" for a commitment, but Jim decided to "trust the clarities" he had. He ended the relationship in the summer of 1990 and the young man left the area shortly thereafter.

As a younger man, Jim would have anguished not so much over the conduct of his relationship as over its very existence. For almost two millennia, natural law theologians have asserted that the existence of two human sexes, and the necessity of each in perpetuating the species, indicates God's intention that men and women exist in a state of interdependence, each supplying what is lacking in the other. Heterosexual unions honor this intention and are therefore moral, the Church teaches. Homosexual unions deny it and are therefore wrong.

But a small, growing school of Catholic intellectuals argue that natural theology actually supports the morality of homosexual unions. If human sexuality, as the Church teaches, is a gift from God, then mustn't God will the existence of homosexuals? Or as Jim puts it: "Why would God make us this way and say 'Uh-uh. You can't.'?"

The Church cites biblical prohibitions to support its position, but Jim found these ambiguous. The destruction of Sodom has long been cited as evidence of God's attitude toward homosexuals, but what stirs God's rage in the account in the Book of Genesis is not homosexuality per se, but the intention of some Sodomites to rape the divine messengers sent to Abraham. To further complicate matters the prophets Isaiah and Ezekiel attribute the city's destruction to its mistreatment of the poor. The book of Leviticus makes homosexuality a capital offense, but it also makes fortunetelling a capital offense, and dictates banishment for couples who have sex while the woman is menstruating. Saint Paul condemns "sodomites," but there is uncertainty among Catholic Scripture scholars as to whether he is referring to homosexuals in general, to those who had sex with prepubescent prostitutes, or heterosexuals who sought novelty.

Jim thought the saint's views were the product of cultural and historical conditioning rather than a direct expression of God's will. "My guess is that he assumed homosexual behavior was a chosen behavior, an alternative to heterosexual love," he said. "He would not have believed you are born into same-sex preference." But that is what Jim believed, and as a biologist he suspected that science might one day bear him out.

But the discovery of a biological explanation for homosexuality would probably not change the Vatican's thinking. In his 1986 letter, "On the Pastoral Care of Homosexual Persons," Cardinal Joseph Ratzinger had gone further than previous Church authorities in acknowledging that homosexual persons did, in fact, exist; that they were something other than failed or deluded heterosexuals. But he argued that because homosexual intercourse was not open to procreation, it distorted "the original harmony between Creator and creatures," and "led to all kinds of moral excess."

In the same document, Ratzinger directed bishops to withdraw support from gay Catholic organizations that did not accept this teaching. In the wake of the letter, Dignity, which had previously enjoyed cordial relations with a number of American bishops, was ousted from Catholic churches across the country.

The cardinal elaborated further on the Vatican's attitude toward homosexuals in the summer of 1992. The United States was then in the midst of a presidential campaign in which candidate Bill Clinton had promised to reverse the federal ban on gays in the military, and Catholic voters in several jurisdictions were faced with ballot initiatives seeking to resolve the legal status of homosexuals. A few befuddled American bishops had written to Ratzinger seeking his help in articulating where the Church stood on these matters, and his response caused a sensation when it was leaked to the press.

The cardinal's comments were contained in a letter which constituted a kind of ecclesial advisory and had no status as Church teachings. Nonetheless, Ratzinger's missive offered a revealing glimpse into the mind of the Church's chief ideologue at a moment when he assumed he was speaking only to his episcopal brethren.

In the letter Ratzinger justified discrimination against gays and lesbians in instances when there was an overriding social interest. Hence, he asserted, it was permissible to discriminate against homosexuals who sought to adopt children, become foster parents, teach school, coach school athletic teams or enter the military. He also justified housing dicrimination when the needs of "genuine families" were at stake.

Whether the cardinal's letter had much effect on the ensuing elections was unclear. American Catholics are of several minds on the issue of homosexuality. According to numerous opinion polls, they solidly oppose the kinds of discrimination that Cardinal Ratzinger condoned. But depending on the survey and the phrasing of the question, they are either evenly divided on the morality of homosexual activity, or narrowly reject the notion that such activity can be moral.

At most times the issue has a relatively low profile within the American Church. Few parishes have gay outreach programs, and Dignity operates almost exclusively out of Protestant sanctuaries. But while gay Catholics maintain a fairly discreet presence within the Church, gay activists are frequently as odds with the American hierarchy. Members of ACT-UP, a radical gay rights group angered by the American bishops' opposition to the distribution of condoms in public schools and clinics, have disrupted liturgies in New York and California. And gay Irish Catholics have waged unsuccessful legal battles against Church-backed opposition for the right to march in Saint Patrick's Day parades in New York and Boston.

Beneath questions of public health and civil rights lies a complex theological issue. A revision of the Church's teaching on homosexual activity would have far-reaching implications. The Church asserts that human beings are incarnated spirits: souls in bodies. An individual's physical structure, it follows, is central to his or her identity. And differences as profound as those between men and women, the Church reasons, must be symbolic of differences in the natures of their beings.

God has created these differences for a reason, the Church maintains. Hence its belief that each sex has a distinctive part to play in the construction of his Kingdom. This accounts for John Paul II's occasional denunciations of feminism, which he believes obscures these differences, and his passion in promoting motherhood as the essential female experience.

If a homosexual orientation is "natural," then the Church has overestimated the extent to which human identity is determined by gender; the body is a much more ambiguous symbol than it has supposed. This would call into question not only Catholic teaching on homosexuality but the ban on women's ordination, for the Vatican argues that women, in their bodies, do not properly "image" Christ.

Many progressive Catholics would cheer these developments. But if the Church were to concede that its interpretation of the human body is fundamentally flawed, and that it had erred in its teaching about what it means to be a woman and what it means to be a man, then it would be forced to admit that it could speak only vaguely about one of the assumptions at the foundation of the faith: that human beings are incarnate spirits, souls in bodies.

Jim Maier was only peripherally aware of the implications of his opinions about Church teaching. For the most part, he had explored the issue on a more experiential level. As his desire for physical intimacy increased, so did his desire to discuss his homosexuality with friends, and so he began to consider how he should volunteer such information—and to whom.

He had given the matter a good deal of thought from a strictly professional point of view. "To the question 'Who has to know?' I'd answer, 'Nobody,' unless your being gay is proving a problem in your ministry," he said. "But the pressure on gay priests is often to feel, 'I want to come clean to everybody,' and then your superior has to know because it affects the kinds of assignments you can take."

For him, the urge to come clean clashed with the urge to spare those who might be devastated by the news. "Coming out is really a hard thing to do, unless you know how somebody will react," Jim said.

He had not told a conservative Jesuit friend to whom he felt particularly close because he was certain the man would be both crushed and angered. Nor had he informed his brother John.

"I wouldn't want to confirm in his mind the idea that my vocation is really nothing, that it was just moving into a life that suited me," he said. "I wouldn't want to confirm in his mind that it is pure naturalism."

The winter of 1993 was not a particularly good time for a priest to admit his homosexuality. A flood of news reports about priestly pedophilia had inflamed Catholics' concern about the integrity of their clergy. Much of the laity did not understand that a gay orientation no more indicated a proclivity to prey on young boys than a heterosexual orientation indicated a predilection to molest young girls.

Holy Trinity had been spared any taint by the scandal, however, and Jim had felt confident enough to inform a handful of parishioners that he was gay. Most were close friends. "I think it enables us to go deeper in relationship," he said.

All, seemingly, had kept his secret. Some had refused to believe him. "They want me to say I'm bisexual or something," he said.

As the end of his tenure as pastor approached, his dilemma intensified. On one hand, he had had a good life in the Society. "I've been really well-rewarded with dignity and confidentiality," he said. "For me it has been a good structure." On the other hand, he wanted to know what it was like to live as a sexually active human being.

Jim was hoping, during his upcoming sabbatical at Loyola Marymount University, to investigate gay life in Los Angeles, to go to a few gay bars, make a few gay friends, and see where this might lead him. But every time he contemplated leaving the Jesuits his mind focused less on the pulse-quickening freedom of new relationships than on practical considerations, like how to make a living, and where a fifty-four-year-old man might find health care.

"I think I am a really good teacher, I'm really good at ministry, the sacraments," he said. "But I can't do that work in the Catholic Church and be in a committed relationship." He was looking into joining the Free Catholic Church or the Metropolitan Community Church, both primarily gay denominations "where I would be acceptable as a gay person and as a minister." But he was in anguish about breaking from the Institutional church.

"It just breaks my heart to think that I, personally, or a group of us, would do something to further fragment the Church," he said. "Somebody told me there are twenty-eight thousand sects. Christian sects. Each of them saying they are the right one. That's crazy. It's crazy. That's why I question working out my personal agenda in a way that breaks with the Catholic Church."

Jim had thought hard about joining Dignity, but that would have brought the cardinal's wrath upon the parish. "For me to do anything more high profile in Washington would be disastrous," he said.

But soon he would be leaving Washington, and all the restrictions his pastorate imposed. And soon parishioners might learn his secret. "Let us suppose that the path I am on at the end of the year leads me to leave the Society and the Catholic Church," he said. "I think people will be really puzzled. Some would say I was being true to my own spiritual journey. But others will see it as a terrible betrayal and rejection of . . . of Christ."

Indeed one doesn't have to look far at Holy Trinity to find such people. "I look at homosexuality as, you have to abstain," said Bill Dombrow, a member of the Young Adult Community. "It's not condoned by God."

"Everybody has problems," said Rosemary Carter, whose husband, Carroll, had questioned the parish's orthodoxy at the forum with Bishop Corrada. "But is Holy Trinity going to be a church where the ideal is raised up? Or do you just say, 'Come on, sinners,' and you don't have to do anything about it?"

Jim gave these objections their due. "I am constantly being bounced back and forth between my conviction that I must do my own thing as well as I can, and the wisdom of centuries that says those who stay within the mainstream of the Catholic Church are ultimately vindicated," he said.

"Can I live the ordained ministry well? There is no question about that; I can. But is it just a question of biting the bullet on celibacy, saying 'This is your cross. This is your road, your road to holiness?' "

He was beginning to formulate a negative answer. "I've imagined writing to people in the parish to tell them I've decided to leave the priesthood," he said. "What would I say? That I loved being a Jesuit, that it was deeply difficult to leave, but that I couldn't live under celibacy. My own struggle has been so long and so pointed at times that I can't ignore that or think it is part of the ascetic path."

But he had still not resolved for himself the issue of whether leaving the priesthood was "going against the will of Christ." At a recent event at Holy Trinity School a little girl told him, for no apparent reason, that she hoped he would always be a priest. "I thought, What a strange thing to say," Jim said. "Is this Balaam's ass? Is God speaking to me through a little kid?"

"Sometimes I think it is just sex. I want sex."

The only thing he knew for certain was how happily he was anticipating his sabbatical in California. "I am very discouraged by the Church, or at least by the East Coast culture of the Church," he said. "I want to give the spirit room to move."

෴

On Holy Saturday evening the church was full at 7:10, though the Vigil mass would not begin until eight o'clock. A blanket of lilies was spread beneath the cross of glory, visible again after forty days behind its burlap screen. Azaleas surrounded the feet of the Blessed Virgin. The lights were low. In the nave, Ellen Crowley moved discreetly through the congregation, making sure that the families of the men and women in the RCIA program had seats from which they could see their loved ones baptized.

At 7:45 the white-robed "candidates" (who had been baptized in other denominations) and catechumens (who had never been baptized) strode ceremoniously up the center aisle. The lights in the church were extinguished and the congregation fell silent. Standing amid the processional party in the rear of the church, Father Maier intoned the question borrowed from the Jewish Seder: Why is this night different from all other nights?

At the lectern a young woman began to read from the first chapter of Genesis. When she came to the words, "God called the light day," Jim kindled the Easter fire, a blue flame at first barely visible above the silver rim of a white bowl. Smoke rose toward the pale blue ceiling and vast undifferentiated shadows danced on the walls.

Slowly he and his acolytes processed up the center aisle, carrying the small ball of flame. Then, for the last time, Father Maier lit the tall white paschal candle, adorned with the outlines of a cross and a risen lamb, that stood beside the lectern.

For the next half-hour, in readings and in song, the people of Holy Trinity followed the course of "salvation history" as it wove from creation through the deluge, from God's promise to Abraham through the Exodus, from the rise of the Jewish nation through its defeat, exile and halting reemergence.

"And then," the young woman said, "Jesus walked among us, telling us not only are we God's people, we are God's sons and daughters." She read from Paul's letter to the Romans: "If, then, we have died with Christ, we believe that we shall also live with him. We know that Christ, raised from the dead, dies no more; death no longer has power over him."

When she had finished, Father Maier rose to the pulpit amid blaring trumpets. The congregation sang the Gospel acclamation so loudly that the pews vibrated. "Alleluia! Alleluia! Alleluia!" The word had not been heard in the church since Ash Wednesday.

The story Jim was about to read was so familiar to the congregation that sometimes he feared its significance was lost. You will die. You will rise. You will live forever. With knowledge of such a promise, how could the world be as it was?

He read solemnly of the women on their way to the tomb, of the displaced stone, and of the man in shimmering garments who told them not to look for the living among the dead. In his white vestment, and with his silvery hair and snowy beard, Father Maier looked plausibly like that man himself.

When he was finished he closed the book, smiled and suddenly relaxed. "Alleluia!" he exclaimed.

"Alleluia," the congregation responded.

"Alleluia!" he said again.

"Alleluia!" they replied.

"Sounds good after forty days, doesn't it?"

That morning, he began, he had looked out his window after he awakened, saw an overcast sky and prayed, "Please don't let it rain."

It was raining.

"You see how good my prayers are?" he said.

The congregation chuckled.

But then he thought of how badly the region needed rain, for crops and gardens, and he changed his prayer: "Let it pour."

"You see how good my prayers are?"

The congregation laughed.

The rain made him think of the seven people who would be baptized that evening. It made him think of Father Ned Hogan, who would be baptizing more than two hundred people that night at his parish in Nigeria. It made him think of his friends at Mary, Mother of the Poor in San Salvador, where the water was always turned off after sunset so there would be enough in the morning.

Water is an ambiguous symbol, he said. Pure, it means refreshment. Contaminated, it brings disease. The ancient Hebrews knew water as a source of life, but also, through floods, as a bringer of death. Like desire, even the desire to follow Jesus, it could both renew and destroy.

Saint Paul had spoken metaphorically about his own destruction in the seventh chapter letter to the Romans, and Scripture scholars have puzzled over what he meant ever since, Jim said. As he spoke of Paul, Jim spoke of himself as well.

"How did he 'die'? Was he cast out of his family? Was he cast out of the temple? Excommunication is death little by little."

Paul said his death was from 'covetousness.' Even after his conversion on the road to Damascus, he still wanted something or "someone" more. "Perhaps he was dying," Jim said, "by commandments he could not keep."

Christ did not come to resolve such struggles for us, he said, but to be with us in our struggling. He promises not triumph but salvation, and sometimes salvation comes through the medium, or the struggle, or the surrender we think will destroy us.

"And so, if you are dead tonight too, you are invited to come to the waters. Christ is about to rise again. And I say, 'Let it pour!' "

A few moments later the candidates and catechumens came forward. They stood beside a small, gurgling pool at the foot of the altar and professed their faith. Standing nearby, friends peered through the lenses of video cameras, capturing the baptisms and the anointings.

In the weeks ahead, families would watch these tapes over and over.

At the end of the ceremony, they would see the last of the candidates step into the silvery baptismal pool. She was a young blond woman with an expensive coiffure, and when Father Maier raised the glass pitcher and poured forth the water, it matted her tresses against her forehead and her cheeks. And if they were paying close attention, they saw, as she wrapped herself in a white towel, that her face shone with something like ecstasy.

CHAPTER SIXTEEN

ᐸᗑᗑᗑᗐ

On Good Friday evening, as the people of Holy Trinity were filing forward to venerate the cross, a small band of parishioners was gathering across town in a basement church with threadbare carpeting, peeling paint and battered pews. Each year, St. Aloysius Gonzaga, one of Holy Trinity's two sister parishes, celebrates the Living Stations, a variation on the Stations of the Cross, which takes worshipers out of the church and into the streets to meditate on the suffering of Jesus in places where his people are suffering still.

St. Al's, as it is universally known, is a poor parish, and the Jesuits who live there have made the neighborhood their cause. The parish runs a shelter for homeless men in the spacious vestibule of the lower church, and operates an emergency food pantry and informal housing and employment services.

Because it stands just one mile north of the U.S. Capitol, St. Al's is a frequent meeting place for activists on the religious Left. During the 1980s and early 1990s, marches and demonstrations against the policies of the Reagan and Bush administrations were organized in its vestibule. All this, and the fact that it is one of the few racially integrated parishes in the city, makes St. Al's a beacon and a refuge for progressive Catholics who believe that fidelity to the Gospel requires a political response.

Where the liturgy at Holy Trinity draws its power from careful planning and artful execution, the shaggier services at St. Aloysius derive their impact from focusing on the world that lays writhing just beyond the church doors. These liturgies are particularly inspiring to the handful of Trinity parishioners who believe that their own parish keeps the poor at arm's length and soothes its conscience by donating 10 percent of its revenues to shelters and social justice programs.

The group that gathered that evening included Kathy Hartley, who was a member of the Holy Trinity–St. Al's prayer group, Rea Howarth and her husband, Tom, who volunteered at the men's shelter, and Marilyn and Paul Nejelski, who chaired the "Twinning Committee," which Father Maier and a brother Jesuit, Father George Anderson, the soft-spoken pastor of St. Aloysius, had formed to deepen the relationship between the two communities.

This deepening was proceeding more slowly than the Nejelskis might have liked. Many Holy Trinity parishioners are simply afraid to visit St. Aloysius, because it stands beside the crime-ridden Sursum Corda housing project. Others are put off by the stark social and economic differences between the two communities.

These differences are embodied in the person of Jesse Dudley, a bald man with brown plastic glasses, who stood at the front of the assembly that night and greeted the crowd of forty worshipers in a thin and not always audible voice. At St. Aloysius, Jesse is the deacon and one of the most respected members of the community. At Visitation, the pricey Georgetown prep school where many Trinity parishioners send their daughters, he is the janitor. The question posed by the sister-parish relationship was whether a common faith, and the good offices of the Society of Jesus, could help the two communities transcend their material and cultural differences and engage one another as sisters and brothers in Christ.

Deacon Dudley, dressed in black work pants and a navy Visitation sweatshirt, led the worshipers down the center aisle and into the vestibule. Behind him strode three young members of the Jesuit Volunteer Corps—a kind of Catholic VISTA program—bearing a wooden cross.

When the deacon stopped amid the homey chaos of the shelter, they stood beside him and held the ten-foot cross erect.

"The first station," Deacon Dudley read. "Jesus is condemned to death. We adore you, Oh Christ, and we praise you."

"Because by your holy cross you have redeemed the world."

As Jesus was unjustly condemned to death, the deacon told them, so the men of this shelter had been condemned to live without homes. And just as the onlookers at Jesus' condemnation were silent in the face of that crime, he said, too many Christians are silent in the face of this one. Then the Jesuit volunteers pushed open the shelter doors and the worshipers followed the cross into a misty rain.

Over the next hour they prayed outside an underfunded nursing home, a struggling social services agency and a crack den. Standing before an outpost of the Veterans Administration they lamented the sin of militarism. Outside a federal printing office they prayed that Congress would embrace more enlightened poverty policies. The dome of the Capitol glowed in the background.

As the group wended its way through the neighborhood, it was joined by a growing band of boys and girls from Sursum Corda. The children were not used to seeing so many white people in their neighborhood, especially at night, and they eyed the procession suspiciously until they spotted the cross.

"What church you all from?" they called, scampering across parking lots shimmering with broken glass. "What kind of song is that?"

The delegation from Holy Trinity was soon playing with the kids and trailing the pack.

Kathy, the Howarths and the Nejelskis could easily live their lives without encountering young people like those who followed them that night. Like almost everyone at Holy Trinity, and like most American Catholics, they live on the comfortable side of the line that separates the haves from the have-nots. But they are among the significant minority who believe that the Gospel calls them to a personal involvement with the poor, and on this score they find their parish wanting.

"Holy Trinity has a class bias," said Tom Howarth, who had recently left the parish for a more politically active church. "It is progressive on issues that cut across economic lines. Environmental issues. Liturgical issues. Sexual issues. But there are other issues it touches nary a bit. It does not confront economic injustice.

"I think the church has caved in to the rich."

This allegation found little support among parishioners at Holy Trinity, some of whom suggested that Father Maier was more interested in St. Al's and Madre de los Pobres than in his own church. In the previous six years, Jim had built up his parish's relationship with St. Al's and founded its relationship with the church in San Salvador. He had supported Ann Marie Santora's efforts to maintain an integrated school and backed Anna Thompson's decision to include community service in the religious education curriculum.

The nature of its relationship to the poor is perhaps the most vexing ethical issue that Holy Trinity faces. In its skirmishes with the archdiocese, the parish can paint itself as the principled underdog, holding fast for freedom of conscience, justice for women, mercy for the divorced and acceptance for homosexuals. But when the issue is economic injustice, Holy Trinity is the establishment.

A glance at the gleaming vehicles in the Visitation parking lot on a Sunday morning, or at the wardrobes of worshipers as they stream into church, confirms that parishioners are accustomed to living well, as does listening to their children recount ski vacations in Vail and Aspen on the weekend after the Christmas holidays. In the language of one of Jesus' best-known parables, Holy Trinity knows less of Lazarus, the beggar who went to heaven, than of Dives, the rich man who went to hell. And how to deal with this discomfiting truth without unduly discomfiting itself has been one of the parish's principal preoccupations.

For most of their history in this country, Catholics have not had to agonize over their relationship with the poor and the outcast, because they were the poor and the outcast. Catholic solidarity, like black cultural and economic solidarity today, had an unassailable logic. Catholics donated what resources they had to their parishes and to their dioceses, which in return gave back to them, in the form of schools, colleges, hospitals and other charitable institutions.

After the G.I. bill, however, Catholics quickly came to educational and economic parity with white Protestants. For the first time, they could imagine themselves camels at the needle's eye, and they began to wonder what was required to pass through.

In the years before the Second Vatican Council, Catholic theologians had begun to articulate a "horizontal spirituality" based on their conviction that there was more to being a Christian than tending to one's "vertical" relationship with God. This idea helped focus Catholics' attention on their suffering brothers and sisters, and on the role they could play in reducing that suffering. At the Council it helped inspire the "preferential option for the poor," the awkwardly named teaching that in making economic decisions the faithful must make the choice most beneficial to the needy.

Like many of the theological innovations of the postwar period, this was actually a work of historical reclamation. The Gospels are replete with manifestations of Christ's concern for the poor. The most forceful of these is the conclusion of the twenty-fifth chapter of Saint Matthew's Gospel, which speaks of a final judgment when the Son of Man will say to the righteous, "Come, you who are blessed by my Father. Inherit the kingdom prepared for you from the foundation of the world. For I was hungry and you gave me food, thirsty and you gave me drink, a stranger and you welcomed me, naked and you clothed me." And when the righteous ask, "When, Lord?" Jesus replies, "Whatever you did for one of these least brothers of mine, you did for me."

The earliest disciples' commitment to this teaching was such that when Peter and the leaders of the Jerusalem Church forged their historic agreement with Paul regarding his mission to the Gentiles, they pressed on him one particular instruction. "We were to be mindful of the poor," Paul recounted in his letter to the Galatians, "which is the very thing I was eager to do."

A sense of kinship with the needy survived into the patristic era, when Saint John Chrysostom wrote, "Not to enable the poor to share in our goods is to steal from them and to deprive them of life. These goods we possess are not ours, but theirs."

But when these words were written, the Church's commitment to the poor had already begun to wane. With the conversion of the emperor Constantine in 312, Roman Catholicism became the state religion, and the Church, which had once been a refuge for the downtrodden, became a tool of the powerful. For the next fifteen centuries, the Vatican was at the center of innumerable European power struggles, and shaped its social teachings to avoid giving scandal to its allies in the nobility and the monarchy.

For most of its history the Church has shown two faces to the poor. It has insisted on the dignity of each individual, no matter how humble, and the worthiness of all work, no matter how lowly. Yet it has resisted or ignored almost every epoch-marking change in the social and political order.

It has inspired legions of compassionate men and women to minister to the needy in times of famine, war and pestilence. Yet it justified the oppression of serfs and the captivity of slaves, and encouraged the murderous dispossession and forced conversion of Native Americans by European conquerors.

No institution in human history can match the scope of the Church's charitable activities. But for centuries the Church helped pacify the poor by preaching that the God who willed their suffering would reward them after death.

Then in 1891, Pope Leo XIII released *Rerum Novarum*, the encyclical that initiated a new era in Catholic social thinking. Attempting to steer a middle course between unbridled capitalism on the right and atheistic radicalism on the left, Leo asserted that workers had a right to unionize, as well as a right to safe working conditions, adequate leisure and a just wage. His successors, particularly John XXIII and Paul VI, developed a more systematic critique of the values of Western capitalism and market ethics, advocating the massive redistribution of wealth as part of a global campaign to eradicate poverty and secure basic human rights.

The popes did not seem to be suggesting a socialist revolution, yet they were exceedingly critical of economic inequalities, and that left many American Catholics puzzled as to how they should respond. Was it enough to vote for liberal Democrats and pay their taxes with a smile? Or were they supposed to behave like Zaccheus the tax collector, who, after having dinner with Jesus, sold half of what he owned and gave it to the poor?

By the mid-1960s liberal Catholics, building on the Church's social encyclicals, had begun to forge a Catholic social justice agenda that sought to humanize free market capitalism through progressive taxation and ambitious social welfare programs. Lyndon Johnson's Great Society was, to many Catholic social thinkers, the embodiment of recent Church teaching.

But the relationship between the Church and the Democratic party was severely undermined in 1973 by the U.S. Supreme Court's affirmation of abortion rights in *Roe* v. *Wade*. This decision split the vehemently antiabortion Church hierarchy from its liberal allies. And as overturning Roe became the Church's primary political focus, new alliances with antiabortion legislators, most of whom opposed the Church's social agenda, took precedence.

The liberal Catholic agenda was further handicapped in the late 1970s by the faltering of the U.S. economy, the precipitous rise in violent crime and the development of a seemingly permanent urban underclass. Compassion suddenly seemed the cause of America's problems rather than their solution. In 1980 and again in 1984, a majority of Catholic voters deserted their Democratic roots and helped elect Ronald Reagan. With much of the hierarchy focused narrowly on abortion and a majority of the faithful supporting a conservative president, progressive Catholics lost their influence in the national debate. Despite the U.S. bishops' impressive pastoral letter on the American economy in 1986, the movement to reassert Catholic social and economic ideals has yet to regain its vigor.

Pope John Paul II is more appreciative of capitalism and more suspicious of socialism than his predecessors. In 1991 he voiced a qualified approval of the free market in his encyclical *Centesimus Annus*. Yet he has continued to speak forcefully against unbridled economic individualism, the exploitation of workers and the denial of basic rights, such as nourishment and health care, to the poor.

In the United States, however, the pope's message is frequently obscured by the vagaries of the broader political debate. Neoconservative intellectuals such as Michael Novak of the American Enterprise Institute have had remarkable success in highlighting the pro-market aspects of John Paul's thinking, and no liberal Catholic of equal notoriety has arisen to challenge them in the American press. The U.S. bishops continue to support progressive economic policies, but they have refrained from partisan debate. As a result, the pope's profound differences with the economic agenda of the Republican party were not fully appreciated until he articulated them himself during a 1995 visit to the East Coast.

In the midst of this confusion, the American Church continues to struggle with the option for the poor. The U.S. bishops operate Catholic Charities, the second-largest private social service agency in the country, and Catholic Relief Services, the second-largest international relief agency in the world. The size of these institutions, however, owes only in part to the largess of the faithful; more than half of their budgets come from government and foundation grants.

But were Church-run relief agencies twice as large, or half as large, they would not provide the best measure of Catholics' commitment to the poor. Observing the preferential option is less a matter of making charitable contributions than of ordering one's economic priorities to lighten the burden of the needy. Proponents of the option argue that this requires a searching moral analysis of every financial decision that an individual or a community makes.

The people of Holy Trinity were forced into such an analysis in 1978, during the most painful episode in the parish's history, when a small and deliberately scruffy band of outsiders challenged the parish's upper-middle-class orthodoxy and reopened the question of whether one can live Dives's life and still reap Lazarus's reward.

By the time he turned up on Holy Trinity's doorstep, Mitch Snyder had already fled a career in advertising, deserted his wife and children, and served time for passing bad checks. He had converted to a rather loose form of Catholicism under the tutelage of his fellow inmate, Father Daniel Berrigan, and been arrested nineteen times for a variety of antiwar and antimilitary activities. But by the spring of 1978 the war was over, and Snyder had fastened on a new cause: the homeless.

The streets of American cities were increasingly peopled with chronic drug and alcohol abusers; with mental patients who had been released during a wave of "deinstitutionalization"; with men whose flophouses had been cleared in the name of urban renewal; with families who just couldn't afford to keep a roof over their heads. No one, at that time, understood the myriad causes of homelessness, but anyone who walked the streets of Washington could see that hundreds of people had no place to lay their heads.

Snyder and his supporters in the Community for Creative Non-Violence (CCNV) cruised the streets on winter nights in a beat-up car, distributing hot baked potatoes and asking people whom they found lying on heating grates and park benches if they needed a place to sleep. Those who said yes, they took home with them.

The group also wrote to churches around the city asking them to open their doors and let the homeless come inside. With the exception of one downtown Lutheran congregation, the churches refused.

Angered but undaunted, Snyder and his friends persuaded the District of Columbia to give them a dilapidated building on Fairmont Street in northwest Washington, not far from their own residence. They planned to renovate it with proceeds from a painting business they had started to keep their rent paid. But it became clear soon enough that

Snyder's heart was not in painting, and that the money would have to come from elsewhere.

Snyder was a friend of Colman McCarthy's, the former Trappist monk who wrote an op-ed column for *The Washington Post*. McCarthy, then a parishioner at Holy Trinity, was well-known for his liberal and pacifistic views. He had once been friendly with Father Jim English, the church's charismatic pastor, and had praised the priest's dynamic liturgies in his column. But in April of 1978, when Father English announced his plan to raise $450,000 to renovate the church, McCarthy became outraged. A parish as wealthy as Holy Trinity, he believed, should not be lavishing its resources on itself. It should be spending them on the less fortunate.

McCarthy suggested to Snyder that Jim English might be able to finance the renovation of the shelter, and Snyder seized on the idea. Holy Trinity was home to a number of prominent liberal Catholics: Senators Edward M. Kennedy and John Tunney, Joseph Califano, the secretary of Health, Education and Welfare and Edward Bennett Williams, the renowned Washington lawyer and part-owner of the Washington Redskins. Surely they could come up with the money he needed.

The fundraising was already under way when Snyder delivered a letter to Father English requesting eighty thousand dollars, and hinting at the dark consequences that befell those who ignored their sisters and brothers in Christ.

When he received the letter, Jim English was at the height of his celebrity. A dapper man with an aristocratic air, he was boyishly handsome, compulsively social and intensely creative. To many in Catholic Washington, he was the very model of what a post–Vatican II pastor should be.

During English's fourteen years at Holy Trinity, every Sunday held the promise of a liturgical happening. He once led half the congregation through the streets of Georgetown to bring the Eucharist to a bedridden parishioner. On another occasion he staged a scene from Paddy Chaefsky's play "Gideon" as part of his homily. Holy Trinity frequently hosted liturgical dancers, and on one spectacular Sunday, Father English invited a troupe of acrobats and built his homily around their routine.

By the late 1970s, the church could no longer hold the crowds that Jim English was attracting. There were not enough exits to satisfy the fire marshal, and the choir loft had begun to sag. Beyond that, the old place, with its cracked plaster and peeling paint, was not a fit symbol for the prosperous and self-confident parish. And so, with the generous backing of some of his wealthiest parishioners, Father English had set about creating a glorious new showcase in the shell of the old church.

It had not occurred to him, or to many others in the parish, that their fundraising should include some provision for the poor. Holy Trinity contributed seventeen hundred dollars to shelters and a food bank that year, and that struck most people as plenty. Father English refused Snyder's request, but told him that if he played his cards correctly, a few parishioners might be willing to help with the shelter privately.

To Snyder, this response typified affluent Christians' obsession with their own extravagant "needs," and he resolved to make an example of Holy Trinity. On the third Sunday in May, he and a few CCNV members began distributing leaflets on the steps of the church, charging that the parish had abandoned the poor and urging it to repent. One of those leaflets found its way to Marjorie Hyer, the religion writer for *The Washington Post*, and for the next six months almost every twist in this unfolding drama was covered by the press.

One month later Snyder and a few supporters began standing throughout every liturgy as a form of protest. Their numbers included four Carmelite nuns active in the homeless rights movement and two members of the Holy Trinity folk group. In late July the protest intensified as Snyder and his supporters began a juice and water fast.

The fast did nothing to budge Jim English, but it caught the attention of the national media. Soon op-ed pages across the country were blooming with moral pronouncements: Holy Trinity was a cold and unchristian parish and Mitch Snyder was a prophet. Or perhaps the people of Holy Trinity were good stewards and Snyder was a parasite.

In truth, neither side was behaving altogether honorably. Snyder had no idea whether eighty thousand dollars would be enough to fix the shelter on Fairmont Street, nor how to go about contracting for its repairs. In the midst of his fast, the building was condemned after the District became aware that he and an untrained repair crew had yanked out a weight-bearing wall. Yet Snyder continued the protest, demanding the parish make some unspecified commitment to the poor before he would take solid food.

That money donated for the renovation of the church could not legally be diverted for other purposes, and that Holy Trinity was otherwise broke, made no impression on him.

Father English, meanwhile, was keeping a troublesome secret. His campaign for $450,000 to renovate Holy Trinity had raised nearly $1 million, and he had decided to spend it all. With the permission of the donors, he could have devoted some of the money to rehabilitating a shelter. He could have made grants to Church-run charities. But these options were never explored.

On August 26 Snyder and three of his supporters upped the ante once again by setting up camp on the parish's schoolyard. By this time their protest was international news. Jim English was receiving clippings about the fast from Italian newspapers, and hundreds of letters were pouring into the rectory, some from as far away as Brazil and the Philippines.

Official Washington was fascinated by the drama. Snyder was receiving free publicity from Colman McCarthy. Father English was receiving free legal advice from a young lawyer named Brendan Sullivan, who would later defend Oliver North. For a brief moment the attention of the city was focused on the nature of Christian responsibility to the poor.

By early September it seemed that the fast, already in its sixth week, might go on indefinitely. With summer vacation ending, it seemed Father English might have to summon the police to remove Snyder and his supporters from the schoolyard. But just before the academic year began, Father Tom Gavigan, who was still in residence in the rectory, received a letter from his friend Father Jim Connor, proposing a compromise.

Father Connor, a former Jesuit provincial and past president of the U.S. Jesuit Conference, had directed retreats for the Social Concerns Committee at Holy Trinity and was alarmed by the public relations beating that the Jesuits and the parish were taking. He suggested that Holy Trinity review its plans after adding two members to the Renovation Committee who were sympathetic to the fasters' cause. In return, Snyder and his friends would leave the schoolyard and end their fast.

Jim English liked the compromise because it allowed him to appear flexible without committing him to do anything. Mitch Snyder may have realized it was his best chance of making some kind of mark on the parish. On September 7, Father English brought the compromise to the Parish Council, and the council approved it.

Afterward the fasters adjourned to Colman McCarthy's home, where Snyder got sick eating too much she-crab soup. The following Sunday they brought doughnuts to the priests in the rectory.

Holy Trinity abided by the terms of the compromise, but the Renovation Committee ultimately decided to continue with its original plans. Snyder felt duped, and in late December he alerted the media that he was undertaking a fast to the death. On the eleventh night of his hunger strike, the Parish Council convened one final time to consider whether it could accede to his now rather vague demands to do something "significant" for the poor.

By this time Snyder was lapsing in and out of consciousness and his body temperature was fluctuating wildly. He intended to continue the fast to the end, but had arranged for three friends to make decisions on his behalf in the event he lost consciousness. These friends watched Jim English announce on the eleven o'clock news the parish's intention to go forward with its renovation plans. They decided that since they could feel no love for the people of Holy Trinity, Snyder's death would not be an act of "pure" nonviolence. They would be letting their friend die simply to punish the obstinate parish, and this, they decided, would be wrong. Just before midnight they called off the fast and rushed Snyder to a hospital.

Three days later, draped over the arms of two friends, Mitch Snyder returned to mass at Holy Trinity. Jim English was preaching, and when his homily was over, a parishioner rose in the midst of the assembly and lauded the pastor for the way he had handled the crisis.

The congregation burst into applause.

Parishioners never learned how much money they actually raised or spent. And though there was some grumbling a few years later when they learned that Father English had neglected to have the roof fixed, they were fairly happy with the outcome of the renovation.

But the Jesuits of the Maryland province had been profoundly embarrassed by Father English's unwillingness to strike a compromise with Snyder. They removed him from Holy Trinity after his term as pastor ended in 1982, denying his request to remain in the parish as Father Gavigan had. Jim Connor succeeded him, and one of his first acts as pastor was to institute what the parish refers to as its "tithe"—the policy under which it donates 10 percent of most revenues to the poor.

In the ensuing years, Father English's relationship with the order continued to deteriorate, and he has not had a prominent assignment with the Jesuits since leaving Holy Trinity.

Mitch Snyder, meanwhile, became a renegade hero. The showdown in Georgetown made him the nation's most recognized spokesman for the homeless. In 1986 he went on another hunger strike, and this time forced the Reagan administration to open a large and well-equipped homeless shelter on the edge of Capitol Hill. Snyder became the prophet of choice for a variety of left-leaning celebrities, and was the subject of a hagiographic television movie, *Samaritan,* in which he was played by Martin Sheen.

But Snyder was a driven man, given to depression, and the depth of these black periods may have been exacerbated by physical weakness owing to his frequent fasts. On July 1, 1990, he called a former member of the Parish Council at Holy Trinity to "make peace" for having tried to manipulate her through his hunger strike. Three days later, Snyder hung himself.

In the thirteen years following the protest, Holy Trinity labored to reconcile its commitment to the poor with its own legitimate needs to maintain its five-building campus, educate its children, pay its employees, and create compelling Christian liturgy. By the spring of 1993, the parish was donating nearly two hundred thousand dollars each year to charitable causes. Its food, clothing and equipment drives were worth nearly as much. Yet it wasn't clear to Tom Howarth and his friends that these efforts caused anyone, beyond a small band of activists, to break a sweat, or reflect more deeply on the plight of the dispossessed.

Jim Maier was particularly avid to move the community beyond its own narrow concerns. Nothing else mattered to him quite so deeply as the parish's fidelity to the option for the poor. But as he waited that spring to learn whom the Jesuits would recommend to succeed him, he sometimes wondered whether he had done enough.

Should he have preached more vigorously on social justice? Should he have woven the sister parishes more fully into the life of his church? Or would these moves have made the parish more contentious, poisoned the nurturing atmosphere, and proved ultimately self-defeating?

It was a perennial pastoral dilemma: to comfort or to challenge? And if to challenge, then *whom* to challenge? The hierarchy? The laity?

It had always been his way to provide his parishioners with opportunities to challenge themselves. But now he was finding that the very people who had risen to those challenges were saying much the same thing as the parish's conservative critics: that the failures of Holy Trinity were rooted in its pastor's timid soul.

CHAPTER SEVENTEEN

⟨∽∽∽⟩

The group from Holy Trinity arrived in twos and threes, stepping out of the soft April evening and into the onion- and cilantro-scented air of a Salvadoran restaurant. There were ten of them in all, too many for a single table, and they were helping the waiters rearrange some furniture when Father Maier walked in and greeted them with a joke about timing his arrival to miss out on the work.

Amid the hugging and handshaking that ensued, a waitress dodged bodies and took drink orders. "Cerveza, por favor," said one of the men, exhausting his command of Spanish. Jim found a seat, and soon the party had settled down to tortilla chips, salsa, menus and conversation.

They had gathered to plan their upcoming visit to Maria, Madre de los Pobres, Holy Trinity's sister parish in El Salvador. Jo Owen, who sat across from Father Maier, would be returning for the sixth time, Jim for the fourth, and Lydia Mendoza, who was organizing the trip, for the second. The others were making their initial visits, and were hungrier for information than for the food they ordered.

Over tacos, burritos and chickpea salads, they discussed logistics, finances, wardrobes and health concerns. Lydia recalled with devious glee how Father Maier had been plagued by diarrhea on a previous trip. The conversation was so lively and so substantive that Jim didn't feel the need to add much. He just sat back and listened as the talk turned to choosing a tour guide and arranging a visit with Reuben Zamorra, the Jesuit-educated intellectual who was the Left's likely candidate in the 1994 presidential election.

If there was one achievement in his pastorate of which Jim should have felt unambiguously proud, it was Holy Trinity's relationship with Maria, Madre de los Pobres. Including his friends at the table that evening, nearly thirty parishioners had visited El Salvador, and several had returned with a new sense of mission.

Dr. Peter Gyves had left his position at the National Institutes of Health and spent three years working at Madre and in the surrounding countryside. Jay Gribble, a demographer, had entered the seminary. Tom Howarth, a lobbyist, began doing pro bono work for the Salvadoran solidarity movement. Retirees Jack and Grace O'Connor joined the Jesuit International Volunteer Corps. Kathleen Conley, who worked at the Federal Reserve Bank, began visiting a pregnant Salvadoran teenager, and Jo Owen had been named to the board of the National Debate for Peace in El Salvador, an ecumenical group founded by the archbishop of San Salvador.

For a man as invested as Father Maier was in the notions of servant leadership and the preferential option for the poor, there could hardly have been a more gratifying response. He could also take quiet pride in being among the few pastors in the archdiocese who had introduced his parishioners to the culture of Hispanic Catholics who composed roughly 15 percent of the American Church. Yet the sister-parish relationship had also been a source of friction at Holy Trinity, first between Jim and parishioners in the U.S. foreign policy community, and later between Jim and a few of his friends who had rallied to the Salvadoran cause.

The experience had been another long and sometimes dispiriting lesson in how difficult it was to focus his parishioners' attention on the moral implications of their affluence. Sometimes Jim feared that in reaction to the harsh and restrictive Catholicism of their youth, the people of Holy Trinity had come to believe in a God who required nothing of them. To his mind, however, God did require something, and it went beyond the rituals of charity; God required a personal commitment to the suffering and the poor.

The necessity of such a commitment was elucidated in the Scriptures, particularly in the book of Isaiah, the Gospel of Luke and the Letter of James. Jim found it elaborated and embodied in the writings and example of Pedro Arrupe, the Jesuits' late father general. And he encountered it in its most radical form, in the work of liberation theologians such as Gustavo Gutiérrez of Peru, Juan Luis Segundo of Uruguay and Ignacio Ellacuria of El Salvador.

For these men, the preferential option for the poor had inescapable political implications. They taught that economic inequality and political repression were sinful, and that Catholics were bound to reform the institutions which perpetrated such sins. Otherwise the faithful were implicated in the suffering of the poor.

Like many American Catholics, Jim was uncomfortable with this rather pointed call to political action. The activism that endows the Catholic Left in Latin America with its prophetic character is found in only a small minority of the parishes in the United States. Sunday worship, in most churches, is about the personal, not the political.

This is partly a matter of historical conditioning. For two centuries, an American Catholic who admitted that the Church shaped his political thinking confirmed the worst suspicions of his Protestant neighbors. To prove their patriotism, Catholics muted whatever differences they perceived between the teachings of Church and the practices of State. By the time they were secure enough to speak out, most had little reason to do so. They assumed the basic justice of a system that had blessed them abundantly, believing, perhaps, that it would lift others' boats as it had lifted theirs.

In the wake of the Second Vatican Council, progressive Catholics attempted to prod the American faithful into examining their economic and political assumptions in the light of the option for the poor. But their success in this venture was limited by their success in another. In disputing *Humanae Vitae*, liberal Catholics had persuaded the American laity that conscience was preeminent in matters sexual. That victory made it extremely difficult to persuade the same audience that Church teaching was preeminent in matters economic and political.

By the time liberation theology received a hearing in the United States, American Catholics were accustomed to plotting their own moral courses. Even abortion, the hierarchy's chief political priority, was seldom preached on in most parishes. The result was a more contemplative Sunday morning, but the faithful received little substantive help in applying the standards of the Gospel to the issues of the day.

Jim Maier had only a limited interest in politics and economics, but he was intrigued by the liberation Church and the depth of its commitment to the poor. In the summer of 1986 he spent six weeks at Maria, Madre de los Pobres—Mary, Mother of the Poor—and found that in ministering to the people of El Salvador, political and economic issues could not be avoided.

The parish was recently founded and aptly named. It sat at the southern edge of San Salvador on land that had once held a garbage dump. The church was built of brick and chicken wire. Wooden posts supported a tin roof. Most people at Holy Trinity had dined in more gracious picnic shelters.

The cinder block parish compound was surrounded by one-room brick and tin houses that sagged against one another along the edge of a much-used railway and the banks of a reeking, polluted river. A civil war was raging, and each day a steady stream of refugees from the "conflicted zones" eddied into the barrio, further straining the meager resources of Padre Daniel Sanchez, the Spanish missionary who had founded the parish.

Daniel was a compact, antic man with gold-rimmed glasses and thinning salt-and-pepper hair. His friends called him the Atomic Flea. By day he and Father Maier, one short and emotive, the other tall and placid, moved through the parish, assessing its staggering needs.

Civic government had all but disintegrated in the neighborhood known as La Chacra, and Padre Daniel knew he would have to provide the most basic kinds of human services: a medical clinic, a dental clinic, a school and a day care center. All of that would come in time. At the moment, it was more important to talk with people, to hear their stories and to share what little food, money and medicine he had, courtesy of international relief agencies.

During the long, hot afternoons, Daniel and Jim listened to accounts of rape, torture, and the most macabre kinds of killings. This mayhem had largely been perpetrated by the Salvadoran military, which was trained and funded by the U.S. government. The military's ostensible opponents were the leftist guerrillas of the FMLN (Farabundo Martí National Liberation Front). But many of the victims were catechists and members of Christian "base communities," small groups which gathered to pray and study the Scriptures. Sometimes in El Salvador, Jim felt that his country was at war with his Church, and he wondered how he would explain that to people back home.

To U.S. foreign policy makers, the civil war in El Salvador was a proxy fight with the Soviet Union, and they backed the anti-Communist forces. But to proponents of liberation theology, the war was an outgrowth of a persecuted people's desire to claim their God-given dignity. Though most deplored the fighting, liberationists believed that the poor had been deprived of their right to be heard, and that war was the inevitable result of such injustice.

The Salvadoran Church was not monolithic in its sympathies. One bishop, a member of the National Guard, reveled in blessing tanks employed by the state. But some priests and nuns openly allied themselves with the rebels. Many Church leaders criticized the military for its attacks on civilian populations. And even among the scrupulously neutral, there were those who spoke against the inequality and repression which inspired the fighting.

The Salvadoran Right responded with violence. In March 1980, Oscar Romero, the popular archbishop of San Salvador, a champion of his country's poor, was shot to death while saying Mass. His execution had been ordered by Major Roberto D'Aubuisson, founder of the Arena party, who had been angered by Romero's call for the suspension of U.S. aid to the armed forces. In December of that year three American nuns and a lay colleague were abducted and murdered by the Salvadoran military. Two of them were also raped.

Cardinal James Hickey knew two of the nuns personally, and he led the U.S. bishops' outraged response to the murders, but most American Catholics remained either unaware of or untroubled by their government's policies in El Salvador. By the time Jim Maier arrived in the country, six years later, Arena controlled the presidency and the legislature. There was a popular slogan on the Salvadoran Right: Be a patriot—Kill a priest.

Lying in bed at night, listening to the trains rumble through the parish and the roosters announce a dawn that was still hours away, Jim wondered how he might bring a piece of his experience home with him, how he might make the Church more universal by linking the desperate valor of El Salvador with the educated affluence of Georgetown. He knew that a handful of his parishioners had read the liberation theologians and followed the Salvadoran war. But he was also aware that Holy Trinity was the spiritual home of employees of the State Department, the World Bank, the CIA and other agencies that shaped or influenced American foreign policy. They would not easily accept him as an expert on Central American affairs. Nor did he feel like one. But he was determined that somehow, Holy Trinity would make at least a quiet stand with the liberation Church.

By the end of his visit, Jim had resolved to begin a sister-parish relationship. The sister-parish movement was a small but growing phenomenon linking North American congregations with churches in the developing world. Typically the two communities exchange correspondence, gifts and, in rare instances, visits. In many cases the North American Church provides financial support. To Jim it seemed the perfect way of aiding the Salvadoran people while staying out of their politics. But his plan encountered resistance as soon as he got home.

A few of the parish's foreign policy experts believed he had been duped by the leftist clergy of Latin America. The sister-parish relationship, they said, was little more than a cover for funneling aid to the FMLN. Other parishioners were wary of unleashing political passions in the parish. And there were many who wondered why Holy Trinity had to go hunting for causes so far from home.

The committee Jim formed to investigate the relationship recommended that he drop the idea. Though as pastor he could have disregarded this advice, Jim decided that it would be politically risky to begin a sister-parish program without some expression of support. The plan languished for more than two years, until the spring of 1988, when Jo Owen gave it new life. In the process, she demonstrated to Father Maier that the real power of the sister-parish relationship was in providing his parishioners with an opportunity to deepen their commitment to Christ.

Sitting across the table from her in the restaurant that night, Jim marveled at how dramatically Jo had changed in the years he had known her. She and her husband, Bruce, an economist, still lived in a lavish home in McLean, Virginia, and counted three U.S. Supreme Court justices among their neighbors. But in fundamental ways, Jo's life had been transformed.

In 1987 her doctors had discovered that she had a malignant melanoma, and though the disease had gone quickly into remission, Jo began to meditate on her mortality.

"I realized I had not lived my life the way I wanted to," she said one noontime, sitting in her living room. "My life had been a sham. It was nothing like the life I wanted. I began to take risks, and in becoming a risk-taker I began to feel alive, really alive. And I began to feel alive through the lives of marginalized people."

These included the gay men she worked with at an AIDS hospice run by Mother Theresa's religious order, the inner city poor she met at St. Aloysius and, eventually, the people of Madre de los Pobres.

Inspired and horrified by the stories Jim told her, she flew to San Salvador in the spring of 1988 as part of a delegation organized by the SHARE Foundation, a Salvadoran solidarity group with left-wing sympathies. She and the other delegates met with members of all the major political parties, with refugees, labor leaders and religious workers of several denominations.

"They didn't tell you what to think," Jo said. "But it was obvious what to think. It was clear the poor were really being persecuted by the military."

When she returned, she began speaking, in her achingly sincere and vaguely ethereal way, about the atrocities of the war and the needs of the Salvadoran people. Several of the foreign service employees in the parish suggested none too subtly that she had been brainwashed. But Jo spoke so passionately to so many people that the sister-parish relationship gradually began to gather support.

By autumn Jim had revived his proposal and asked her to present it to the Parish Council. Jo was befuddled. If Jim really believed in the idea, and he seemed to, then why didn't he present it himself? He was a much better speaker than she.

But Jim did not want to be perceived as forcing his pet project on the parish, and so he remained silent throughout her presentation and offered no assistance when the question-and-answer period became contentious.

One cautious council member thought the parish would be asking for trouble by starting a sister-parish relationship in a war zone. He wanted no part of it. Another sought to redirect the plan by suggesting Trinity find a sister parish in Africa, where he had served in the Peace Corps. A third proposed finding a relationship in Mexico, because it was a more sensible and convenient country in which to vacation.

Jo handled these objections as best she could, steering clear of political issues and returning again and again to the hospitality, the unselfishness and the deep faith of the people she had met. In the midst of one response she remembers looking at Jim and thinking, "Why won't you speak?"

The sister-parish plan passed by a healthy margin, but Jo remained skeptical about Jim's commitment to the new relationship.

In May 1989 the first official delegation from Holy Trinity departed for Madre de los Pobres. Among its six members were Jim, Jo, Lydia, Ted Tschudy and Peter Gyves. For one week they did much the same thing as Jo's initial delegation, meeting with politicians, diplomats, archdiocesan officials, rural pastors and the foreign-born nuns who seemed to be the glue of the Salvadoran church.

Within a few days they had heard each side in the conflict state its well-rehearsed case. The government was fighting to save the country from Communism. The guerrillas were fighting to reverse centuries of economic oppression. They also tasted something of the fear of war. Each night as they lay in bed, they could hear army helicopters hovering over the parish. Each day they were struck by the omnipresence of soldiers and armaments. At a village in the countryside their sleeping quarters were patrolled by rifle-toting men of indeterminate sympathies.

Though they spent much of the trip trying to grasp the political and economic forces fueling the Salvadoran crisis, in the end these were obscured by the poignancy of the parishioners of Madre de los Pobres, whose hope seemed so much stronger and whose faith seemed so much deeper than their own.

Whatever the reasons for the war, it seemed obvious to the delegation from Holy Trinity that God did not will these brave people to suffer, and that the delegates and their fellow parishioners could help alleviate that suffering. Yet when they returned home, they found they could not communicate, even to their spouses, why their visit had moved them so deeply or why the parish should commit new resources to Madre de los Pobres.

A new divide began to open within the parish. There were those who had been to Madre and those who had not. And when the subject of El Salvador arose, it was as though they had no common language.

The delegation had been home for five months when the FMLN launched a major military offensive. In the midst of the fighting came news that on November 16, Ignacio Ellacuria, the rector of the University of Central America, five of his brother Jesuits, their housekeeper and her daughter had been murdered by the Salvadoran military.

For Tom Howarth, an oval-faced, heavyset man with dark hair, dark eyes and a dark mustache, Ellacuria and the other Jesuits had offered a model of Catholic witness in wartime. They had spoken out against the excesses of both sides, encouraged a negotiated settlement, worked among the poorest campesinos and laid a strong statistical base beneath their moral indictment of Salvadoran society.

Tom was a Washington lobbyist. He had volunteered in George McGovern's presidential campaign, lobbied for the labor movement, and served on the staff of Senator Frank Lautenberg, the Democrat of New Jersey, before entering a private firm. He was also a member of the Parish Council, a CCD catechist, and one of the organizers of Camp Trinity, the parish's annual family getaway weekend. For much of the previous five years he had endeavored, with mixed results, to put his professional skills at the service of his faith. The murder of the Jesuits spoke to him on both levels. It was further evidence that U.S. policy had failed and that the Salvadoran military was out of control. But beyond that it was a challenge to complacent American Catholics to commit themselves to the struggle of the Salvadoran poor.

In the days after the murders, Tom presented Jim with a three-part proposal: that Holy Trinity hold a memorial service for the Jesuits; that it host a presentation of the movie *Romero*; and that it convene a panel of Latin American experts to discuss the situation in El Salvador at a town meeting.

But the murders of his brother Jesuits had not changed Jim's thinking about the sister parish program. Despite his personal anguish, he wanted no part of an ideological fight, and he intended to keep the relationship with Madre de los Pobres politically neutral. He was convinced that that was the best way to protect it from being undermined by those who had opposed it to begin with.

Jim declined Tom's suggestions, and Tom took his ideas elsewhere.

St. Aloysius hosted a memorial service for the Jesuits and Georgetown University sponsored an open forum on El Salvador. Though pleased with his success, Tom remained puzzled about his pastor's apparent timidity. He thought he was enlisting in Father Maier's favorite cause, and hoped their collaboration might constitute the basis for a friendship. Now he, like Jo, wondered about the nature of Jim's intentions.

These doubts did not deter Tom from joining Jo and Father Maier on the parish's second official delegation to El Salvador in January 1991. Tom was in the midst of making the Spiritual Exercises with Natalie Ganley when he departed, and he meditated frequently on St. Ignatius' admonition to free one's self of attachments to "earthly things." This trip, he thought, might teach him to do that.

From the moment he stepped off the plane and into the tropical heat, Tom's mind and body moved as though in a different dimension. He had never seen such poverty, nor experienced such hospitality. Everywhere he went, people were destitute, and all of those people offered him something to eat.

Tom was particularly captivated by the children of the parish, who seemed so joyful despite their poverty and despite the war. Sometimes in his prayers he imagined them playing on the lap of Jesus. Other times he imagined them crucified, and himself in the quiescent crowd.

One morning he meditated on the conquistador in the film *The Mission*, who tried to scale a mountain while dragging his armor and possessions on a rope behind him. What was it that he himself would have to let go of before he reached the mountaintop? Tom wondered. Friends? Financial security? Perhaps his reputation as a reasonable man?

An old man in El Salvador had said to him, "You will be our voice," and Tom took the informal commission to heart.

Not long after their return, he and Jo met with Jim to discuss the next step in the sister-parish relationship. In El Salvador, the three had spent a great deal of time together, but now the two lay people found their pastor distant and distracted. Worse, he seemed to have no intention of mobilizing his parishioners on behalf of the Salvadoran poor.

What neither Tom nor Jo realized was that Father Maier was under quiet pressure from various pillars of the parish community to distance himself from the sister-parish program, to keep it small and relatively inconsequential so that it did not become a breeding ground for activists who would force a divisive political agenda upon the parish. Holy Trinity already sent ten thousand dollars to Padre Daniel each year, these parishioners pointed out. Wasn't that enough?

Jim did not think so, but he was unsure how to reconcile his own commitment to Madre de los Pobres with the resistance of an influential minority and the lukewarm response of the parish at large. He was constantly weighing how to advance the sister-parish relationship—Was a slide show about Madre too little? Was a Salvadoran craft sale too much? He could sense Tom and Jo's disappointment with his restraint, but they, as lay people, were free to indulge their passion, while he, as a pastor responsible for the harmony of his community, was not.

Tom Howarth returned to El Salvador in November of 1991 for a mass commemorating the second anniversary of the murders at the UCA, and came home feeling more acutely than ever the need to atone, as an American, for the sins of his government. He wrote a reflection on his trip for the *Holy Trinity News*, and asked Father Maier for an opportunity to address the entire parish. Jim refused, but allowed Tom to give the adult education lecture on the Sunday before Christmas.

On that brisk morning, Tom delivered a speech informed by passion and frustration. "One of the greatest sins in El Salvador and in the U.S. . . . is holding the truth captive," he told the eighty people who had gathered in the theater. Father Maier, he continued, was committing that sin. He could have put the news about what was happening in El Salvador before thirty-five hundred people, simply by giving Tom an opportunity to speak at the liturgies. Instead, he had chosen to limit the audience to those willing to attend Tom's lecture.

"If what I have to say about El Salvador and our country's policies, which, as I wrote, brutalize the poor, is false, then it should be challenged and rejected," Tom said. "If it is debatable, it should be debated. But if it is true, then it should be proclaimed to all that have ears to hear."

But many in the parish did not want Tom's newfound passion thrust upon them. Even members of the Parish-to-Parish Committee, which oversaw the relationship with Madre de los Pobres, were put off by his zeal. Whenever he suggested that the group draft a letter to Congress or the State Department, someone would protest that they met to facilitate an international friendship, not to pick political fights.

By November of 1992 Tom was planning his third trip to El Salvador in eighteen months, and serving as the Parish-to-Parish Committee chair. He was also acting as an informal consultant to the presidential campaign of Reuben Zamorra. He, his wife Rea, and their two daughters had befriended a family of Salvadoran immigrants in Arlington. They were helping the teenage son get into a community college while they nursed his sister through a long surgical convalescence.

In the heat of his passion for the Salvadoran people, Tom regarded Jim Maier and the Parish-to-Parish Committee as sodden wood. By the time he returned from his trip, Tom had decided that his commitment to Holy Trinity and his hopes of a friendship with Father Maier were what he needed to let go before he could reach the mountaintop. He resigned his chairmanship of the Parish-to-Parish Committee and his membership on the Parish Council, and left the parish.

There was no final confrontation with pastor or parishioners, simply a quiet parting. An uncontested divorce, as Tom put it. He found refuge at a South Arlington church where the pastor shared his belief that the Gospel required Catholics to make a political commitment to the cause of the poor.

Jim Maier was sorry to see him go. But perhaps the parting was inevitable. Tom wanted to mold the Parish-to-Parish Committee into the vanguard of a movement; Jim believed it would survive best as a band of pilgrims.

By the evening that Jim's group convened at the Salvadoran restaurant, Tom Howarth was planning another return to El Salvador, this time as part of an American delegation that would be trained as poll watchers for the upcoming election.

It was odd, Jim thought, but both Tom, whose views were strongly liberal, and Peter Schaumber, who was staunchly conservative, wanted the same thing from him: a declaration to parishioners that something was required of them, that certain actions were owing before they could consider themselves real Catholics. For Tom the moral imperative was struggling with the poor against the powerful; for Peter it was submitting to the authority of Rome. But Jim, with his distaste for pastoral pronouncements, his aversion to confrontation and his faith in the spiritual integrity of his parishioners, would not satisfy either man. It was the paradox of his position that by embracing a progressive pastoral style— by inviting rather than commanding—he aroused the ire of liberals and conservatives alike.

To Peter, with whom he disagreed on most important issues, Jim could offer little. But to Tom, whose concerns were so close to his own, he offered the example of his annual return to Madre de los Pobres, and wished it were enough.

Being a pastor, it seemed to him, was less about full-throated testimony to the truth than about venturing what one could when one could, and trying to live with one's equivocations.

CHAPTER EIGHTEEN

◊ΠΠΛϿ

She stood in the bare sanctuary, dressed in the veil and tunic of first-century Palestine, gazing out at the crowd in the church before her. Her name was Sarah, she said, and she was the wife of Simon, the Galilean fisherman whom the world came to know as Peter.

He was the leader of the Apostles, the hero of Pentecost and perhaps the most important figure in Christian history save one. But to hear this feisty, oracular woman tell it, he was not much of a husband, at least not after he met the carpenter from Nazareth. That was when the traveling began, and the fishing tapered off. Food got scarce, and money, too. Peter became consumed by devotion to his new master and had time for little else. Including her.

Sometimes it seemed that God did strange things to men, and then men did strange things to women. But she had not come to lament her life. It was her place in history that concerned her. Or her lack of a place in history.

Everyone knew that Peter had a mother-in-law. In the eighth chapter of Matthew's Gospel Jesus heals her, and the woman rises from her bed and begins to wait on him.

But where was Peter's wife? Where were the wives of the other Apostles?

Were they disciples? The Gospels do not say. Did their husbands abandon them for missionary pursuits? Again, the Gospels are silent.

I have come to break the silence, Sarah said, stepping to the edge of the altar platform and peering into the faces of those near the front of the church. About myself and all those women whose absence leaves holes in Christian history. My husband has written his epistles; this is mine.

Standing in the rear of the church, Rea Howarth was prepared to declare the evening a success, even before "Sarah" finished her introduction. There were 450 people in the building, and enough money in her cash box to cover the cost of the program and allow for a few small donations to charity. More to the point, the message that she and the rest of the Working Groups had been laboring to convey for almost a year was at last being articulated from the altar.

When the groups had first discussed inviting the actress Roberta Nobleman to perform her one-woman show at Holy Trinity, even its own members doubted whether they could pull it off. Too controversial, some warned. Too costly. But now here they were, on the last Saturday in April—Rea, Kathy Hartley, Ray McGovern and the others—at what amounted to their coming-out party. *All That I Am*, as the show was called, was their initial attempt to offer the parish something more than protest. And if the turnout was any indication, the parish was welcoming them with open arms.

At the front of the church, Nobleman had changed costume and character. Now she was Maria Van Wedemeyer, the fiancée of Dietrich Bonhoeffer, the great Lutheran pastor and theologian. At the outset of World War II, he had chosen to return to Germany and speak out against the Nazis rather than remaining abroad and beginning a new life with her. As the piece opens, he is in an internment camp, and she is teetering on the edge of madness.

Her jagged monologue is spoken to an unseen visitor, and it tells the story of her courtship. Maria would like to give it a happy ending, but the longer she speaks, the clearer it becomes that she is preparing for the blow that is about to fall. Dietrich is going to die. His sacrifice will be her sacrifice. But only he will be remembered as a hero.

The audience sat in silence as Nobleman stepped to the rear of the sanctuary and, in a flurry of fabric and elbows, departed the twentieth century for the sixteenth. Cradling a baby, Anne Donne, the wife of Anglican priest and poet John Donne, took a seat at her fireside and began telling her tale amid numerous interruptions from her vast brood of offspring.

She and John had married when she was seventeen, and she bore him twelve children. Parishoners who were following the performance in their programs knew that she died in childbirth at thirty-three. Those who were not could observe that her collapse was imminent.

Overwhelmed by the demands of her sick and unruly children, struggling to feed a dozen mouths on a priest's wages, she was unraveling beneath her exertions. Nonetheless, Anne was unwilling to summon her husband from his writerly solitude, and he was unable to perceive the domestic passion unfolding in his own home. This did not diminish him in her eyes. He was about the Lord's work, and what were her sufferings when measured against that?

Jim Maier, who wrote a little poetry himself, watched the piece on Donne with particular interest from his seat near the rear of the nave. In his six years as pastor, Holy Trinity had never hosted a dramatic performance in the church, and he was enjoying the novelty of the experience. Some parishioners had suggested that with the choice of his successor still pending, it was foolish to stage a feminist disquisition on Christian history. But Jim disagreed.

Sponsoring *All That I Am* was precisely the sort of gentle challenge to Church authority with which he felt most comfortable. The show was thought-provoking though hardly unorthodox. It would hearten the many feminists who crowded the church that night without contradicting the teachings of the magisterium. In pastoral terms, the program had perfect pitch.

In the four weeks since the open forum, Jim had been wondering how to move the discussion about sexism and the Standing to a less contentious plane. As he watched Nobleman change character once again, he thought that perhaps presentations such as this one were the answer. If the Working Groups felt they had a platform from which to address the parish, perhaps they would persuade Ray McGovern and the other protestors to sit down, if only to ensure access to such substantial audiences.

In the sanctuary, Hilde of St. Bremar, the fictional wife of a twelfth-century priest, had just learned that the Vatican was preparing to enforce the long-ignored celibacy laws. Her husband would have to leave her. In Nobleman's portrayal the woman was resigned rather than bereft, wondering how her husband would get along without her, and how Rome, in its wisdom, had determined that breaking up her household was essential to the good of the Church.

In a moment, Hilde yielded to a woman referred to only as "The Mistress." She was the lover Saint Augustine had cast off before converting to Christianity and embracing the celibate life. Little is known of her historically, other than that she bore Augustine a son, Adeodatus, whom he took with him into the monastery.

In *All That I Am*, she is a servant in a fourth-century way station, speaking with a traveler about his visit with the great man. He does not know of her former relationship with Augustine, and does not notice the effect his words are having upon her. In passing he mentions that the saint is grieving. Adeodatus, not yet twenty years old, has died in a monastery.

The Mistress's face contorts, and her body doubles in pain. When at last she is alone, her sorrow overwhelms her and she dissolves in tears. To lose her child once was outrageous. To be cast as a barrier to his salvation was humiliating. But to be denied the opportunity to mourn him is inhuman.

Was this the harshness of Augustine's God? Or was this the harshness of the saint himself? Did the Lord ordain her maternal exile, or had Augustine bartered her pain for his purity? Sometimes God did strange things to men, and then men did strange things to women.

Ray McGovern rose to his feet, cheering appreciatively when the performance ended. Much of the audience did the same. Listening to the ovation he felt, for a moment, as though he were being washed in a tide of fellow-feeling, as though the parish was finally willing to embrace his cause as its own.

This, he realized, was wishful thinking. There would be no more protestors at mass the next morning than there had been on any of the previous Sundays. After one emotionally draining year, the Standing was becoming an increasingly lonely endeavor. In recent weeks, even his friends seemed to have turned against him.

Throughout the winter, Rea and Kathy had plotted strategies to gain the Working Groups wider acceptance in the parish. But with every initiative, they encountered an undercurrent of resistance. Much of the 9:15 community silently supported Ray's protest; many people were indifferent. But enough influential parishioners were angry to fluster the Parish Council and jeopardize the existence of the groups.

It was time to make a choice, the two women had told him, either continue the Standing for its own sake or move beyond the protest to pursue a broader agenda. By spring, most of the remaining handful of protestors had decided to sit down, or move to the side aisles where they would not obstruct the view to the altar. Only Ray and a high school student named Devon Franklin remained standing in the middle of the nave. Since Devon seldom attended the groups' meetings, Ray was left to defend his position alone.

It was ironic, Ray thought, that his friends were now advancing their opponents' arguments. They told him he had to sit down for the good of the community—the community in this case being the groups rather than the parish. They told him his protest was hurting his cause. They told him it was time for new tactics.

He had heard it all before, he responded, and it sounded no more persuasive from allies than from adversaries. By late April a few members of the Working Groups regarded Ray in much the same way as his more dispassionate critics, as a stubborn and self-righteous man made lonely by an obsession with his integrity.

But *All That I Am* blew through Holy Trinity like a summer thunderstorm, trailing temperate weather in its wake. The success of the performance convinced Kathy and Rea that there was a large audience for the programs they hoped to sponsor, whether Ray sat down or not. And Ray came to realize that it would be better for the groups, and easier for him, if they stopped talking about the Standing and moved on to other issues.

This convergence produced a compromise. At their first meeting in May, members of the Working Groups on Sexism agreed to disagree about the protest that had brought the groups into being.

"We have reached a consensus," Rea wrote to Father Maier and Carl Sylvester, the president of the Parish Council. "Whether persons feel called to stand or wear symbolic stoles or ribbons during worship is a matter of individual conscience. We believe we must respect conscience, but not necessarily join in any particular witness. We also respect those who oppose such witness and encourage their participation in the overall mission and objectives of the group."

In a more forgiving atmosphere, this conciliatory statement might have earned the groups the grudging goodwill of their opponents. But with the future of the parish still in question, these adversaries were not in a forgiving mood. Shannon Jordan, Paul and Cathy Quinn, Mike and Pam Hall and their allies wanted the protest stopped and all institutional support for the protestors dismantled. The Working Groups, whatever their official philosophy, would have to go.

That spring, as he monitored the deteriorating relationship between the two sides, Jim Maier realized that the struggle over the Standing might outlive his pastorate. Ray could conceivably go on standing for years, and his opponents, frustrated by their inability to force a resolution, might gradually begin to inflict whatever damage they could on the causes of his allies. As it was, members of the two camps reliably opposed one another on whatever was being debated in the parish. This kind of infighting, Jim feared, would do more lasting damage to Holy Trinity than the most reactionary pastor that Bishop Corrada could dig up.

Alone in his room at night, he could find only two consolations in the midst of this contention. One was the fact that most of the parish was oblivious to the strife created by the Standing. Ray's protest had never really spread beyond the 9:15 community, and so roughly two thousand of the thirty-five hundred worshipers who thronged Holy Trinity each weekend were utterly undisturbed by it. The other was that even in such angry times, there remained certain things that almost the entire parish could agree upon, certain people whom everyone wished well. And on the first Sunday in May, as though to force a momentary armistice, two of them were getting married.

⌒⍫⌒

To her surprise and delight, Christine Flanagan's annulment had materialized during Holy Week. There was no explanation of why it had been held up for more than two years, or on what grounds the Church had decided that her marriage of eighteen years had never been valid to begin with. But she didn't care.

With summer approaching, Christine had almost given up on the hope that she and Tim could get married at Holy Trinity. He would soon be heading to Connecticut to begin his graduate work, and she was already making regular trips to Kansas City, where she had been named chief administrator of a large hospital. Soon neither of them would have any ties, beyond those of affection, to the parish where they had fallen in love. Now, however, with her annulment in hand, she could begin her new life in the midst of the community that had helped make it possible.

Newcomers to the church that Sunday must have been surprised when the 9:15 mass began with the procession of Tim and his attendants, the middle-aged members of Trinity's Saturday morning men's group. One man carried a rough-hewn staff and another beat an Indian drum as they traversed the middle aisle, mixing a bit of Robert Bly into the Roman Catholic proceedings.

Christine and her attendants followed in outfits that were both festive and sensible, a perfect reflection of the bride's personality. Behind them walked Father Maier; Father Joe Koury, a former moderator of the Separated, Divorced and Remarried Catholics group, and Margaret Costello, who would be joining Jim in the two-part homily.

Because the Catholic Church does not have a rite of remarriage, Holy Trinity had created one of its own. After "Morning Has Broken" gave way to "Lord of the Dance," and "Lord of the Dance" to "Canticle of the Sun," Father Maier greeted the eight hundred people wedged into the church that morning and explained to them the unusual liturgy they were about to celebrate. Then Tim and Christine began the penitential rite.

Usually this prayer, based on either the old Confiteor ("I confess to almighty God, and to you my brothers and sisters . . .") or the Kyrie ("Lord, have mercy. Christ, have mercy. Lord, have mercy.") is led by the priest. But for their wedding, Tim and Christine had prepared a text of their own.

"This is a day of new beginnings and great happiness for us," they said in unison. "But we come here as two people whose faults and failings have hurt others. Like all human beings, we bear the burden of human sinfulness and are in need of forgiveness. We especially ask the forgiveness of our former spouses . . . for anything we have done which contributed to the failure of our prior marriages and which caused you grief and pain. Let us all assembled ask for each other's forgiveness and ask God to heal us."

There were other subtle personal touches sprinkled throughout the liturgy. After the first reading, the congregation sang the psalm that had meant so much to Christine during her most difficult times: "As the deer longs for flowing streams, so longs my soul, for you O God. . . ."

In their homily Jim and Margaret spoke of hope and fulfillment. "Jesus does not promise that we will live happily ever after," Margaret said. "He does not promise that our lives will be a fairy tale if we believe in him. Jesus came 'that we might have life and have it to the full.' To the full of all of the experiences—the joys and sorrows—of human life.

"If we are companions on the journey with Jesus . . . we will travel home in safety to God together. As you listen to Tim and Christine make their vows to each other and to Jesus, please choose to be a companion."

By Catholic standards, the vows were unusual only in that they were being witnessed by the couple's children. Afterward, Christine and Tim exchanged gold bands cast from the melted mixture of their original rings.

At Communion, the bride and groom served as eucharistic ministers, pressing the body of Christ into the palms of their family and friends, and handing them the chalice of consecrated wine. The choir sang:

When love is found and hope comes home,
Sing and be glad that two are one.
When love explodes and fills the sky,
Praise God and share our Maker's joy.

After Communion, in a departure from the usual wedding ceremony, Tim and Christine anointed one another with holy oil.

"May we touch each other as healers, tending to the wounds inflicted in a broken world," Christine said, making the sign of the cross in chrism on his forehead. "May we touch each other as lovers, experiencing the bonding and transcendence of the sexual embrace."

"May we touch each other as friends, offering a helping hand to assist each other on the journey," said Tim, repeating the gesture. "May we touch each other as Christ, with ardent respect for each other's destiny as one called by God."

They exited to a trumpet tune and stood on the sidewalks in front of the church, as people whom they had never met before streamed up to greet them, offering congratulations and thanks for the moving ceremony. Inside, several disgruntled people approached Father Maier, asking why two divorced people had been allowed to get married in a Catholic church, let alone in the middle of Sunday mass.

Jim's explanations did not seem to satisfy them. They seemed not to understand that the Church did not prohibit remarriage, only remarriage without an annulment. They seemed not to care that the Church permitted weddings at Sunday masses. For Jim it was a brief reminder of why change is so difficult in the Church; people find security in rules, repetition and the belief that there is only one proper way to praise God.

Nearly 250 people turned up at the Quinns' home in nearby Falls Church later that morning for the reception. The garage was festooned with flowers and the dogwoods were in bloom. Christine felt as though all creation was blessing her marriage.

In the midst of toasts and feasting, Tim, whose ancestors came from Scotland, presented her with the sash of his clan. As he did, a bagpiper, whose performance was Christine's gift to him, appeared at the top of the Quinns' long driveway and made his way, pipes wailing, into the throng.

Among the crowd was Ray McGovern. He was a friend of both Tim's and Christine's, and he had sought their advice about standing at the wedding. They had requested that he continue his protest, but move to the side aisle, and Ray, against his better judgment, had agreed.

After mass, Rea Howarth had rushed up to embrace him. "See, you do listen," she said. But Ray was already regretting his momentary compromise. "On a day like this, everybody wants to say, 'See, things are all right,' " he said. "But things are not all right."

Jim Maier, eating and making merry in the soft spring afternoon, harbored more ambivalent feelings. This was another moment in which his parish had demonstrated perfect ecclesial pitch. Holy Trinity had done everything the Church allowed to meet the needs of Christine Flanagan and Tim McLaren, from sponsoring the Separated, Divorced and Remarried Catholics group, to advising them on their annulments, to throwing them perhaps the most joyous celebration in the church outside of Triduum. Yet in no way had it violated the Church's teaching against divorce or suggested that it was proper to do so.

If it were always possible to find this sort of middle ground to meet the needs of contemporary Catholics without traducing the ancient norms of the Church, Jim would have been a happy man and a contented priest. But his own internal struggle told him that it was not.

As the end of his tenure neared, he found himself thinking more frequently about his sabbatical. He had decided to keep his Jesuit identity a secret from the students at Loyola Marymount. He wanted time away from his ministry to contemplate his vow of celibacy, to make gay friends and to decide whether he should leave the Society.

In the meantime, he had resolved to make one final effort to repair the breech in his parish that had opened over the Standing. The following Sunday was Mother's Day, which seemed to him the perfect time to address the status of women in the Church. He would not, of course, be stating his own views on the matter. That was still too dangerous. Rather, he would seek to attain the perfect pitch that had characterized the wedding and the one-woman show.

One week later, he stood in the pulpit clad in the white vestments of the Easter season. As he looked down at Shannon Jordan and her family in one of the front pews, Paul Quinn and Mike Hall supervising the ushers in the rear of the church, Ray McGovern upright in the middle of the nave and Kathy Hartley and Rea Howarth with their blue stoles draped around their shoulders, he wondered if there was anything he could say to bring them together, make them trust one another, to turn back parish time.

But before the Standing there had been an ordeal over the parish's financial plan, and before that the campaign to initiate the sister-parish relationship in El Salvador, and before that a particularly vituperative battle over who would choose the music for the 11:30 mass. There had never been a peaceful time at Holy Trinity, not during his pastorate, not during Jim English's, not during Tom Gavigan's. Probably not since Vatican II.

Was that because his parishioners were more argumentative than others? Probably. But it was also because the Church *was* an argument, a continuous reexamination of the values embodied by Jesus as he is portrayed in the Scriptures, the dogma articulated by the Church through two millennia and the spiritual insights of the community that gathered to celebrate the Eucharist each week.

The people of Holy Trinity took their faith seriously. Hence, they fought. What he hoped to offer them that morning was a piece of paradoxical advice: fight in peace.

The epistle that morning was from the first Letter of Peter, and it had spoken of a royal priesthood. In preparing his homily, Jim lit on that phrase as his theme. "What does it mean to say that we are a royal priesthood?" he asked, eyes moving over the sea of faces before him. "What does it have to say to women to whom the doors of holy orders and the exercise of the presbyterial ministry of prayer and service are closed? How are women and men to relate in our Catholic community? Here at Holy Trinity?

"The women and men witnessing in our community through standing and the wearing of blue ribbons and stoles are saying that something is wrong here in our church, at Holy Trinity and in the Great Church— that we are not treating one another justly; that we are victims of the "-ism" of sexism.

"As with the question of clerical celibacy, Pope John Paul II has discouraged discussion of the question [of women's ordination], yet it breaks out continually in discussion among Catholics, threatening even to create schism among us. Are *you* trying, through conversation and reading and lecture, to understand his point of view? That's one way we can deal with sexism, one way we can become better Catholics."

But then, having urged respect for the pope's position, Jim subtly changed course. "Our bishops are trying to continue, after the failed pastoral letter [on women in the Church], to reflect on the issues and invite us to do the same." But how can we do this? he asked. How can we make women feel more welcome and more appreciated in our Church?

We can use the female pronoun when referring to God, he said. We can support the people working to eradicate sexism at Holy Trinity, and we can be sensitive to the suffering that sexism has caused.

"We know that our sexist practices are sinful; our bishops have said that forcefully. We cannot tolerate these practices in ourselves or others. Unless we seek conversion, we can scarcely become the royal priesthood that Saint Peter dreamed of."

He closed the cover of the folder that held his homily, left the pulpit and crossed the sanctuary to the presider's bench, which sat beneath the Cross of Glory. There was a long moment of silence, and then the congregation burst into applause. The ovation lasted for almost a full minute, but it was hard to say why people were cheering.

Jim's statement had been highly qualified, carefully nuanced. He had asked many questions and offered no answers, calling his parishioners only to a continuing struggle against sexism in its many forms. Perhaps his assertion that Catholics could imagine a feminine God had triggered the applause. Perhaps it was his tacit admission that the laity need not be silent simply because the pope commands them to be. Perhaps it was the parishioners' relief that their pastor had finally articulated some sort of view on the subjects of sexism and the Standing, even though they might not have been able to say precisely what that view was.

Whatever the reason, the 9:15 community had cheered and, standing in their midst, Ray McGovern felt better about his parish and his protest than he had for many months.

"The homily was a high point," he said later. "It was a real shot in the arm. I was particularly glad my daughter was there to hear it. There was that electric silence when you could hear a pin drop, and then all that applause. I was moved to tears."

Shannon Jordan was less enthused. She felt the homily had legitimized the disruption of the Eucharist, and the following weekend, at a party at her home, she took Jim aside to say so. People milling through the house could see him leaning against a doorpost, studying her face and nodding occasionally, his arms crossed in front of him, a soft drink in one hand.

Kathy Hartley could not understand what all the fuss was about. Except for a fairly firm stand in favor of inclusive language in the liturgy, Jim's homily was a mist of good intentions, a ringing endorsement of being as just as the unjust magisterium would allow. As for the reaction of the congregation, it struck her as fairly typical of what Holy Trinity was becoming, a parish so impressed with its good intentions that it felt no need to act on them.

Jim enjoyed the applause. He hoped his homily and the reception it had received might make Ray and the Working Groups feel less defensive, while rendering their high-profile opponents a little less certain of their oft-repeated contention that they spoke for the majority of the parish. Beyond that, he was not much concerned about people's evaluation of the homily.

Ed Glynn had promised him that he would be out of the parish by August, and as summer approached, Jim began to worry less about Holy Trinity's future than his own. He was preparing for a long period of study and meditation, and he sensed that regardless of what he decided about his future as a priest, his life, in some fundamental way, was about to be transformed.

It was odd that after all these years of guiding Jesuit novices and lay people along their particular spiritual paths, Jim now felt rather lost himself. He was seeing a therapist for advice on how to begin separating from people at the parish. He was praying as fervently as he ever had in the hour he set aside for meditation each day. Yet he had the feeling that he was edging toward the unknown.

For solace, Jim would sometimes contemplate the example of a friend who had recently concluded her own long examination of the unknown. And he found in this woman's grace and bravery something of the sustenance he needed.

Hattie Kennedy was eighty-two years old in the fall of 1990 when she and her pastor became friendly. She had recently been diagnosed with terminal cancer and informed that she had no more than six months to live. Under Jim's guidance and that of Father Jerry Campbell, she began preparing to die.

Though she attended mass most mornings, Hattie had long been dissatisfied with her spiritual life—"I never feel I go deep enough," she'd said—and that winter she made a weeklong retreat with Father Maier.

After four days, Jim thought the retreat was going wonderfully. He enjoyed the spirited old woman's tart, incisive analysis of her own failings and those of the biblical characters on whom she was meditating. But before their final session together, Hattie climbed the stairs to his office, peered around his doorpost and said in an exhausted voice, "I have nothing to say." Then she disappeared.

By the time Jim got up from his chair, she was at the bottom of the stairs. "What did I do?" he called. But Hattie did not answer him. She left the parish center, went into the church, sank into a pew and remained utterly still.

There were children from the parish elementary school in the building that morning, and they stared at her. She knew she must have looked strange to them, a white-haired woman with a sharp nose and probing brown eyes who sat motionless for so long that she lost track of the time.

Hattie was thinking of St. Ignatius, and how he sat on the banks of the River Cardoner near Manresa in northeastern Spain until the realization that changed his life dawned slowly upon him.

Then her own revelation came.

"You know how after a storm the sky becomes extremely clear?" she would ask later. "All these words were just blazoned across that sky—the words from the Bible that I had always read—and I said, 'Oh!

That's what they mean. This is what these words are. This is what this is all about. This is all a beautiful new world.' "

The experience "changed my whole life," she told Jim later. "Suddenly everything became clear. Before, I think I was dutiful. I had what might have been vestiges of love. But what I had then, I think, was a realization of God's presence."

Her spiritual revelation was not the only blessing Hattie received that winter. To her doctor's surprise, chemotherapy defeated her cancer, and the disease did not recur for two years.

Hattie lived those years as the gift she believed they were, resuming her career as a sculptor, volunteering as a Communion minister at Georgetown University Hospital, spending nights at a homeless shelter and making the Spiritual Exercises of Saint Ignatius with Father Campbell.

It is difficult to know what makes one person seem "spiritual" to another, especially in a parish like Holy Trinity where people are distrustful of conspicuous piety. Perhaps it was the remission of her cancer, or perhaps it was word of mouth about her experience on the retreat. Whatever the reason, Hattie Kennedy came to be seen by some of her fellow parishioners as a holy woman.

One friend told her, "Hattie, I know when you are in church. I don't have to turn around to know you are there."

"I thought, 'Come off it.' I am not conscious of my *aura*," she said, and smiled wickedly.

Shannon Jordan invited her to speak about her spirituality one Sunday morning after the 9:15 mass, a time generally reserved for professors of theology. "No way I can stand up in front of people and talk about this," Hattie told her. But she did receive the visitors that Jim sent to her, people facing personal problems but reluctant to explain them to a counselor or a priest.

"I don't know what he expects me to do for them," she would say. But she must have offered them something beyond hot tea and a quiet place to sit, because several kept coming back.

When her cancer recurred in the winter of 1992, Hattie took the news with a dazzling equanimity. In the last months of her life, she seemed to be living with one foot in this world and one in the next. There was nothing ethereal about the manner in which she did this. She was too aware of and too inconvenienced by her body's decay to pretend she was pure spirit. She was too passionate in her concern for the parish to pretend that she was above earthly affairs. And yet, perhaps because of her illness, Hattie seemed to project a constant awareness of God's presence.

For Jim, her courage was the substance of things hoped for, the proof that God accompanied his people through their most excruciating trials. And if she could find solace in that knowledge as she prepared for death, then he could find solace in it as he contemplated a new life.

Hattie died in Georgetown University Hospital on April 28, 1993, and was buried a few days later in a private ceremony attended only by Fathers Maier, Campbell and Sobierajski, and by her son Peter.

On the morning after Mother's Day, Jim presided at her memorial mass, which drew more than two hundred people to the church. In his homily he recalled how Hattie had defied limits and conventions, how she had befriended Mitch Snyder during his campaign against the renovation of the church, how she wrung extra years from her life, how she had pursued her spiritual journey unstintingly and how she had become an inspiration for him and for others.

After Communion he read "The Handshake, The Entrance," a poem by John Berryman. It spoke of a long, lonesome journey, and the heartbreak of departure, but it ended with these hopeful words:

Through the ridges I endured,
down in no simple valley I opened my eyes,
with my strong walk down in the vales & dealt with death.
I increased my stride, cured."

CHAPTER NINETEEN

᭰᭰᭰

Throughout that spring, at a desk in his Baltimore office, Ed Glynn reviewed the files of the men in his province, hoping that an obvious choice for the pastorate at Holy Trinity would leap out at him.

It would not have been easy in the best of times to give the people of Holy Trinity a pastor as distinguished as Jim Maier or his recent predecessors. And these were not the best of times.

Once, the Jesuits of the Maryland province had had so many priests, they could barely find posts for them all. But now the Society, like almost all religious orders, was contracting dramatically. There were fewer names in Ed's provincial directory, and fewer colleagues rattling around the utilitarian offices of provincial headquarters.

Father Glynn knew he had to find a man who was more comfortable exerting pastoral authority than Father Maier was; the cardinal would insist on that. Yet Ed was committed to protecting the Jesuits' achievement at Holy Trinity and to ensuring the laity's right to full participation in the sacramental and administrative life of its church. He needed some-

213

one strong-willed enough to persuade Cardinal Hickey that the Jesuits had taken his concerns seriously, yet progressive enough to preserve the pastoral tone of the parish.

The person he had in mind was Father Larry Madden, a vigorous man in his late fifties, who had been a part-time associate pastor at Holy Trinity for almost fifteen years. Father Madden was a man of medium height, but his bald pate, pink complexion, slate blue eyes, and neatly trimmed mustache gave him a gnome-like appearance. A devoted sailor who liked to spend his free time on the Chesapeake Bay, Larry ran his small liturgical think tank as a tight ship. He had neither Jim's qualms about exercising pastoral prerogatives nor his patience with those who claimed the prophet's mantle.

If Father Maier embodied the pastor as spiritual guide, Father Madden was the pastor as enlightened CEO. The two men shared a vision of the Church as a people on pilgrimage. But the pilgrimage, Larry thought, should be orderly and well run.

Father Madden was just the sort of man, and just the sort of administrator, to instill confidence in the cardinal, Ed Glynn thought. Theologically speaking, however, he might be a tougher sell.

Father Madden's liturgy center, officially known as the Georgetown Center for Liturgy, Spirituality and the Arts, was progressive in its orientation. Larry and those who worked for him were committed to implementing the liturgical reforms initiated at the Second Vatican Council but incompletely realized in the decades since.

The center sponsored workshops along the eastern seaboard to train lay people for liturgical roles, from reading Scripture and distributing Communion to designing the liturgical environment and planning the mass. At the invitation of bishops around the country, Larry and his staff also conducted workshops for priests whose pastoral duties did not allow them to keep pace with the latest developments in liturgical scholarship.

These workshops for the clergy were not always well received. There is a joke familiar in Church circles—Q: What is the difference between a liturgist and a terrorist? *A:* You can negotiate with a terrorist— and indeed, some liturgists seem to believe the Mass has been celebrated incorrectly for centuries and is in need of their particular interpretive touch to render its mysteries comprehensible to the benighted faithful. And, for that matter, to the benighted priest.

This attitude is particularly galling to conservative priests who believe that silent, self-emptying adoration is the proper response of the Catholic laity to the reenactment of their Savior's sacrifice. They find that the new Mass, with its contemporary musical idiom and its emphasis on "participation," makes this fervent state impossible to achieve. That the reforms include the laity on a more equal ceremonial footing and thereby establish the symbolic foundation for more representative Church governance only enhances these men's opposition.

Larry had been in the vanguard of the liturgical reform movement in the archdiocese, but he was sensitive to parts of the conservative critique. He, too, worried that liturgical music written in recent years was becoming so dominant that it obscured the Church's medieval, Renaissance and classical heritage. He, too, believed that many priests were inappropriately casual in their liturgical behavior. (Though the self-consciously regal style of the "take back the Church" crowd seemed the greater liturgical offense.) And he worried that progressive Catholics, with their tendency to measure all things by their material impact on the poor, were losing their capacity to appreciate the spiritual value of the sublime in art, music and architecture.

In one view, however, Larry had never wavered. The Mass did not belong to the priest alone; it was the prayer of the community, and as such it had to involve, indeed, to transform, the community. That involvement, ideally, would be contemplative as well as responsive, but the latter could not be sacrificed to the former. By responding in the liturgy, Christians manifested their commitment to respond in life to the preaching and sacrifice of Christ.

If greater involvement of the laity in the liturgy threatened the status of his fellow priests, if it offended the sensibilities of those who thought the peasantry should not be allowed to participate in the rites of court, then so be it.

This conviction had earned Larry his share of enemies in the Washington archdiocese. Among them were Bishop Corrada and some of his allies who favored liturgical regression in the service of a more conservative Church. If the Mass could be returned to the capable hands of priests, deacons and quasi-clerical functionaries, they seemed to believe, the laity would soon come to appreciate its true place in the power structure.

Father Glynn knew that the auxiliary bishop would oppose Larry's candidacy, but he believed that the cardinal was not as conservative as

Corrada in these matters. Cardinal Hickey was certainly fond of incense and elaborate ceremony, but he accepted the existence of liturgical variety, and he was such a stickler for liturgical rubrics, he was unlikely to deny Larry the pastorate over what amounted to differences in aesthetics and interpretation.

Larry was not only the provincial's choice, he was the people's choice as well. In his fifteen years at Holy Trinity he had presided at their weddings and their loved ones' funerals. He had baptized their children and kept the kids interested in the Mass with his preaching partner, Mr. Blue.

Some were leery of his autocratic tendencies, and a handful doubted his commitment to the parish's social ministries, in which he had never taken an active role. Yet even those who were underwhelmed by Larry regarded him as the devil they did know, and much preferred him to the devil they did not.

Of course it was possible, Ed Glynn recognized, that the cardinal had absorbed so much misinformation about Holy Trinity that he would insist that its new leader be a man unsullied by previous experience with the parish. And so, as he contemplated the various scenarios that might unfold after he named his candidate, he decided to hedge his bet and offer the cardinal three names instead of one.

The other two men were Father Joe Sobierajski, the most theologically conservative of the priests at Holy Trinity, and Father Dan Gatti, director of pastoral care at the Georgetown University Medical Center, who occasionally said Mass at the church.

Father Sobierajski was an introverted man who had neither the taste for the enormous administrative strain of managing the parish, nor the desire to deal with contentious parishioners. Joe longed to return to teaching art at Loyola College in his native Baltimore, and allowed his name to be sent forward only as a last-ditch effort to save the parish for the Society.

Since no one believed the cardinal would appoint Father Sobierajski under these circumstances, the parish's fears focused on Dan Gatti, an aloof and handsome man whom few parishioners knew. He was reported to have shared an 'embrace with Bishop Corrada, his seminary classmate, on the night of Father Gavigan's funeral, and that was enough to foster conspiracy theories in the anxious parish. He was the stealth candidate, people said, the reactionary in moderate's clothing.

For much of that spring, Father Madden projected the air of a man amused but otherwise unaffected by the rumors that swirled around him. When Ed Glynn first approached him about the pastor's job in the fall, he had been reluctant to have his name put forward. Being pastor would divert him from the liturgy center just as he was being invited to give workshops and retreats in the large and theologically conservative archdioceses of New York and Philadelphia. But as he and the other Jesuits at Holy Trinity began reviewing the list of potential pastoral candidates, and as they watched the best men request and receive other jobs, they became increasingly concerned. It had taken Tom Gavigan and his successors almost three decades to build Holy Trinity, but the wrong pastor might ruin it in a tenth of that time.

For Larry, there was also a question of self-interest. If Holy Trinity changed its pastoral course, he would be left without a parish at which to test his ideas and showcase his innovations.

The longer he thought about the job, the more he believed that he might actually enjoy it. He began to ruminate on how he might instill a more professional spirit in his staff, to speculate about modernizing the parish's administrative procedures, and to dream of building the new parish center, which parishioners had been considering for several years. Almost in spite of himself, Father Madden's cautious openness was transformed into frank desire.

In mid-May Ed Glynn relayed his choices to the archdiocese, with Larry's name at the top of the list. But Cardinal Hickey was in Rome, and the decision would have to await his return.

◠ᴥᴥ◡

Father Maier sat on a makeshift stage dressed in black pants, his Roman collar and a white cardigan sweater. He was changing his shoes. "Hello boys and girls," he intoned, in a plausible imitation of a much-parodied voice. "I'm so glad you came to play. It's a beautiful day in the neighborhood. My neighborhood is called Georgetown. Can you say that? Georgetown. I thought you could."

Sitting on lawn chairs, reclining on blankets and leaning against stout trees, the fifteen hundred people who had gathered for Holy Trinity's annual parish picnic burst into laughter. The picnic, which was held each year on Trinity Sunday, brought parishioners from Holy Trinity and St. Aloysius to the stately grounds of Visitation School, where they celebrated the liturgy and partook of hot dogs on the rolling grassy hills.

There were booths where the children could have their faces painted, a piñata sponsored by the Parish-to-Parish Committee, and free-form games of softball and soccer. But the high point of the afternoon was always the entertainment. This was largely because the priests of Holy Trinity and St. Aloysius were goodnatured enough to risk making fools of themselves.

"Do you like to play?" Father Maier continued in his best Fred Rogers tone of voice. "My friends come over all the time. They are called parishioners. They tell me how to spend my money. I have lots of friends."

For parishioners who were new to the picnic and had imagined that Father Maier spent all his time in ethereal contemplation or an administrative sweat, it was disarming and delightful to watch him shed his seriousness. It was as though he was giving them permission to have a good cleansing laugh, and he did not care whether it came at his expense.

For all its frivolousness, the entertainment at the picnic served an essential function. It was the one occasion on which the people of Holy Trinity coaxed levity rather than anxiety from the foibles, misunderstandings and disagreements that separated them from each other and from the larger Church. Laughter cut their apprehensions down to size, assured them that despite everything, it would be all right. And perhaps because they were no longer certain that this was so, the entertainment that Sunday was more spirited than ever.

After "Father Maier's Neighborhood," the CCD catechists sang a ditty set to music from *A Funny Thing Happened on the Way to the Forum* by Stephen Sondheim. It was called "Orthodox Tomorrow, Trinity Tonight," and had been adapted by parishioner Herbie Di Fonzo.

> Something sagacious, something flirtatious,
> We've got both smarts and sex at Trinity Tonight!
> Something that teases Archdioceses,
> Bishops are welcome here at Trinity Tonight!
> Parents take heed! Get your son or daughter.
> This show is rated: No Imprimatur.
> Straight up to glory. No purgatory.
> We keep Ignatius in our sights.
> Orthodox tomorrow. Trinity tonight!

Next came the "Jim Maier Look-Alike Contest," with various parishioners parading across the stage in snowy felt beards and ill-fitting silvery wigs. Then Jim appeared, wearing a tattered cloak and carrying a huge staff. His hair was unruly, his face lined with wrinkles. He was supposed to resemble Saint Ignatius as a hermit, but he looked more like a refugee from the *Mad Max* movies. Later, Father George Anderson, the pastor of St. Aloysius, who looked like a cross between Mr. Chips and Saint Francis of Assisi, danced a soft-shoe.

It was as festive a picnic as anyone could remember, perhaps because Trinity parishioners realized it was the last time that they would all be together with the pastor they had come to love so well. Jim would be leaving on his sabbatical in mid-August whether the cardinal had named a successor or not, and though there would be other smaller gatherings in the intervening weeks, the picnic amounted to his official farewell.

As the program drew to a close, he sat sheepishly on the stage and listened to one speaker after another laud him for his courage, his leadership and his gift for making them feel the presence of God.

Finally it was his turn to speak.

He had stood before them many times, to ask for money, to challenge them with the Gospel, to suggest that they contemplate their sinfulness and their mortality. Almost always, he had found the proper words. But on this occasion Jim discovered that he had nothing to say. Or nothing he could say.

He could not inform them of the status of the search for his successor. Nor could he speak of his own slowly solidifying plans, and so he took refuge in greeting-card sentiment. He had loved being their pastor, he said. God would continue to lead them, as he hoped God would continue to lead him. They would grow in Christ, through the Spirit. Farewell.

People cheered. They had more to eat. It was only that evening or the following day that parishioners learned what Jim had not wanted to tell them.

That weekend, Cardinal Hickey had rejected all three of the candidates Ed Glynn had proposed to him. He had rejected these men without interviewing them, without studying their curricula vitae and, in Larry Madden's case, without reviewing his published writings. And he had rejected them without a word of explanation.

Father Maier was crestfallen. This humiliation seemed directed more at him than at the candidates themselves. After six years, to have his stewardship evaluated so harshly that no one affiliated with him was thought suitable for the pastorate wounded and enraged him. It also persuaded him, for the first time, that the Jesuits' two-hundred-year tenure at Holy Trinity might soon come to an end.

A few weeks earlier he had polled his brother Jesuits about whether they would be willing to stay in the parish and work with an archdiocesan pastor. No, they had said. Nothing against the man, whoever he might be, but they were Jesuits and wanted to live and work in a Jesuit community.

That settled it, then, Jim thought. He had lost Holy Trinity for the Society.

Ed Glynn did not take the rejection quite so personally, but he was livid nonetheless. The Jesuits had followed proper procedures. They had selected priests whom they deemed to be the best candidates and they had taken the unusual step of offering the cardinal three choices. But Hickey had dismissed these men in a way that suggested he had determined to do so before he even knew who they were.

If that was the case, Glynn wondered, why hadn't he bypassed the Jesuits altogether and made the appointment himself? That night at the Loyola College graduation in Baltimore, Father Glynn ran into Dennis and Pam Lucey, two Trinity stalwarts. In a fit of temper, he said: "If he wants the parish that badly, he can have it."

Those words were soon burning on the parish grapevine. Rumors about the advent of either Bishop Corrada or Father Vaghi resumed in full force. Meanwhile some normally prudent parishioners were beginning to consider radical action.

The Catholic laity has no legal standing to challenge the decisions of the hierarchy. It has no ecclesial forum in which it can make itself heard. Its only recourses are protest and freelance boat rocking.

Catholics in other dioceses, angry over the closing of a parish or the consolidation of schools, have occupied their churches or staged demonstrations. The people of Holy Trinity, who counted among their number many influential political operatives, were considering more bureaucratically nuanced moves.

There was talk of forming an escrow account for all contributions to the parish and the cardinal's annual stewardship campaign. There was talk of putting pressure on the cardinal through the political and philanthropic machinery on which the archdiocese relied in its lobbying and its charitable work. There was talk of bringing the parish's story to *The Washington Post*.

But though they could have made life miserable for James Hickey, parishioners seemed to understand that they could not, in the end, overpower him. They understood that whatever kind of campaign they launched might quickly turn vindictive, and that any aggressive action would ruin whatever slim hopes they might have for a reconciliation with the archdiocese.

The proud and self-consciously prominent parish felt itself at the cardinal's mercy, and hoped that he might reach an agreement with the Jesuits. Yet they feared that in rejecting the names put forward by Ed Glynn, Hickey had signaled his intention to "purify" the archdiocese, to define a narrow band of opinion as truly orthodox and to rout all who disagreed.

Ed Glynn, meanwhile, had determined to sit tight. If the cardinal were trying to send him a message, then it was time for him to make his meaning clear.

Father Glynn was in his office a few days later when Hickey called to say that he was concerned about the impasse at Holy Trinity. He wanted to suggest a few names.

Glynn did not know whether to be delighted or apprehensive. Perhaps the cardinal was not going to take over the parish after all. Or perhaps he was maneuvering the Jesuits into a corner. Perhaps he would request the services of men whom he knew he could not have, and then use their unavailability as grounds for installing a diocesan pastor.

But when the cardinal listed his names, Father Glynn was suddenly hopeful about the fate of Holy Trinity for the first time in several days. Hickey's candidates were Jim Devereaux, a former provincial who was now a pastor in Charlotte, North Carolina; Joe Michini, who had once been stationed at Holy Trinity and now served in Philadelphia; and Paul Cioffi, who lived at Georgetown University and had recently founded the one-man Institute for Priestly Renewal.

Cardinal Hickey knew each of these priests personally. All were intelligent men with nuanced views. None was a member of the "take back the Church" crowd. When left to his own devices, it seemed, James Hickey was not nearly as alarmed about Holy Trinity as some of the priests who had his ear.

The trouble was that two of the men were committed to long-term appointments in other dioceses, and the third did not want the job.

Paul Cioffi was the cardinal's personal favorite. An oval-faced man in his early sixties, he had a Roman nose and a receding hairline. In profile, he bore a passing resemblance to Pope Pius XII. In accent, he was pure Brooklyn.

Father Cioffi was the kind of priest who reveled in the trappings of the priesthood. He loved the ritual of Sunday morning, the company of his fellow Jesuits, the solemn proprietary quality of even the most mundane ecclesial transactions. His vision of the clergy was as men set apart, purified and elevated by the strenuous path they had chosen. He was High Church in his liturgical tastes. The cardinal liked that.

But Father Cioffi's traditionalism was tempered by modestly liberal theological views. He favored the use of inclusive language in liturgical and scriptural texts. He had preached against the Gulf War. The preferential option for the poor was among his most frequent homiletic themes. In extolling its social concerns programs, he had once referred to Holy Trinity as a "city on a hill."

But he was not an admirer of Jim Maier's pastorate. "Authority is part of the priestly charism," he said one spring afternoon over lunch in the Jesuit dining room at Georgetown. "I am embarrassed by that, but there it is." The involvement of so many lay people in the decision making at Holy Trinity had thrown the parish into disarray, he believed. The profusion of committees was a sign that the church was being run on an ad hoc basis.

The thought of warring on a nightly basis with the members of those committees filled him with dread. But that was not his principal reason for avoiding the pastorate.

One year earlier he had founded the Institute for Priestly Renewal, from which he hoped to shore up the sagging morale of the American presbyterate. He had sacrificed a tenured teaching position at Georgetown to begin the project, and wanted to devote the rest of his active ministry toward making it grow. He hoped the cardinal would not force him to abandon these plans.

But James Hickey, with whom he had worked preparing seminarians for the priesthood at the North American College in Rome, was a friend as well as a superior, and so on a mid-June morning Father Cioffi drove across town to the archdiocesan pastoral center in suburban Prince Georges County.

He had been waiting only a moment when the cardinal, tall, thin and white-haired, emerged from his office. Hickey had round, ruddy cheeks and a sharply pointed nose. In public he often projected a beaming opacity, but the cardinal was warm, if not exactly relaxed, in the company of his favorite priests.

The two men greeted each other like the old friends that they were. Father Cioffi felt himself being borne along on a solicitous tide. Why was it that Jim Maier had never developed a rapport with this man?

"My intention is to twist your arm a little," Hickey said jokingly, after they had seated themselves in his office. It was a big, sunlit room with dark wooden furniture and winged-backed chairs. Well-chosen religious art hung from the walls, and Father Cioffi felt comfortable in these warm if slightly formal surroundings.

We have a problem, Hickey continued.

The people at Holy Trinity are not being taught the faith in simple and straightforward terms, the cardinal said. They are being served by priests who are not preaching the truths of the faith and not exercising the leadership entrusted them by the Church. They need a firm hand to guide them back toward orthodoxy.

Much as he wanted to defend the Jesuit parish, Father Cioffi had to acknowledge some of the cardinal's concerns. He wondered, sometimes, if the people of Holy Trinity understood that discipleship required certain sacrifices, or if they simply came together to enjoy the pleasure of one another's company. He remembered Tom Gavigan telling him, during the Mitch Snyder controversy, that Holy Trinity was becoming "the ha-ha parish with the la-la spirituality."

Yet he was at pains to remind Hickey that at least some of what he had heard about the parish was simply incorrect, particularly in regards to the liturgy, which was extremely lively, yet generally by the book. They do need a man who can keep them in line, Father Cioffi agreed, but they don't need a complete theological retooling.

You would be just the man for the job then, the cardinal said.

Wishing, perhaps, that he could have been elsewhere in that moment, Father Cioffi began to make the case against his own candidacy. Being considered for the pastorate at a church as prominent as Holy Trinity was an honor he had never anticipated, he said. And obviously, if the cardinal ordered him to assume the post, he would do so, not only out of obedience, which he had vowed as a Jesuit, but out of respect.

Then he reached into his jacket pocket and withdrew a flyer for the Institute of Priestly Renewal. "But what about this?" he asked the cardinal. "Shall I give it up?"

Cioffi knew that the shortage of priestly vocations and the declining morale of American priests were among Hickey's principal concerns, and he hoped this would be enough to keep the cardinal from ordering him to take the job.

The cardinal looked at the pamphlet, and then at his friend. He was aware of the sacrifices Cioffi had made to found the Institute, and of his capacity for inspiring young priests. Won't you at least think about it? he asked in a resigned tone of voice. Won't you at least pray over it?

Of course, Father Cioffi said.

And will you look over the men of your province and see if you find any suitable candidates? Hickey asked.

When he heard those words, Cioffi knew he was off the hook. The cardinal was not going to force him to take the job. But if he did not become pastor at Holy Trinity, who would?

That afternoon he did as the cardinal requested, paging through the Jesuit annual and mulling over the pastoral possibilities. In truth, he thought he already knew the best man for the job. It was Larry Madden. And his cursory research only deepened that conviction.

Larry was the only person he could imagine controlling the parish's fractious committees and its independent staff. He would surround himself with sensible, patient people. He would restore a sense of order. He would persuade the parish that the Church changed slowly and that the faithful had to bear with it.

He and Ed Glynn had voiced this opinion to one another in a meeting shortly before Cioffi's appointment with Cardinal Hickey. Now their job was convincing the cardinal to give Larry a chance.

When he phoned the cardinal the following morning, Father Cioffi said that his survey of the province had unearthed several potential candidates, all but one of whom were unavailable. Then he raised Father Madden's name.

The cardinal replied that he had heard various rumors which indicated that Larry might not be wholly reliable.

But those rumors were baseless, Father Cioffi said, and the men who had conveyed them had been forced to admit that. If the cardinal would meet with Father Madden, he would see how loyal Larry was to the institutional Church and how little inclined he was to rock its boat.

Cioffi did not tell the cardinal that Larry was a member of the Women's Ordination Conference, because he did not know it. Nor did he remind Hickey that it was Larry who drew a rousing ovation twenty-five years earlier when he defied Cardinal O'Boyle and gave an oblique defense of Tom Gavigan's objections to *Humanae Vitae*. Instead he stressed how "sound" Father Madden was, and how "mature."

Ed Glynn also stepped up his campaign on Larry's behalf. In conversations with the cardinal, Ed reminded Hickey that he had received a good deal of false or deliberately misleading information about Holy Trinity, and that much of it had come from his auxiliary bishop, Alvaro Corrada.

"I have no faith in his judgment," Father Glynn said.

It was a risky tack to pursue with a man like Hickey, who reveres the ecclesial power structure, but the remark struck home. The portrait of Father Madden painted by the Jesuits was so radically different from that sketched by Bishop Corrada that the cardinal felt compelled to examine the difference himself. In the second week of June he requested a copy of Larry's curriculum vitae and several of his publications. Finding nothing in these that alarmed him, he asked his secretary to make an appointment with Larry for the morning of June 23.

On the night his name had been rejected Father Madden had been presiding at a wedding in Pennsylvania. "I can see why the cardinal would be afraid of me," he said bitterly to some friends. "I brought Joseph Campbell back from the dead."

Of all the Jesuits at Holy Trinity, Larry had the surest institutional touch. He knew how to make the Church, the Society and the parish serve his ends. In rejecting his pastoral candidacy, the cardinal had denigrated not only his ministry but his organizational savvy, and it was hard to say which hurt more.

Yet Father Madden knew it would harm his renewed candidacy to make an issue of his wounded pride, and so he arrived at the pastoral center in as upbeat a mood as he could muster. Father Cioffi had done the heavy lifting and gotten him the interview, he told himself. All he had to do was persuade the cardinal that he was trustworthy.

Inside his first-floor office, Hickey received his guest with wary cordiality. The cardinal had sparred so often with Ed Glynn and the priests at Georgetown that his suspicion of Jesuits was practically reflexive. Yet he was determined to give Father Madden a fair hearing. He sensed, however, that they had something to resolve before their conversation could begin in earnest.

No sooner had Larry seated himself than the cardinal asked whether he had been angry about having his initial nomination rejected so abruptly.

"Yes," Father Madden said bluntly. "I was."

Hickey did not respond directly to this admission, but it seemed to clear the air between them. Each man relaxed, if only slightly, and the interview began in a more friendly fashion. The cardinal asked his questions with a touch of amused curiosity, and Larry responded as though eager to tell his superior what he wanted to hear.

They spoke of the pastor's duty to represent the bishop to the people of his parish, and of the spiritual riches of the liturgy. Father Madden believed he was off to a fast start. But then Hickey asked whether he accepted the Church's teaching on women's ordination.

"I accept it," Larry said quickly. This was true in the narrowest sense. Father Madden thought the teaching was in error, but he accepted that it bound him as a priest.

"But I think in twenty years we are going to have a big problem," he added. "There just aren't going to be enough priests."

Might the drop in vocations not be a passing fad? the cardinal asked.

No, Larry said. American Catholics had come to new understandings about the natures of authority and sexuality. These were behind the plunge in vocations, and they would not be easily reversed.

He could not tell from the cardinal's expression what Hickey thought of this reply.

"Will you uphold the magisterium in your preaching?" the cardinal asked.

Again Larry chose his words carefully. As a liturgist, Larry believed that homilies should always be based upon the themes articulated in that day's Scripture readings. The American bishops had said much the same thing in a pastoral letter on preaching in the late 1980s. But the Scriptures say nothing about such contentious issues as abortion, artificial contraception, priestly celibacy, women's ordination or papal authority. And neither, when he could avoid it, did he.

Our preaching flows from Scripture, Larry said. "I will preach the Gospel."

It was an elusive answer, but Hickey did not press him on it. Perhaps he was giving Father Madden the benefit of the doubt. Or perhaps he was waiting for what he had not heard.

They had been quiet for a moment when the cardinal asked Larry for his views about the Standing.

At last, Larry thought to himself, a softball, a question he could answer by saying precisely what the cardinal wanted to hear. Protest had no place in the Mass, he replied. He would do everything he could to stop it.

By the end of this examination, Cardinal Hickey seemed to have taken a liking to Father Madden. Larry was thoughtful, committed, and less prone than Jim Maier to err on the side of weakness. He understood the need for authority, and for following teachings one did not necessarily agree with.

The cardinal may have been aware that if he dug a little deeper he would find areas on which he and Father Madden differed. Larry was clearly influenced by theologians on the left wing of ecclesial debates, yet he seemed sound enough for all that. Perhaps Glynn and Cioffi were right, and his own people were wrong. Perhaps Father Madden was his man.

Larry drove back to Georgetown feeling optimistic, yet occasionally uncertain. He thought things had gone well. Yet he couldn't be sure he had said everything that the cardinal wanted to hear.

At the parish center he conferred briefly with Jim and a few other colleagues. Then the Jesuits in the rectory and the staff in the parish center began their vigils near the phone.

Early that evening, the call came in to the rectory. Cardinal Hickey offered Father Madden the pastorate of Holy Trinity parish. Father Madden accepted.

The long uncertainty was over. Holy Trinity would remain in Jesuit hands.

The following morning staff members filed into Larry's office and congratulated him with high fives. Parish phone lines burned with the news.

There would be no need for protests, no need for escrow accounts, no need to find a new spiritual home. Holy Trinity would survive as that rare and cherished piece of ecclesial ground: a place where the laity could discuss, dispute and progress in their faith, a place where questioning Catholics could continue to *be* Catholics. And that was reason for rejoicing.

In her office at the parish center, Margaret Costello did just that.

Much of what she knew about the liturgy, she had learned from Father Madden. He was her field supervisor in one of the classes she was taking at the Washington Theological Union. They were in almost perfect accord on most of the issues that confronted her as interim director of the liturgy, and it seemed certain that he would recommend to members of the recently formed search committee that they appoint her to the job on a permanent basis.

The lay people who preached in the parish also rejoiced. Larry's appointment assured the continued existence of the parish retreat programs, as well as the vespers and reconciliation services at which they were sometimes offered the chance to preach.

Paul and Cathy Quinn celebrated the news, as did Mike and Pam Hall, because Larry was a more moderate man than Jim Maier, and because he was on record as an opponent of the Standing.

Ray McGovern was among the few people not gladdened by the choice of the new pastor. He was relieved that his protest had not caused the cataclysm that other parishioners had predicted. But he feared that Larry Madden would adopt confrontational tactics to end the Standing.

Indeed, just days after his appointment, Larry announced his intention of meeting with the Working Groups on Sexism, which were convening the following week. According to one rumor, he was coming with a compromise. According to another, he bore an ultimatum.

Jim Maier, who would nominally remain pastor until his departure in August, cared only vaguely what Larry was planning. When Larry was named as his successor he felt his burden lift, and not merely in the metaphorical sense. The muscles in his shoulders loosened. He felt lighter. Despite the Standing, the suspicion against his female staff members, the protest against the CCD program, and his "softness" on homosexuality, the parish had survived; he had handed it over to a brother Jesuit, a man whom he respected and trusted.

His ordeal as a pastor was over, and the time for confronting his personal dilemma was at hand. He would begin in El Salvador, where the Spirit had always seemed to him a particularly powerful presence.

CHAPTER TWENTY

From the air, the mountains of Guatemala appeared to buckle, one into the next, like a green and rocky accordion. Gazing out the window as the plane ascended from Guatemala City, Jim could see the volcano of San Salvador—The Savior—in the distance, and the ocean beyond. This was his fifth trip to El Salvador, and he realized that it might be his last.

In front of, beside and behind him sat the other nine delegates from Holy Trinity, six women and three men, most of them white-collar workers in their mid-thirties to mid-fifties. Only four spoke decent Spanish, and only two had previously visited El Salvador.

In the seven years he had been making his own pilgrimages, Jim had known people to make the trip for a variety of reasons—spiritual, personal and political—and that morning after he had celebrated Mass for the group at Dulles Airport in a small room where model airplanes hung on the walls, he wondered about the motivations of his companions.

Some were self-evident. Jo Owen and Lydia Mendoza, mainstays of the sister-parish program, were eager to renew old friendships. Kathleen Conley and Jay Gribble were the new leaders of the Parish-to-Parish Committee. Kathy Hartley had been drawn south by her interest in liberation theology, and Mary Gravalos, at seventy-two the oldest member of the group, had acquired an interest in U.S. involvement in the region during her career as an analyst at the CIA.

But there were others in the group whose interests Jim could not quite place, who seemed hot on the trail of something they had not yet identified, and their presence made him wonder how well he understood his own reasons for returning to Madre de los Pobres. Did he imagine that he might come to a sudden decision about his future? Or was he eager for a morally acceptable means of putting the matter out of his mind? Perhaps he thought the matter would resolve itself while his attention was elsewhere.

One thing he was sure of: life in El Salvador seemed more real and more urgent than life at home. The needs were many, obvious and immediate. Doing good, at least as a visitor, seemed almost a matter of reflex. At home it was seldom that simple.

On their first night at Madre de los Pobres, the delegates called at the convent of the Sisters of the Assumption, who taught at Fe y Alegría (Faith and Happiness), the parish-sponsored elementary school. Most of the nuns were Spanish, and though their small residence sat along a dirt path employed primarily by pigs and chickens, inside a vestigial European formality reigned.

Madre Adela, the school's principal, received them in a small, neat and sparsely furnished sitting room. She was a dark-haired, olive-skinned woman whose sturdy physique was well-suited to the rigors of ascetic life. Her expression was intense, but her manner light. She was a woman who took her work more seriously than she took herself.

Seated at a simple wicker desk, she thanked them for the two thousand dollars that Holy Trinity had sent her the previous year. She had used it, she said, to buy shoes for the children who came to school barefoot. Enrollment had risen after the end of the war in 1991, but many families could barely afford the forty-dollar annual tuition.

With peace, she told them, had come a gradual understanding of how costly the conflict had been. There were hundreds of orphans and war widows in the parish. Domestic violence and alcoholism were almost as pervasive as unemployment, illiteracy and malnutrition. Still, she added with a sad but grateful smile, it was better than before.

Studying his speechless colleagues, Jim wondered if they were feeling the curious rush of emotions that had overtaken him in similar instances during his first trips to El Salvador. The sufferings of the Salvadoran poor seemed so vast and deeply rooted that they moved him beyond anger and beyond pity, to the edge of despair. Yet the example of Madre Adela and others like her filled him with admiration, with awe and, finally, with hope. In El Salvador, a friend had once told him, you were constantly meeting Christ crucified, and constantly meeting Christ risen.

After the meeting, they walked along the railroad that bisected the parish. Shacks stood close to the tracks, and children, who were expert at divining when a train was coming, played along the rails. They were dressed in ancient Jethro Tull T-shirts, ragged Minnie Mouse jumpers and other North American hand-me-downs, yet the desolation of their surroundings had yet to invade their souls. Several of the delegates were carrying cameras, and the children streamed toward them in bunches crying, "*Una foto? Una foto?*" When Kathy and Kathleen obliged them, they struck poses as studiously dignified as those in a nineteenth-century studio portrait.

A bridge bore the railroad over the river, and the delegates stood in the middle of it, peering down between the ties at the gray and acrid waters. On either side, single stalks of corn sprouted from tiny indentations in the sheer cliffs, and they wondered how these had been planted and how they would be harvested.

It was only 9:00 P.M. when the delegates returned to their bunk houses—the six women in one large cinder block room and the four men in a slightly smaller one—but they were unanimous in their exhaustion. Already Jim could feel the group struggling with the same question that always haunted him when he came to El Salvador: how to respond to the suffering they were seeing without becoming overwhelmed by it.

He wondered how many were entertaining the romantic dream that he had once nursed, of leaving behind his former life and giving himself over to the cause of the poor. As recently as last winter he had considered requesting a teaching assignment at the University of Central America, where his Jesuit brothers had been murdered. But in the months since then, he had come to the humbling realization that he was not equal to the task.

Burdened by his sexual dilemma, he had neither the will nor the energy to begin a new job in a foreign country. It had nonetheless been a difficult dream to surrender, for it meant acknowledging that his greatest contribution to the Salvadoran struggle—the establishment of the sister-parish program—had already been made. It also meant acknowledging that until he resolved his own problem, he would be of little use to anyone else.

In the next three days he and the other delegates visited every cranny of Padre Daniel's cinder-block empire: the day care center, the medical and dental clinics, the bakery and the struggling carpentry shop. They bought brightly colored stuffed birds at the sewing cooperative and played softball with the children on a field beside the church.

At midweek they left for Guarjila, a tiny village in the mountains of Chalatenango province, where they spent two days with the campesinos who had resettled the area at the end of the war and were now waiting to see if they would be given title to the land. Here, too, there were people like Madre Adela and Padre Daniel, who had made the Salvadorans' struggle their own: Jon de Cortina, a Jesuit engineer and architect who lived in the village and had designed a makeshift bridge made of discarded materials over the Sempul River; a young doctor and his wife, who had come to spend a year at the village clinic, and John Giuliano, a former Jesuit seminarian, who had lived in a one-room hut in Guarjila since 1987 because, as he put it, "This is the only place where I can pray and it still makes sense."

On their last full day in the country, they drove to the campus of the University of Central America and followed the narrow road that wound between the school's small and simply designed buildings to the chapel where the murdered Jesuits were interred. Though they had been expecting to find their experience there a wrenching one, the delegates were utterly unprepared for the savage beauty of the small church.

On the rear wall of the chapel, in lieu of more traditional Stations of the Cross, hung fourteen haunting pencil drawings of the tortured, tongueless, bullet-riddled bodies of Salvadorans for whom the civil war had become a personal Calvary. To the right of the main altar hung a portrait of the eight dead—six Jesuits, their housekeeper and her daughter—their sober countenances hovering over a Chagall-like landscape of destruction. To the left, beneath a formal portrait of Archbishop Romero, the tiled floor gave way to a rectangle of gravel and greenery. This was where the priests were interred.

The delegates moved about individually and in silence. Despite the almost palpable presence of lingering evil, the atmosphere in the chapel was one of anguished peace. Light streamed through the wrought iron that formed the two side walls, falling on pews and altar pieces of simple blond wood.

Beside the chapel stood the building behind which most of the eight had been killed. Inside, a conference room had been turned into a small museum. The delegates entered in the same silence they had observed in the church. Along the right wall stood glass cases holding theology books ripped in two by machine-gun fire, a portrait of Romero singed by a flamethrower and jars containing blood-soaked earth taken from beneath the bodies of Ignacio Ellacuria and the others.

They exited through a back door, climbed a short staircase and stood in the yard where the bodies were found. There, the UCA's groundskeeper, husband and father to the two murdered women, had planted a rose garden.

It was a warm afternoon in the rainy Salvadoran winter, and a single crimson flower was in bloom.

Later that afternoon the delegates drove to the Hospital of Divine Providence and celebrated Mass in the chapel where Oscar Romero had been murdered. On one side of the altar stood a statue of Our Lady of Mount Carmel, patron of the nuns who operated the hospital. On the other, a small, square piece of marble jutted from the linoleum floor, marking the spot where the archbishop had fallen after having been shot through the throat while saying Mass.

The intensity of the day was almost too much for the group by that point. Their responses to the prayers were muted, almost whispered. Jo and Kathy delivered their readings in the wrong order, and Jim gave a brief talk that was more a request and confession than a homily.

Oscar Romero had devoted his priesthood to serving the poor, he said. The members of this group had encouraged him to do the same. They had supported him when he was in trouble and remonstrated with him when he faltered. He wanted to thank them for that, and to pray that each of them might find their own particular way of serving God by serving the poor.

He asked that they offer similar prayers for him.

Flying home the next day, Father Maier felt as he often felt at the end of such trips, that the Church in El Salvador was immersed in the work of God, and that the Church in the United States was dissipating its energies in fruitless struggle over abstruse theological points. After his earliest trips, this feeling had been so strong that he'd felt alienated, upon his return, from his parishioners and their seemingly petty concerns. But as his own sexual dilemma intensified, he had come to see a link between the struggles of those whose dignity and sense of worth were diminished by sexism and homophobia and those whose dignity and survival were imperiled by violence, a repressive government or the vicissitudes of the global economy.

Injustices of the latter kind struck him as more compelling than injustices of the former. Yet that was no reason not to combat both. The danger for middle-class American Catholics, such as his parishioners, was that they would become so caught up in their battle against whatever beset them at the moment that they would become merely self-indulgent—obsessed by rights but ignorant of responsibilities.

As he continued contemplating his future, Jim realized he faced this danger himself. Soon he would be losing his pulpit, and his authority to allocate the resources of an affluent community. He would have to find some other way of honoring his commitment to the poor as he sought to resolve his dilemma as a gay priest.

⟨ℳ⟩

Jim returned from the heat and humidity of El Salvador to the heat and humidity of a Washington summer, and a parish preoccupied by a single question: What was Father Madden going to do about the Standing? Many parishioners assumed, correctly, that Larry's opposition to the protest had been central to his appointment as pastor. Some assumed further that a quid pro quo existed between Cardinal Hickey and Father Glynn: a Jesuit pastor in return for an end to the Standing.

In the week after his appointment, Larry Madden dropped in on a meeting of the Working Groups on Sexism. Though the fifteen or so people who had gathered in the lower-school cafeteria that evening had never viewed him as a friend of their cause, they received him warmly nonetheless. Larry was their deliverer, the man who had saved the parish from an assault on its liberal traditions, and for this they were deeply grateful.

They were also aware that the future of their group rested in his hands. After Jim's departure in early August, Larry would be the man to decide whether they could continue to meet on Holy Trinity's property and publicize their activities in its bulletin. Those who had been searching for a way to distance the groups from the ordination protest and move on to other topics were also hoping that he might somehow resolve this issue for them.

After the opening prayer, Rea Howarth turned the floor over to Father Madden, who segued smoothly into his sales pitch. He wanted them to know, he said, that he shared their desire to improve the status of women in the Catholic Church. He supported the concept of a female priesthood and he recognized that sexism was a sin of which the Church was frequently guilty.

Where matters became complicated, he continued, was in working to eradicate that sin. Should the future of the entire parish be risked on a quixotic gesture like the Standing? Or should Holy Trinity make the argument for women's equality in a more meaningful way: by serving as a model of how the Church benefits from feminine energy, talent and leadership?

They should make no mistake that this was the choice before them, he said. They had very nearly lost the parish, and the Standing was the principal reason. They might lose it yet. If the protest did not end, "The cardinal could pull me out of here," he said.

Larry paused to take a quick reading of the room. Though the group was largely impassive, he sensed that it accepted his assessment of the situation. Now came the hard part.

I have come with a compromise, he told them. If those of you who are protesting will sit down from the beginning of the readings until the end of Communion, I will allow you to remain standing during the rest of the mass. This arrangement might not satisfy liturgical purists, he went on, but it will satisfy me. And, in all likelihood, it will lay the controversy over the Standing to rest.

Heads nodded as Father Madden outlined his plan. Relief played across Rea Howarth's features. Kathy Hartley looked judiciously pleased. Here was a small symbolic victory and a ready escape from the morass of bitter feelings and recriminations which the Standing had loosed upon the parish in general and upon themselves in particular.

Margaret Costello made no effort to mask her enthusiasm. If Ray would sit down, perhaps opponents of the Standing would cease to view her every initiative as another front in McGovern's war. Larry's compromise seemed on the verge of carrying the night.

But in the Standing, as in the Vatican, only one man's opinion truly counted, and that man was unimpressed. Ray McGovern saw no value in Larry's plan. He was disturbed, he said, by his colleagues' rush to embrace it. Couldn't they see that aside from the few moments following Communion, he would be standing only when others were standing? His protest would become all but unnoticeable. And for what? Holy Trinity was not becoming more hospitable to women. It was frozen, as the rest of the Church was frozen, by the self-elevating dicta of the Roman hierarchy. Until those dicta were challenged and changed, the "progress" people spoke of regarding women's role in the Church was just so much embroidery.

When Ray finished speaking an uneasy silence descended upon the room. It was as though the other participants in the meeting had reached an immediate and unspoken consensus: McGovern had gone too far. He had not simply defended his position, he had challenged the integrity and commitment of those who disagreed with him.

For Margaret Costello, this was too much to bear. Over the course of the protest she had become increasingly irritated by Ray's attitude. Although he pretended to be striking a blow against patriarchy, McGovern, to her mind, was engaging in fairly typical male behavior: he was playing the knight errant; the lone ranger. It was all just a bit too self-aggrandizing.

Worse, he had acceded to himself the right to make decisions which might determine the future of the entire community. He had assumed the worst traits of the hierarchy he opposed, and in so doing he had destroyed the atmosphere of respect and trust which had previously allowed parishioners of differing viewpoints to reason together toward common ends.

Perhaps no one felt this more keenly than she. If Margaret suggested that a lay woman, such as Linda Arnold or Natalie Ganley, preside at vespers or a reconciliation service, it was assumed by opponents of the Standing that she did so because she had an agenda to advance rather than because she believed these women had something valuable to say. When she suggested that Holy Trinity include "lay listeners" along with priestly confessors at its reconciliation services, it was assumed that her interest was in blurring the line between the ordained and the nonordained rather than in providing partners for spiritual conversation to those parishioners who were not seeking absolution.

Parishioners who objected to inclusive language, women preachers, women altar servers, contemporary liturgical music or the use of a variety of new Church-approved prayers vented their wrath upon her. And they vented it in language they might not have directed at someone wearing a Roman collar.

After nine months as interim director of the liturgy, Margaret had become accustomed, if not inured, to the whispering campaign against her. Much of the time, she still loved her job. She thrilled when Linda, Natalie or another lay person delivered an excellent homily. She drew quiet satisfaction from hearing the prayers she had rendered in inclusive language read from the altar. She was energized by the sheer numbers of women, more than two hundred, who served in some kind of ministerial position at Holy Trinity.

But none of these advances had been accomplished without struggle. How dare Ray McGovern characterize them as window dressing?

I resent that, Margaret said curtly, looking Ray momentarily in the eye. We've worked very hard to invite women into ministry in this parish, and we've been more successful than anybody in the archdiocese. Yes, we are confined by sexist doctrine. Yes, we are policed by a sexist hierarchy. But we are making progress, and you seem to be one of the only people who doesn't recognize that. When this protest began, I felt supported by this group, she concluded. I don't feel that way any more.

Margaret's remarks gave the few members of the Working Groups who still supported the Standing reason for pause. It was one thing for the protest to splinter the parish; some resistance was to be expected. But alienating one's natural allies was another matter. One by one, they voiced their support of Larry's plan. He is offering us a way out, they told Ray. Declare victory and let's move on.

But why should we let ourselves off the hook when discrimination against women is still so blatant? Ray asked. What gives us the right not to resist?

As the evening wore on, Father Madden saw his chances for winning a compromise dwindling. He foresaw the possibility that the Standing could become a constant headache for him just as it had for Jim Maier, and he lashed out at the one person obstructing a solution.

"Why don't you just leave [the Church]?" he barked at McGovern. And when Ray attempted to respond, Larry said again, "Why don't you just leave?"

It was not clear, by the end of the evening, whether Ray had a single supporter among those who had gathered that night. But it was clear that Ray was not going to sit down, and that Father Madden would need to employ methods other than persuasion if he expected a speedy result.

The meeting adjourned on a discordant note, and the one hopeful development of the night was more or less forgotten. Before the conversation deteriorated, Larry had expressed a vague willingness to include a prayer in the liturgy lamenting the evil of sexism, and Ray, with equal vagueness, had suggested that such a prayer might persuade him to reexamine his position.

This possibility had particular appeal for McGovern, who was eager to institutionalize his protest, and he attempted to explore the matter more fully in a letter to Larry two days later. If the parish would adopt "a very strong prayer condemning sexism" he wrote, then he would stand at the side of the church, where he would no longer block parishioners' view of the mass.

It was the first time Ray had shown the slightest willingness to compromise, and Larry was initially enthused. But as he read the sample prayer that McGovern had composed, his optimism evaporated:

> Creator God we acknowledge our sinfulness, particularly the evil of sexism by which we subordinate women and deny them full equality, even here at this liturgy. Before bringing our gifts to the altar we seek to be reconciled with the women here and also with those who choose not to be here because it is too painful to them to be treated as second-class citizens. We ask their forgiveness and yours too, for the intolerable injustice that we tolerate.

The prayer posed several problems. Theologically it was suspect for elevating sexism above other evils and for urging the reconciliation of men and women, rather than the reconciliation of each to the other and all to God. Of more practical concern, opponents of the Standing would be outraged if Ray were allowed to dictate the terms of his partial surrender. And the cardinal would order an end to the prayer as soon as he learned of its existence.

For Father Madden, the prayer was evidence that further conversation with Ray was fruitless. The two men had been meeting to discuss the Standing for longer than most parishioners realized. They had begun three months earlier, when Ray contacted Larry after their dispute at the open forum on women's ordination. On that occasion they had had lunch in a Georgetown restaurant, and Larry had attempted to counsel Ray in patience.

"You know this is going to happen, don't you?" he said, referring to the eventual ordination of women priests.

"That's the wrong question," Ray replied. "The question is what are you doing to make it happen?"

That exchange captured the critical difference between the two men. Both Ray and Larry were known for their bluntness, their stubbornness and a romantic devotion to their Irish heritage. Perhaps most significantly, each was accomplished at maneuvering for advantage within a large and powerful institution—the Church in Larry's case and the CIA in Ray's.

But in his professional life McGovern had wearied of this game and begun to regret the compromises he had made to remain a player in the agency. He took early retirement, fell hard for the new and more intuitive theology being taught at Georgetown and other American Catholic universities, for the feminist critique of American patriarchy and for the virtues of a simpler and more emotional way of living his life.

Larry, on the other hand, found plenty of room to maneuver within the Church. He had imbibed progressive theology at an earlier age than Ray, but its influence was balanced by his conviction that celebrating the liturgy was the most profound act a person could perform. It was imperative, therefore, that he maintain his viability as a priest. Whatever his private disagreements with the magisterium, he was a creature of his institution.

Had the future of Holy Trinity not been at stake, Ray and Larry might have remained friendly verbal sparring partners, but Father Madden felt that the situation was forcing his hand. After he was named pastor the two men met privately once again, and this time Larry went on the offensive. When Ray told him that this protest was a matter of conscience, Larry reminded him of the September day in 1649 when a man with a similarly clear conscience led an army into the Irish village of Drogheda and slaughtered many of its inhabitants.

The reference was to Oliver Cromwell, the great Puritan persecutor of Ireland, and Ray, who knew his Irish history, was offended by what he regarded as a wildly inappropriate comparison.

"You better sit down," Larry continued. "The cardinal is angry about this."

"Excuse me, Larry," Ray had said. "You are the one who has taken the vow of obedience. Not me."

As testy as that meeting had been, the two men had managed to pray together before Ray left. But Father Madden was beginning to realize that maintaining a decent relationship with McGovern wasn't getting him anywhere. It was time to do something. And so, during the first week of July, he began to review his options.

Calling the police was out of the question. It would begin his pastorate on a disastrous note, and leave him with a divided parish for the duration of his tenure.

He could demand from the pulpit that Ray sit down. But if Ray didn't sit down, that got him nowhere. He could ask for a show of hands: How many people think Ray should sit down? But what would happen, Larry wondered, if he didn't command a majority? Or what if his majority was slim?

Perhaps he could preach a homily against the Standing and leave it at that. But that might simply underscore his powerlessness.

As Larry considered what to say that Sunday, word began circulating in the parish that he and McGovern were edging toward a confrontation at the 9:15 mass.

News of the impending clash found Ray in a deepening dilemma. He had begun to accept that the Standing might never galvanize a broader protest, and to weary of the strain it placed on him and his family. His wife, Rita, a cradle Catholic, had stopped attending church some years earlier, put off by the all-male hierarchy and its preoccupation with issues of gender and sexuality. Their son Joseph, now a college sophomore, shared many of his father's ideals; he was considering work as a lay missionary upon graduation, but he disapproved of the protest for the unwelcome notoriety it brought to his family. Even Christin no longer stood with her father, though she continued to support him and to sit by his side.

As a former intelligence officer, the thought of being arrested was painful to Ray, and though many in the parish believed him impervious to public opinion, he took criticism quite personally. To be chastised by the pastor from the pulpit would be a humiliating experience. Yet no one, in the eighteen months of his protest, had said anything to change his mind about the need to confront injustice.

The church was full, as usual that Sunday morning, 800 people jammed into a space that comfortably accommodated 650. When Larry processed to the altar, he passed the pew where Ray was standing. The score of parishioners who knew about the rupture between the two men prepared for another episode in the saga of the Standing.

Father Madden greeted them in the Name of the Father, the Son and the Holy Spirit. He led them through the Penitential Rite. He sat and listened to the Scripture. Then, as the choir sang Alleluia and the congregation rose to its feet, he stepped to the lectern to proclaim the Gospel.

The reading was from the eleventh chapter of the Gospel according to Matthew. Larry rendered it in a clear, steady voice: "Come to me, all you who are weary and find life burdensome, and I will refresh you. Take my yoke upon your shoulder and learn from me, for I am gentle and humble of heart. You souls will find rest, for my yoke is easy and my burden light."

When he had finished, the congregation seated itself, all except for Ray, who, as usual, was the most noticeable figure in the church. But Larry did not look at McGovern. Rather, his eye swept over the entire assembly and he began to speak of the heavy burden of expectation that modern men and women placed upon themselves by virtue of their desires to be successful, or wealthy, or otherwise impressive.

God wants to relieve us of these burdens, Larry said. And as he began to speak of humility and self-knowledge, it became clear that he was not going to chastise Ray McGovern. He was not going to talk about the Standing. He was not even going to acknowledge its existence.

From the pulpit he could see the relief, disappointment and confusion on the faces of those who had come expecting a confrontation. Later he would explain that he had decided not to make a martyr of McGovern, but to marginalize him gradually. What he did not say was that he, like Jim Maier, had found no satisfactory means of dealing with the Bartleby in their midst.

A few weeks passed before Larry responded to Ray's letter:

"If I thought there was a way other than what we've discussed, that you and I could solve this issue, I would be so glad. But there really isn't one. I have done what I promised to do, Ray. I have asked the director of liturgy to plan how we can bring sexism, the sin of sexism, into our liturgical prayer. But the liturgy belongs to the Church, Ray, and there are limits to what you or I can legitimately do to it. I do not think that given your last suggestion and prayer, any prayer that I could support would meet your demands. . . . I truly do not understand why you won't compromise . . . and I have no hope that more talk will clarify things. Sadly, that's how I feel."

Larry was prepared to put the Standing behind him, even though it was not over. It was a cagey strategy, but it ignored one mitigating factor. Opponents of the Standing were too aggrieved to put the issue to rest. Ray, to their minds, had politicized the liturgy, and now they were prepared to politicize any changes to the ceremonial life of the parish that Larry or Margaret suggested. Someone had to pay for the havoc Ray had wreaked, and if he was out of their reach, then his purported allies and protectors would do.

To complicate matters further, Father Madden learned in mid-July that Cardinal Hickey himself would make his first visit to Holy Trinity in more than six years to preside at the mass at which Larry would be installed as pastor. And how he would respond if Ray was still standing was anyone's guess.

❦

Though he was still nominally the pastor of Holy Trinity, Jim Maier surveyed the drama of that July with a disinterested eye. He doubted that the cardinal would remove Larry as pastor, no matter what Ray did. Hickey seemed willing to let the tempest of the Standing swirl in the teapot of Holy Trinity, as long as it did not threaten to spread. And so, with the future of the parish relatively secure, he began to focus on more personal concerns.

On the first Sunday in August he was leaving for a vacation on the Outer Banks of North Carolina with a group of Jesuit friends who rented the same beach house every year. From there he would fly to upstate New York to visit his brother. After he returned to Washington in mid-August, he and another Jesuit would drive cross-country to Los Angeles. At Loyola Marymount he planned to read, write poetry and try to make sense of his conflicting desires.

One of his fondest hopes was that he would enjoy anonymity sufficient to allow him to explore gay life in Los Angeles. Though he knew what it was like to have a romantic relationship with another man, he had no idea how it felt to move in the secular gay milieu, and he suspected that his comfort in that culture would greatly influence his decision about the priesthood.

He had also decided to explore ministry in the American Catholic Church and the Metropolitan Church, both of which permitted openly gay priests. At the same time, he had resolved to examine his options should he choose to remain a Jesuit. In El Salvador he had begun to question the Society's custom of ministering to the poor from within the security of large institutions. Perhaps he should do as Daniel did and work in the streets, where life was more raw and the needs more immediate. Los Angeles, he knew, would provide many opportunities for such ministry.

Happily, the Jesuits were not pressuring him to make up his mind. His service as a teacher, novice master and pastor had earned him a bit of leeway, and he planned to use it.

As some parishioners knew, he would be back in Washington in six weeks to perform a few marriages. As fewer were aware, he had also promised to say a "mass of thanksgiving" in Chicago in November after the wedding of his former colleague, Ed Dougherty, and Ellen Kerley.

Ed and Ellen had resumed their friendship as soon as Ed left Holy Trinity, and they quickly became romantically involved. After several months they were living together, and by late spring they had decided to get married. Because Ed had not been released from his vows by the Vatican, their marriage could not be sanctioned by the Church. But it was not uncommon in such instances for a sympathetic priest to offer a "mass of thanksgiving."

In the new year, Ed and Ellen would be returning to Washington because of a change in her job. Knowing Ed's low opinion of liturgy elsewhere in the archdiocese, Jim assumed they would once again worship at Holy Trinity, but he was not sure that this would be wise. Ed could not count on everyone receiving him well. And even if the parish was kind, his own feeling of being out of place might be so strong that it would make true worship impossible.

Jim was glad that he would be examining his own relationship with the Church at a great remove from Holy Trinity. But he would miss the place, and he hoped people would miss him. "I would like to think they might say that during a time when the parish was in a real phase of growth, which was somewhat chaotic, we had a great pastor who helped us with spirituality," he said one late July morning as he packed up his office. "I think that's perceived as my main gift, being a really kind person who made time for everybody ... a kind, compassionate man who cared about people, who really encouraged people spiritually."

Perhaps because his departure was imminent, he was willing, that morning, to speculate aloud about the news his parishioners might hear from Los Angeles when the year was over.

"I am going out there with an open mind," he said. "But if I had to bet right now, it would be that I would leave."

A few days later, on the first Sunday of August, he was packing his car in the lot behind the rectory. Though he would be returning in several weeks to make some additional preparations for his trip to Los Angeles, this was, in effect, his last day in the parish. Because he wished to avoid saying any additional goodbyes, he did most of his work while parishioners were at mass. But as he crossed the lot on one of his last trips, he heard Jo Owen call his name.

When he turned, she seemed surprised, and at first he could not think why. Then it came to him. A few days earlier, he had shaved his beard. She was looking at the new Jim Maier.

CHAPTER TWENTY-ONE

On the Sunday after Labor Day, the people of Holy Trinity found a new prayer printed on their song sheets:

> We confess to Almighty God, and all assembled here, that we have sinned against God, our sisters, our brothers and Creation.
> Through our thoughts, and through our words, in what we have done, and in what we have failed to do.
> Through our structures that oppress human beings and violate human dignity.
> Through our systems that stifle freedom and impose inequality.
> And through our cultural and religious symbols,
> that we allow to mask the evils of war, consumerism, racism, classism and sexism.

> Merciful God, we are heartily sorry for our selective blindness.

We firmly resolve, with the help of your grace, to confess our
      sins, to do penance, to open our eyes to sinful structures,
      systems and symbols.
And to become responsible stewards of Your Creation.
Amen.

Those few who worshiped occasionally at St. Aloysius had recited
these potent if inelegant words before, but the prayer was unfamiliar to
most of the Holy Trinity congregation, which rendered it hesitantly and
in inexpressive tones.

The St. Al's Prayer, as it came to be known, constituted Father
Madden and Margaret Costello's last effort to defuse the Standing before
Cardinal Hickey's visit to the parish in mid-October. Kathy Hartley and
a few others had called it to their attention during the summer, and they
had seen its virtues at first glance.

Because it explicitly addressed the issue of sexism, the prayer had
the potential to mollify Ray McGovern. But in enumerating other sins,
it avoided the error of elevating one ism above another. Beyond that,
the prayer made a useful theological point: one was culpable not only in
the evil one did but in the evil in which one acquiesced. Ray had been
saying the same thing for more than a year, and Larry and Margaret
assumed he would be delighted to have his point made as part of the
Penitential Rite.

The new prayer set the conversational agenda for the 9:15 coffee
hour. Margaret had scarcely stepped into the upper school that morning
when people began offering their opinions. The members of the Working Group were unsurprisingly pleased; even Ray acknowledged a step
in the right direction, though he refused to say whether the step was
big enough.

But the emphasis on structural sin struck some parishioners as a
veiled critique of capitalism, and that upset a few people who owned or
managed businesses. Others who supported the prayer's sentiments disliked its language; they thought it sounded more like a party platform
than an act of contrition.

Margaret had expected some debate about the St. Al's Prayer, and
she was prepared to make modifications, but she assumed that most of
the parish would accept it with few qualms. The following day, however,
she received a long, impassioned letter from Stephen Skousgaard, Shannon Jordan's husband-to-be, a former professor of philosophy and a man

with a formidable intellectual reputation in the parish. He accused her of tampering with the language of the Church to advance her liberal, feminist agenda. The St. Al's Prayer constituted a breach of faith, he wrote, an abuse of power, and an affront to orthodox believers.

Margaret was taken aback by the hostility of the letter. Stephen seemed to be unaware that the Church allowed for variety in the Penitential Rite; the sacramentary instructed the congregation to pray "in these or other words."

But as much as she resented what Stephen had written, Margaret could not put it out of her mind. If he were upset, that would mean Shannon and perhaps Paul Quinn and the other opponents of the Standing were upset, and these were people whose concerns she had to take seriously. Perhaps unconsciously she *had* allowed her political agenda to compromise her professional judgment. It was at least worth seeking an outside opinion.

Later that week she met with Father Ken Himes, a professor of moral theology, at the Washington Theological Union. She handed him a copy of the prayer, and Father Himes read through it slowly. What was the problem? he asked.

People are saying it's the agenda of the Democratic party, Margaret said.

It is the agenda of the Catholic Church, he replied.

Margaret relayed the arguments of her opponents, but Father Himes waved them off. I know you have to choose your battles carefully, he said. But I would go to the mat on this one.

She drove back to the parish examining her mixed emotions. Happy as she was to have her judgment affirmed, and satisfying as it would have been to refute her critics, she wondered whether Holy Trinity could stand further controversy. However sound its theology, a penitential rite was ineffective if it caused division rather than reconciliation.

Margaret stuck with the St. Al's Prayer for two more weeks, but the opposition did not subside, and Ray McGovern did not budge. And so, in late September, she reinstituded the previous Penitential Rite.

Now it was Ray's turn to be livid. His sole liturgical achievement had been snatched away by the protest of a small and, to his mind, theologically backward minority. Why should he sit down, he asked, when political pressure was all that parish leaders understood? His friends in the Working Groups asked the same question.

Once again, Margaret felt besieged from both sides. To Stephen,

Shannon, the Schaumbers and their allies, she was a radical who trivialized the liturgy to score cheap political points. To her former friends in the Working Groups, she was a traitor, co-opted by her desire to be named director of liturgy on a full-time basis.

The wonder of it was that she still wanted the job. Had she found herself in a similar situation even one year earlier, she would surely have walked away. But in that year her commitment had been strengthened, her conviction that she was making a difference had been increased. She wanted the liturgy job because, aside from her family, nothing mattered to her as much as the mass.

It was Margaret's good fortune that neither the Working Groups nor their increasingly conservative opponents were represented on the search committee that Father Maier had appointed to select the new director of liturgy. The group was composed almost entirely of men and women who had served long terms on liturgy planning teams. They knew Margaret as an easy person to work with, a thoughtful conversation partner, and a woman who seldom cast herself in the most prominent liturgical roles. Her interview had gone well, and she had heard, via the parish grapevine, that the focus of the search had been narrowed to herself and one other candidate.

As she waited for news of her future that fall, Margaret immersed herself in the details of Larry Madden's pastoral installation. Everyone in the parish seemingly wanted to be part of the liturgy that day. There would be a children's choir and an adult choir. There would be guitars and a piano, trumpet and organ. There would be special duties for Larry's family and special duties for prominent parishioners. On top of all that there would be the complicating presence of Cardinal Hickey.

The cardinal's view of liturgy was rather different than Holy Trinity's. He enjoyed pomp. His masses at St. Matthew's Cathedral and the Basilica of the Immaculate Conception had more in common with medieval pageants than with a supper that had taken place in first-century Palestine. Everything seemed designed to *distance* the laity from the mystery unfolding on the altar, and to elevate the few lavishly robed men who stood near the table.

Making *his* mass the community's mass would not be easy. But in this, she found Father Madden of invaluable assistance. Larry had a knack for blending tradition and innovation in his liturgies, for creating a mass which was formal yet energetic, elegant but not off-putting. He was expert at using old forms to speak new truths.

This was most evident in their conversations about the composition of the processional party. Usually, at a pastoral installation, the cardinal and the candidate were preceded to the altar by whatever priests, deacons and altar boys had been amassed for the occasion. But this presented an almost entirely clerical (and entirely male) vision of the Church. For Larry's mass, they decided, the procession should include the entire staff, from the top pastoral aides to the maintenance men and the payroll clerks. It would be one of their few opportunities to assert in symbol that the Church was the people of God.

To Margaret's chagrin, every step in the liturgical plan had to be approved by archdiocesan officials who behaved as though anal retention were the essential Catholic virtue. There were seemingly arbitrary rules for everything: who could stand where, who could move when, and who could carry what. Hickey's aides made him seem a dowager empress. He would need a deacon, of course, and a master of ceremonies. Bishop Corrada would be on hand, too.

As she watched the number of ordained men on the altar rising, Margaret wondered if women would fit anywhere within this celebration. Larry's sister was to read from the Scriptures; Margaret herself would read the prayers of petition; and Barbara Perez, who was the cantor at the 9:15 liturgy, and Barbara Conley Waldmiller, who worked with Larry at the liturgy center, would lead the singing. But the cardinal's assistants made it clear that these women were to be seated in the nave, or with the choir, and to enter the sanctuary only to discharge their liturgical duties.

The men of the archdiocese had also informed Margaret that contrary to Holy Trinity's custom, the girls who walked in the entrance procession would not be allowed to wear albs. She called each of the girl's parents with this news, and told them that she would understand if they decided to remove their daughters from the procession. Her only consolation was that none did.

CHARLIE

The mass was to begin at 9:30 on that October morning. It was 9:10 when Ray McGovern and his daughter Christin arrived and found a pew off the center aisle. Ray sat to slip his blue stole over his shoulders, then stood in prayer. The church filled up around him. There were two others standing, both of them high school students: Devon Franklin and Keara Depenbrock.

At 9:20, the children's choir, fifty-five strong, processed up the right aisle, assembled around the piano and sang a heartfelt if quavering rendition of "O Day of Peace."

In the rear of the church Cardinal Hickey stood with Bishop Corrada and Father Glynn, each resplendent in white vestments.

"I want to thank you for coming," the Jesuit provincial said.

"This is my way of saying that you were right and I was wrong," the cardinal replied.

Soon the organ prelude faded and the opening strains of the entrance hymn filled the church. From beneath the balcony, the processional party began its solemn progress up the center aisle. Behind the girls in their dresses and jumpers walked the altar boys in their albs. Two wore special mittens for handling the cardinal's miter and crosier. Behind the boys marched the janitors and maintenance men, and behind them the women who kept the parish's bills paid. They were followed by Margaret, Anna Thompson, and the rest of the pastoral staff. Next came the Jesuits who lived in the rectory, and finally, Larry, Cardinal Hickey, and his attendants.

When they reached the front of the church, the lay people filed into pews while the priests, deacon and altar boys ascended to the altar. Then, in a moment of irony that parishioners could not help but savor, Bishop Corrada, their great nemesis, stepped forward and read the letter in which Cardinal Hickey officially designated Father Madden as pastor of Holy Trinity Church.

It was an unremarkable document save for one sentence: "He must be solicitous for those who have been alienated from the church." Not everyone gathered at Holy Trinity that morning believed that James Hickey understood what he was urging, but they were tickled that he had put the words in Bishop Corrada's mouth.

When the bishop had finished, the congregation rose in a standing ovation. On the altar, Larry embraced his fellow Jesuits.

The mass proceeded at a stately pace. The choir performed a meditative, chant-like *Gloria*, and parishioners, though accustomed to joining in a more jubilant variation of this great hymn of praise, sat listening appreciatively. It was as though they were attempting to persuade the cardinal that he and they had more in common than he supposed.

After a short, bearded deacon proclaimed the Gospel, Hickey stepped to the lectern and looking down, saw Ray, Devon and Keara standing before him.

He was glad to be visiting "this wonderful parish," the cardinal said, for he had been eager for a chance to "reflect prayerfully" with Holy Trinity parishioners on what was "most basic" in their community.

His eyes strayed from his text to the place where Ray and Devon were standing, but he did not break his homiletic stride. For the next twenty minutes he explained the role of the pastor in "teaching, preaching and sanctifying." His bloodless prose was enlivened by a pleasant, sincere delivery.

If the cardinal intended to lambaste McGovern or threaten the parish, he was working up to it gradually. Whenever he looked up, his eyes seemed to find Ray's, but his words made only oblique reference to the Standing.

"The faith the church professes is not a mere ideal, still less a set of arbitrary rules. It is God's revelation," the cardinal said. "At the Eucharist, the barriers, pretensions and entanglements that separate people from one another are broken down."

But McGovern and his young companions still stood silently, as if to assert that this mystical unity could not be achieved without Hickey's repentance.

"I am giving Father Madden a challenging responsibility," the cardinal said in closing. "I ask your support. Work with him for the unity, the harmony and the faith of this unique parish family." Then he turned and walked to his seat behind the altar.

There had been no showdown.

In a few moments the cardinal and Father Madden came to the front of the sanctuary where Larry was to take the oath of fidelity. As they rose, Mary Tschudy, whose daughter Megan had been treated so poorly by Bishop Corrada at the Bad Confirmation, hurried up the left aisle to get a good photographic angle. She was planning to present Larry with a collage of her pictures.

Mary was kneeling on the floor, looking through her viewfinder, when she realized that there were no women in her frame. Lowering the camera from her eye, she realized that there were none on the altar. After she had taken her pictures, she returned to her pew and remained standing.

Other parishioners were less offended by the scene in the sanctuary than by the words of Larry's oath.

With firm faith I believe everything contained in God's word, written or handed down in tradition and proposed by the Church, whether in solemn judgment or in ordinary and universal magisterium, as divinely revealed and calling for faith. I also firmly accept and hold each and every thing that is proposed by the Church definitively regarding teaching on faith and morals. Moreover, I adhere with religious submission of will and intellect to the teachings which either the Roman pontiff or the College of Bishops enunciate when they exercise the authentic magisterium even if they proclaim those teachings in an act that is not definitive.

The oath seemed demeaning and unreasonable. In its long history the Church had advanced many teachings which it now deems erroneous, such as the legitimacy of holding slaves. A nineteenth-century pastor under the oath Larry had just recited would have had to accept that teaching, regardless of the prompting of his own conscience. After two millennia of mortal errors—from the torture and execution of heretics, through the demonization of Jews, the Catholic hierarchy seemingly persisted in the belief that everything it taught was incontrovertibly true.

Thankfully, the oath was brief and the mass resumed. Lay people brought forth the congregation's gift, including the weekly financial offering, food for a local hospice, and the bread and wine that would be consecrated for Communion.

A few lay people were permitted in the sanctuary long enough to assist in the distribution of Communion, but the task was handled primarily by the great clerical party on the altar. When it was over, and the final meditative strains of the Communion hymn had faded, Father Madden walked to the lectern. This time there was silence rather than applause.

What point would he put before them on this ambiguous day? What could he tell them, in the cardinal's presence, about the future of their church?

Father Madden addressed neither of these questions. At least not directly.

Today was the day of what a boy at Holy Trinity School had called his "pastorizing," Larry said, and he was honored that they had shared it with him. He offered his special thanks to the cardinal, to his family, and to Margaret Costello and Barbara Conley Waldmiller, whose names drew vigorous applause.

He reminded them of all those who were with them in spirit that morning, and all those who had labored to make their parish a spirit-filled place. Then, very subtly, Larry raised Holy Trinity's flag.

"You know," he said, "Father Tom Gavigan would have been eighty-three today. And I can think of no more wonderful human presence that could be evoked over this affair."

With equal subtlety he framed the question that separated the man who sat behind him on the altar, wearing his miter, from the people who sat—and stood—before him in the pews. The most important part of his job, Larry said, was "preaching the Word." It was a sentiment to which no one in the church would have objected, yet it defined their divisions.

For the cardinal the Word was a series of laws and customs based on a definitive revelation and codified by Church-sanctioned experts down through the ages. It was the surest means of guiding ordinary people, who lacked the ability to determine complex theological and moral matters for themselves, into the saving presence of their God.

But for the people of Holy Trinity the Word was the scriptural example of Jesus Christ, who said little about the issues that obsessed the hierarchy, but much about the extravagant love and forgiveness of their God, the necessity of opening oneself to the Holy Spirit and the imperative of finding God in one's neighbors, particularly the poor.

These differing interpretations had led the two camps into conflict before. Lay Catholics, claiming to be led by the Spirit, sought recognition of their spiritual growth and their intellectual independence; the hierarchy, claiming the authority of the Apostles, attempted to reassert the validity of its teachings and its right to dictate sweeping terms to those who professed the faith.

"The Word of God is the best thing we have to show us the glory of our lives," Father Madden said. "It is what God gives us to help us be that piece of the Kingdom that he desires right here on our street."

Which Word he proposed to preach at Holy Trinity he did not say, but the congregation sang him out with resounding joy.

After mass most of the worshipers streamed along Thirty-sixth Street to the Car Barn, a former trolley garage which had been converted into a reception and conference facility with expansive views of the Potomac River.

The cardinal and his party were among the last to arrive. The morning had gone reasonably well from their perspective. The liturgy had been lovely. There had been no rebellious excess on the part of the Jesuits or the parish staff, and the protest, though distracting, had been limited in scope. Perhaps Holy Trinity was not in such bad shape after all.

Larry took off the skipper's cap he had donned after mass and showed the cardinal to a seat. No sooner was Hickey comfortable than parishioners began lining up to greet him. The cardinal spent the next hour shaking hands and wishing people well, beaming with sincerity but seldom engaging in serious conversation.

Near the end of the line stood Ray McGovern, and as he drew closer one of the cardinal's aides began edging toward Hickey to ask whether it might not be time to go. But the aide was a polite man, and he found himself detained in a series of conversations, so that by the time he reached the cardinal's side, Hickey was already shaking McGovern's hand.

"I have a question for you," the cardinal said. "Don't you get awfully tired standing throughout the service. I'm concerned about that."

"No," Ray said. "I don't get tired. But thank you for asking. Now I have a question for you." He pointed out that contrary to Holy Trinity's usual practice, no women had been allowed to sit in the sanctuary that day, and the girls who walked in the entrance procession had not been wearing albs. "I was wondering if that was your doing," McGovern said.

"We cannot give women the notion that they have an official function in the Eucharistic liturgy," Hickey replied. "So we really can't allow that sort of thing."

But a number of prominent theologians believed that women *had* performed official functions in the Eucharistic liturgies of the early Church, Ray told him.

"Oh, theologians will say all manner of things," the cardinal responded. "It is what the Holy Father says that matters, and the Holy Father has been clear on this."

Sensing he had reached a dead end, McGovern changed the subject, reminding Hickey that eleven months earlier, when the American bishops had rejected the third draft of the proposed pastoral letter on the role of women in the Church, they had also passed a resolution calling for further discussion on the subject. "I am wondering when that will start in our diocese," he said.

The cardinal replied that he was a busy man. "And when the pope had been so clear, I don't think we need to take up our time," he said.

When McGovern heard Hickey invoke the pope for the second time in their brief conversation, he understood that he and the cardinal had reached the limits of their discourse. Ray hadn't expected to change Hickey's mind, but he had hoped to engage him in debate. But that would be impossible if the cardinal's every argument was based on the importance of fealty to the pope.

As the reception eddied around them, the two men spoke for another five minutes, but try as he might, McGovern could not induce the cardinal to abandon the solicitous, condescending tone he habitually employed with the laity.

Though Ray was frustrated, some of his ambivalent supporters, watching discreetly from around the room, were cheered. McGovern had taken his argument with the hierarchy *to* the hierarchy; he had made Hickey hear him. Whether such quiet confrontations would eventually achieve the conversion of the Roman hierarchy, or whether persistent and pervasive dissent would ultimately breed an American schism, they could not say. But for that one morning there was honor in standing, however metaphorically, with a man who had made the hierarchy acknowledge what it preferred to deny.

But it was only one morning.

On the following Sunday, Cardinal Hickey stood, wreathed in incense, on the altar at St. Matthew's Cathedral, celebrating a mass so coldly baroque that it seemed less an expression of a living faith than an abstruse piece of performance art.

Meanwhile at Holy Trinity, the church was full, the singing was boisterous and Ray McGovern was standing in his familiar place.

EPILOGUE

ᕙᕗ

On Ash Wednesday 1996, Jim Maier attended the 6:20 A.M. mass at his parish church in suburban Los Angeles. On his sweater vest he wore a small pin proclaiming his membership in Dignity. By his side was John Turk, an antique store owner, who had been his companion for almost two and a half years.

In official terms Jim was still a Jesuit on a leave of absence and still a priest, but he had been living as a lay person for just over two years. The previous fall, he and the Society had forwarded papers to Rome requesting that he be released from his vows. They were expecting word of the Vatican's decision by spring.

In the meantime, Jim presided, once each month, at liturgies sponsored by Dignity/Los Angeles. It was an arrangement he assumed would continue even after Rome relieved him of his priestly faculties, for the men and women of the congregation did not believe that living in a monogamous gay relationship should disqualify one from the ministerial priesthood.

"It's like having my cake and eating it, too," Jim said one unusually chilly California afternoon a few days after the service. "I am able to pursue this relationship, and I'm still able to continue in the sacramental ministry which I deeply love."

Two years earlier, after requesting a leave of absence from the Jesuits and moving out of the community at Loyola Marymount, he had begun work as a bilingual counselor for a call-in service operated by AIDS Project Los Angeles, acting as advisor to and advocate for people with AIDS or HIV-related symptoms who were experiencing financial problems or having difficulties finding housing or obtaining health care. It is very much the sort of face-to-face, or at least voice-to-voice, involvement with the suffering that he found so compelling in El Salvador.

When Jim accepted the position, one of his supervisors explained to him tactfully that many of his gay and lesbian coworkers harbored a deep distrust of the Catholic Church, and that perhaps he should be discreet about revealing his background.

"It was like a looking-glass world," Jim recalled. In Washington as a priest he had had to make a secret of his homosexuality. In Los Angeles, among other homosexuals, he had to make a secret of his priesthood.

He met John after mass one Sunday evening. They fell into conversation, and John invited him to join a group that was going to dinner at a Chinese restaurant. Jim later reciprocated by inviting John to dine with the Jesuits at Loyola Marymount. Their growing attraction and his refusal to live any longer in the closet precipitated his request to leave the community.

Jim took a small, furnished apartment four blocks from John's. He says he has few qualms about the direction he has chosen. "The kind of questions I have now are questions about my relationship," he said. "Where is it going? Am I supposed to have a life partner? Should we buy a house together? Is he the one?"

Since leaving Holy Trinity, he has disclosed his homosexuality to his family and most of his close friends, and though some of these conversations were stressful, he has met with little rejection. Jim still struggles, at times, with the morality of having forsaken his vows, of having broken the promises he made to the Society and to the Church, but his guilt is assuaged by his conviction that he has chosen a more honest way of life, and by his ability to continue doing what he considers God's work. After a few months on the job, he and a colleague began a spirituality support group for gay men who are HIV positive. In Lent of 1996, it was beginning its fourth ten-week session.

In the office where Jim works, there are large bowls of male and female condoms for clients who come in to meet with their case managers. Sometimes, when supplies run low, he takes it upon himself to replenish the stock. Then, with his hands submerged in latex, he thinks to himself, "If Cardinal Hickey could see me now."

ᑐᗰᗰᕬᑐ

Among Jim's most frequent visitors from his old life is Ray McGovern, who has business in Los Angeles a few times each year. They've met for dinner on several occasions, and at their first reunion, Jim asked Ray if he was still standing.

Ray said that he was.

Good, Jim replied.

By Ash Wednesday of 1996, McGovern had been standing at the family mass for almost four years. Though many worshipers remain aggrieved, the furor surrounding his protest had subsided significantly. But this comparative tranquillity is a recent phenomenon.

In April of 1995, on the third anniversary of the Standing, members of the Working Groups on Sexism had distributed flyers inviting other parishioners to stand in acknowledgment of Ray's efforts. Between fifteen and thirty people did so, at one point or another, precipitating an immediate backlash. In letters to Father Madden and the Parish Council, opponents of the groups renewed their demands that Ray be removed from the church and that the Working Groups be forbidden to meet on church grounds or participate in parish programs. Many prominent opponents of the protest, including Shannon Jordan, Cathy Quinn and Carole Farrell, were members of the council, and it appeared, for a time, that despite having no formal authority, Ray's adversaries might be able to force Father Madden's hand.

At one particularly volatile meeting, one of McGovern's antagonists suggested arresting him.

"Arrest him," another seconded.

"Yeah," said Jo Owen, Ray's only supporter on the council. "And then let's crucify him."

In the end, the council formed a committee to study a response to the Standing. In December 1995 it produced its report, in the form of an open letter from Father Madden to the parish community, explaining why the Standing was liturgically and theologically incorrect.

"When we celebrate the Eucharist," Father Madden wrote, "we anticipate our existence in heaven; we taste that communion in God when there will be no Jew or Greek, no male or female, no rich or poor, no old or young. It is the time when all divisions cease. . . . This is why it is inappropriate for divisions in the Christian community to be emphasized at the Eucharist."

In a public forum Ray might have replied that it was the Church which compromised the meal of the Kingdom by emphasizing divisions between male and female. And in a private conversation, Father Madden might have agreed. But since Larry's letter seemed to satisfy opponents of the Standing, McGovern saw no reason to provoke them with a response. He simply went on standing.

He was, however, almost entirely without company. His daughter Christin, a junior at the University of Virginia, worships at an Episcopal Church when she is home on vacation.

Brian Depenbrock and his daughter Keara have also left Holy Trinity. "I was feeling a little more radical than what they wanted to do," Brian said of his departure from the Working Groups on Sexism.

He and Keara worship sporadically at St. Augustine's, a boisterous African-American community in inner-city Washington, but both feel increasingly alienated from the Church. Nor has his wife, Martha Manning, who wrote in *U.S. Catholic* of Keara's impending confirmation, and has recently published a memoir of her Catholic girlhood, returned to the Church.

Peter and Kathie Schaumber have also left Holy Trinity, though for different reasons. "As I became more active in the parish I got a better sense of what was going on behind the scenes," Peter said. "There is an atmosphere of dissent there which isn't good for my faith." The Schaumbers now attend mass at the Georgetown University Hospital chapel.

Peter's bête noire, Anna Thompson, resigned as director of religious education for personal reasons not long after Father Madden's installation, and returned to her native New Zealand. The Good Choices Program was abandoned by her successor for reasons more pedagogical than doctrinal. In January 1996, however, a group of eleven parish families, disappointed with the moral decision-making component of the new program, contacted Susan Keys and asked her to offer the program to their children in their homes. Susan, who is now assistant professor of counseling and human development at Johns Hopkins University, agreed.

Most of the other players in the controversies that shock Holy Trinity remain active in the parish.

On February 14, 1994, Margaret Costello was named full-time director of liturgy, and she continues in that position.

Shannon Jordan is a member of the Parish Council, where she has raised frequent complaints about the Working Groups and the parish's liturgical orthodoxy.

Kathy Hartley serves on Holy Trinity's delegation to the Washington Interfaith Network, a church-, synagogue- and mosque-based organization working on issues of housing, education and crime prevention.

Ellen Crowley continues to lead the RCIA program, and Paul and Cathy Quinn remain among the most active people in the parish, as do Pam and Mike Hall. Paul occasionally preaches at non-Eucharistic services, as does Linda Arnold, who is now director of campus ministry at Trinity College, a women's college on the northeast side of town.

Natalie Ganley preaches at non-eucharistic services, too. But her preaching at mass has come to an end. She gave "reflections" at the 8:00 A.M. weekday mass for one week in Advent of 1993, and one week in Lent of 1994, before her activities were reported to Cardinal Hickey. The cardinal did not demand that she cease, but he told Father Madden that he thought Holy Trinity was "fudging," by allowing a woman to preach at mass.

Natalie decided to stop. "I didn't want the bishop to close my parish because I preached," she said. "I didn't think that was the ditch we ought to die in." She continues to write for homily services and Catholic periodicals, and to offer spiritual direction on the parish retreat team.

Ed Dougherty and his wife, Ellen returned to Washington in June 1994. He works for a health care consulting firm; she is a legal recruiter. They live in northern Virginia.

The Doughertys sometimes worship at Holy Trinity, where Ed says he has found the community "loving and hospitable," but he has trouble with his own "comfort level."

"Sometimes I'm looking for a way to worship anonymously," he said. "I don't want to be an issue for anybody. I don't want to be a red flag."

He and the Maryland province of the Society of Jesus have twice forwarded papers to Rome requesting that Ed be "laicized," but both times his request has been denied.

Father Ed Glynn completed his term as superior of the Maryland province of the Society of Jesus in 1996, and was offered the presidency of the Jesuit-operated Weston School of Theology in Cambridge, Massachusetts. But the position requires a *nihil obstat*, a declaration from the Vatican that "nothing impedes" the candidate from assuming the job, and in Glynn's case, despite the support of American cardinals Joseph Bernardin and William Keeler, this declaration was withheld.

The Congregation for Catholic Education did not disclose the reason for its decision, but many of Glynn's Jesuit colleagues believe that Cardinal James Hickey, still irked that Glynn had not ordered the Jesuits at Georgetown University to expel a now-defunct undergraduate abortion rights group from their campus, had blocked his appointment.

The cardinal declined to comment on Glynn's situation, and within six weeks, Father Glynn had accepted an offer to become president of Gonzaga University, a Jesuit college in Spokane, Washington. The school does not have a pontifically-approved faculty, and hence the position does not require a *nihil obstat*.

Christine Flanagan and Tim McLaren have moved to the Midwest. Theresa Marino and Gary Cosgrove remain parishioners at Holy Trinity.

ᏂᎷᎧ

Of the many activists at the Georgetown parish, Rea Howarth, who heads the Working Groups on Sexism, has had perhaps the most direct experience of the passion, indeed the hysteria, that attaches to issues of Church reform.

In the fall of 1994, she and Charlie Davis, another Holy Trinity parishioner, helped found the Northern Virginia chapter of Call to Action, the leading Church reform organization in the United States. Shortly after the group's first meeting, Rea began receiving harassing phone calls. One night a man she did not know kept her house under surveillance.

"He sat out there watching, and I watched right back," Rea said.

The group's third meeting, at a Catholic parish in Alexandria, Virginia, was disrupted by a small contingent of antiabortion activists who shouted down the scheduled speakers. Before its next meeting, at a Catholic church in Sterling, Virginia, Rea notified the Loudoun County sheriff's department that demonstrators might be present. On the night of the meeting, the sheriff's department arrested the seven most unruly members of a large and angry crowd, which disconnected the public-address system in the auditorium where the meeting was being held, shouted down speakers and menaced participants.

Six of the seven were convicted of trespassing and given suspended sentences. At their trial one of the protestors claimed that she had informed Father Robert Ripey, chancellor of the Diocese of Arlington, of their plans, and he had told them to "do what you have to do."

Father Ripey did not testify.

Call to Action/Northern Virginia now holds its meetings in non-church facilities. A presentation on Church reform in February 1996 drew more than one hundred people.

Holy Trinity has been somewhat calmer during the first three years of Father Madden's tenure than it was during the last eighteen months of Jim Maier's. Larry's cordial relationship with Cardinal Hickey has quieted fears of an impending crackdown, as has the fact that Auxiliary Bishop Alvaro Corrada now oversees another jurisdiction within the archdiocese. But Father Madden's tenure has had its trials nonetheless.

In the spring of 1995 Larry launched a $5 million capital campaign to shore up and dramatically expand Holy Trinity's crumbling parish center, which is also the original church, and the oldest remaining place of Catholic worship in the nation's capital. Unfortunately, the campaign was launched before parishioners had an opportunity to view the plans or discuss the scope, cost and necessity of the project. It was the first fundraiser at Holy Trinity since the Mitch Snyder incident that did not, from the outset, commit 10 percent of its revenues to the poor, and this provoked additional opposition.

After a series of meetings early that summer, Father Madden agreed that in conjunction with the capital campaign, Holy Trinity could conduct a "companion campaign" to raise money for building projects in its sister parishes. (In the interest of disclosure, I should say that I helped conceive and solidify support for this compromise, but was disillusioned by the zeal with which the parish leadership committed itself to fundraising and the prominence that the campaign was accorded in the liturgy. My family left the area for nine months after the fundraising began, and on our return we joined another parish.

By the spring of 1996 Holy Trinity had raised roughly half of what it needed for its new parish center. Some forty-five thousand dollars had been contributed to the companion campaigns.

Despite Father Maier's departure, a small core of parishioners remain committed to the relationship Jim initiated with the parish in San Salvador. In January 1994, the Parish-to-Parish hosted a week-long visit by three members of *Maria, Madre de los Pobres*, and several months later instituted a "village bank," to provide loans to aspiring "micro-entrepreneurs" in Padre Daniel's community. That summer Ted and Mary Tschudy led a delegation of teenagers, including their daughter Megan and Shannon Jordan's son Matthew, on a visit to their sister parish where they helped build a basketball court.

Jo Owen has also deepened her commitment to the Salvadoran poor. While visiting Chalatenango with other delegates from Holy Trinity in the summer of 1993, she met a young man from a peasant family whom several American aid workers said would make an excellent doctor. She and her husband Bruce are currently putting him through college and medical school in San Salvador, with the written understanding that he will return to serve the people of his native province.

Tom Howarth continues to visit El Salvador once or twice a year, and he and Rea remain in almost daily contact with a large family of Salvadoran immigrants they befriended six years ago. Tom now worships at St. Aloysius and volunteers one night each week at its men's shelter.

⌒〰〰〰〰◎

Though their anxieties about the future of their parish have abated, parishioners at Holy Trinity realize that the struggle for control of the Roman Catholic Church in the United States and around the world has intensified.

In October 1993, Pope John Paul II released the encyclical *Veritatis Splendor*, which asserted not simply the existence of absolute moral truths, a point on which he might have found widespread Catholic concurrence, but the Roman hierarchy's unerring ability to divine such truths and command assent. The document seemed a thinly veiled attack on the moral theology taught at most seminaries and graduate schools in the United States and in Europe since Vatican II.

Some months later, Rome released troubling news about the soon-to-be released English-language version of the *Catechism of the Catholic Church*. A committee of American bishops and scholars, under the direction of Cardinal Bernard Law of Boston, had originally rendered the book in what is known as "horizontally" inclusive language, meaning that the word "humanity" was used rather than "mankind," and the designation "men" was forsaken for "men and women." But even this small gesture toward American sensibilities and current English usage was deemed subversive by the catechism's principal author Cardinal Joseph Ratzinger, prefect of the Congregation for the Doctrine of the Faith. The catechism was rewritten using only masculine pronouns, and now includes several instances of unintentional humor such as: "everyone, man and woman, should acknowledge and accept his sexual identity."

The necessity of combating feminism in the Church also prompted the apostolic letter *Ordinatio Sacerdotalis*, which was released in May 1994 and is perhaps the most controversial writing of John Paul's papacy. Timed to coincide with the ordination of one thousand women by the Anglican church, it was intended to settle the question of a female priesthood once and for all. "I declare that the Church has no authority whatsoever to confer priestly ordination on women, and that this judgment is to be definitively held by all the Church's faithful," the pope wrote.

But the letter only stirred further controversy. Some scholars were perplexed by the wording of the document. What did it mean to say that something must be held "definitively"? As in *Veritatis Splendor*, the pope seemed to be creating an entirely new category of Catholic truth— teachings not so certain as to be declared infallible but which commanded unquestioning assent nonetheless.

Other partisans in the debate over women's ordination noted that *Ordinatio Sacerdotalis* advanced no new arguments to support an all-male priesthood. This was troubling, because the existing arguments had been badly undermined. The letter, as a result, seemed merely an exercise in authority.

As Sister Mary Collins had explained at Holy Trinity, the Pontifical Biblical Commission had informed Paul VI in the late 1970s that the question of a female priesthood could not be resolved by appeals to Scripture. That left the argument from tradition—which holds that an all-male priesthood must represent the will of God because it is the unbroken custom of the Church—and the argument from image—that females cannot act as the liturgical personification of a male Christ.

But the argument from tradition is so weak as to be seldom advanced. Until the late nineteenth century, the Church taught that slavery was morally justified. It denied a right to religious freedom until 1965. That the Church has been in error on an issue for centuries is not a credible reason for its remaining so.

The argument from image is a more slippery affair. It is true that the Church has long compared the relationship between Christ and itself to that of a bridegroom and his bride. But Christ spoke of the relationship between himself and his followers in many metaphorical ways—vine and branches, food and hungry—which bore no reference to gender. Why one figure of speech is codified as doctrine and others are not, particularly when the effect of that codification is discriminatory, is far from clear. As are the reasons for giving greater symbolic emphasis to Christ's masculinity than to his humanity, especially since it is the latter on which salvation is predicated.

A few months after the release of *Ordinatio Sacerdotalis* the Vatican spoke out on another issue of great importance to the American Church. In October, Cardinal Ratzinger reiterated the Church's teaching that divorced Catholics who had remarried without an annulment could not receive communion. Though his position was unsurprising, Ratzinger advanced an unusual argument in defending it. The notion that an individual's conscience was the final arbiter in determining fitness for the reception of Communion was a "mistaken conviction," he wrote.

But that conscience is always the final arbiter in any moral decision has been the bedrock of Catholic moral theology for centuries. The cardinal, perhaps, was searching for a forceful way to say that as a Catholic one could not simply do as one pleased, that one was bound by certain teachings. But in doing so, he ignored one of the teachings by which he, himself, should have been bound.

Cardinal Ratzinger intensified his campaign against progressives and moderates in the American Church in December of that year when he decreed that the New Revised Standard Version of the Bible, could not be used in the liturgy because it contained horizontally inclusive language. At the same time, he rescinded his earlier approval of the Psalter drawn from that Bible.

The NRSV had already been cleared by the American and Canadian bishops, and in overruling them, the cardinal seemed to be saying they had only as much teaching authority as the Vatican permitted them.

The Church, however, teaches that the bishops are successors of the Apostles. The Roman curia, on the other hand, has no roots in Scripture or in early Christian tradition. Why the latter enjoyed authority over the former, the cardinal did not explain. Nor did the German-speaking Ratzinger elaborate on his competence to judge an English biblical translation performed by the best Scripture scholars in North America.

Ironically, the biblical citations in the Pope's best-selling book, *Crossing the Threshold of Hope*, were taken from the NRSV.

In March 1995, John Paul released *Evangelium Vitae*, perhaps the longest awaited of his many encyclicals. It proclaimed human life inviolable from its earliest moments, before implantation of the fertilized egg and before individuation at two weeks. He condemned euthanasia, said capital punishment was seldom if ever moral, urged Catholic politicians and voters to enact laws forbidding abortion and suggested there were instances in which it was sinful to support candidates who would not vote to curtail abortion rights.

As in *Centesimus Annus*, his 1991 encyclical on work and the economy, the pope presented in *Evangelium Vitae* a vigorous moral argument on some of the most perplexing issues of the day. As such it was welcomed and debated in the United States as few encyclicals are. But some American Catholics who were in substantial agreement with the pope's views questioned the wisdom of describing the world as caught in a struggle between the "culture of life" and the "culture of death." The designation seemed to suggest that there was something vaguely murderous in questioning John Paul's sweeping intellectual arguments. It also radically raised the rhetorical stakes in the already overheated culture wars that gripped the western democracies.

It may have been tempting for papal loyalists to believe that obedience to the pontiff made the choices between the forces of life and those of death abundantly clear, but as students of the papacy soon discovered, even the pope made decisions that were morally ambiguous at the very least. This was dramatically illustrated by the selection of a new archbishop for San Salvador in the spring of 1995.

With the civil war over, the Vatican was eager to establish a less confrontational relationship between the local Church and the right-wing Arena government, which had maintained its hold on power in the first post-war elections. But Arena was the party whose founder had ordered the murder of Oscar Romero, and whose leaders had organized, financed and covered up the torture and murder of priests, nuns and lay people in the liberation church. It was also the party whose oppresive political and economic policies had earned it the frequent censure of Romero's succesor, Archbishop Arturo Rivera y Damas who had died the previous year.

How far would Rome go in courting a party with an abysmal record on human rights, but a potential ally at the United Nations and in other international bodies?

In May 1995 the pope named Fernando Sáenz Lacalle, a member of *Opus Dei* and former vicar of the Salvadoran armed forces, to the see once occupied by Romero. Among Lacalle's first public statements was that liberation theology no longer had a place in the Salvadoran Church.

The Vatican's campaign against the moral and intellectual sensibilities of progressive Catholics reached a high point a few months later when Cardinal Ratzinger released a letter to bishops, responding to questions he had received about *Ordinatio Sacerdotalis*. In it, he proclaimed that the teaching John Paul described as "definitive" was, in fact, infallible.

For a doctrine to be declared infallible, however, it must be either explicitly designated by the pope or universally accepted by the entire body of Catholic bishops as divinely revealed. Neither was the case in this instance. John Paul II approved the release of Ratzinger's letter, but he cannot transfer his infallibility.

This document, like the catechism, had its moments of unintentional humor. "You must consider that the priestly ministry is a service and not a position of power and privilege above others," wrote the cardinal in demanding that Catholics conform their thoughts on this matter to his own.

In Europe, these aggressive tactics have provoked a strong backlash. More than 1.5 million German Catholics signed petitions opposing priestly celibacy and the Church's traditional sexual teachings. In Austria, roughly half of those who attended mass each Sunday, some five hundred thousand people, signed petitions supporting the ordination of women, an end to mandatory priestly celibacy, and more liberal teaching on homosexuality. And in Ireland, despite a direct appeal by the pope, a small majority voted to legalize divorce.

The Church in the United States is outwardly more peaceful. Catholics continue to profess their admiration of the pope as they continue to disregard his teachings. Even those who profess their fealty on sexual issues, and dismiss those who do not as "cafeteria Catholics," have not taken up John Paul's call to work for an end to the arms trade, the virtual abolition of capital punishment, or the forgiveness of Third World debt. In this, they are cafeteria Catholics themselves.

When the pope speaks, American Catholics listen, but they do not reflexively obey. This is due in part, no doubt, to the difficulty of what he demands of them. But in larger measure it flows from their conviction that on many issues, particularly those of gender and sexuality, he is simply mistaken.

Raised on the freedoms of the First Amendment, steeped in the empiricism of the marketplace and suspicious of elites of every kind, American Catholics are unwilling to live their lives entirely by the directives which a clerical caste has wrung from a speculative metaphysical system developed in a prescientific age. Especially when these directives seem in opposition to the compassionate spirit of the Gospel. It is not that they doubt their own humanity, and therefore their inclination to sin. They simply understand that the Church is a human institution and therefore sinful too.

⚮

On Ash Wednesday 1996, Ray McGovern, Kathy Hartley and perhaps eighty other Catholics gathered outside St. Matthew's Cathedral in downtown Washington at noon. As hundreds of other worshipers from scores of downtown offices streamed into the church for the lunchtime service, the group began its own liturgy at the foot of the wide stone stairs.

It was a simple affair: hymns, prayers and Scripture readings that spoke of the need for repentance. Kim Lamberty of Holy Trinity recited the opening prayer. Kathy read the first reading, and all joined in the chant: "We call the Church to repentance for its sins against women."

At the climax of the ceremony, the worshippers filed forward to have the sign of the cross traced with ash upon their foreheads, "We all take upon us this sign of our repentance proclaiming as we do that we are nothing if we are not yours," they prayed. A phalanx of Washington, D.C. police officers, summoned by the archdiocese, looked on.

The service was nearly over, when Ray and some forty others dipped their thumbs in a dish of ashes created by burning copies of Cardinal Ratzinger's letter on *Ordinatio Sacerdotalis*. Climbing the cathedral stairs, they stood before a gleaming door, and marked it with signs of the cross.

ACKNOWLEDGMENTS

This book would not have been possible without the generous coopera-tion of the people, priests and staff of Holy Trinity Church, particularly Father Jim Maier. They gave graciously of their time, their insights and their memories. I am also grateful to the people of Maria, Madre de los Pobres in San Salvador, and of St. Aloysius in Washington, D.C., for their hospitality and cooperation.

I hesitate to thank my teachers, for fear they will be held accountable for my mistakes. With that said, I learned a great deal about the theology of Karl Rahner and his influence on the Second Vatican Council from conversations with Father Jim Connor. My understanding of the Church in El Salvador was deepened considerably by talks with Father David Blanchard. And my knowledge of the Christian spiritual tradition was enriched by Fathers Xavier Seubert and Pat McMahon.

Two individuals whose deaths I recount inspired me with examples of courage, humility, humor and love. If I did not have sons, I would have dedicated this book to the memories of Father Tom Gavigan and Hattie Wise Kennedy.

Catholics in Crisis would not have come into being without the efforts of my agent David Black. I'd like to thank Elizabeth Perle McKenna for making the original commitment to the project, William Patrick for sticking with it, and most especially, Sharon Broll, my editor, for seeing it sensitively into print.

The manuscript benefited from the comments of Thomas Frail, Julia Ketcham, William Powers and Charles Trueheart. Dan Froomkin provided some last minute research help.

For various kinds of spiritual and emotional support, as well as recreational opportunities, I'd like to thank Father Jerry Campbell, Barbara Connor, Mike Connor, Ellen Crowley, LeRoy Friessen, Natalie Ganley, John Kastor, Mae Kastor, Julia Ketcham, Howard Mansfield, Sy Montgomery, Alice Naughton, Frank Naughton, Enid Rubin, Isaiah Rubin and Arthur Stein.

My trip to El Salvador was enriched by the companionship of Kathleen Conley, Mary Gravalos, Jay Gribble, Kathy Hartley, Luke Hester, Lydia Mendoza, Jim Maier, Sally Outman and Jo Owen. Zoila Benavides, Father Dean Brackley, Francisco Calle, Jorge Ramirez Cuchia, John Giuliano, Padre Daniel Sanchez and Reuben Zamorra helped make our stay pleasurable as well as challenging. Rosemary Lyon, Grace and Jack O'Connor, and Mary and Ted Tschudy were essential in making this opportunity available to me and to others.

Several people, especially Pat D'Amico, Henry Hockeimer, Anne Murphy, Sally Outman and Mary Jane Owens, shared with me stories of personal conversion which did not ultimately find a place in the book, but which greatly enhanced my appreciation of the spiritual life of the parish. I would also like to thank Ellen Crowley, Sister Elizabeth O'Connor and the candidates and catechumens who entered the Rite of Christian Initiation of Adults in February of 1993 for allowing me to follow them through the inquiry process.

The following people sat for at least one interview, and many for several. This list is not exhaustive, however, and should not be used as a key to the identities of pseudonymous characters or confidential sources: Julianne Aaron, Sister Rosa Alvarez, Father George Anderson, Rosemary Anton, George Arnold, Linda Arnold, Mary Barnds, Zoila Benavides, Father David Blanchard, John Borelli, Father Dean Brackley, Marie Brown, Father Greg Budha, Father Walter Burghardt, Father Richard Burton, Father William Byron, John Cairns, Mary Cairns, Mary Calanan,

Father Jerry Campbell, LaSalle Caron, Carroll Carter, Rosemary Carter, Barbara Cebuhar, Joan Challinor, Father Paul Cioffi, Joe Clark, Susan Classen, Judy Miller Clear, Mary Connelly, Father Jim Connor, Father Jon de Cortina, Margaret Costello, Ellen Crowley, Father Bob Curry, Father Peter Daly, Pat D'Amico, Ed Dougherty, Charles Davis, Brian Depenbrock, Keara Depenbrock, Bill Dowbrow, Maureen Dowling, Father Regis Duffy, Father Avery Dulles, James Dyson, Father Ray East, Father Jim English, Fred Farmer, Carole Farrell, Ron Farrell, Carol Fennelly, Father Joseph Fitzmyer, Peter Foley, Linda Formella, Sister Maureen Fotz, LeRoy Friessen, Fred Ganley, Joseph Ganley, Natalie Ganley, John Giuliano, Bishop Medardo Gomez, Jay Gribble, Barbara Gryzmala, Tom Gryzmala, Ed Guinan, Mike Hall, Pam Hall, K. T. Haroun, Alberto Harth, Kathy Hartley, Diana Hayes, Henry Hockeimer, Father Ned Hogan, Mary Ellen Holm, Tom Howarth, Rea Howarth, Thomas Jenkins Sr., Mary Helen Jones, Carmel Kang, Franz Kaps, Michael Kelleher, Mary Agatha Kelly, Father Ray Kemp, Pat Kennedy, Susan Keys, Father Joseph Komonchak, Danny Kuhn, Ruth Kuhn, Father Joe Lacey, Mark Lee, Dennis Lucey, Pam Lucey, Richard Lucht, Ann Waters Lydanne, Mary Catherine Lydanne, Father Larry Madden, Father Jim Maier, Martha Manning, Pat Markun, Herb Martin, Ann McBride, Colman McCarthy, Sheila McCarthy, Father Rob McChesney, Adoreen McCormack, Paul McElligott, Ray McGovern, Father Dick McSorley, Laura Meaghar, Father Mark Mealy, Ann Miskovski, Milan Miskovski, Father Frank Moan, Tony Moore, Father John Mudd, Anne Murphy, Mary Gay Mutino, Father Joe Nangle, Marilyn Nejelski, Paul Nejelski, Meigs Newkirk, Katherine "Kitty" Nolan, Margaret Nolan, Susan O'Connell, Sister Elizabeth O'Connor, Grace O'Connor, Jack O'Connor, Bridie O'Donnell, Larry O'Rourke, the parents of Father Octavio Ortiz, Bob O'Sullivan, Sally Outman, Jo Owen, Mary Jane Owens, John Page, Darlene Palmer, Michael Petite, Cathy Quinn, Paul Quinn, Tim Ragan, Lin Romano, Rosemary Ryan, Ann Marie Santora, Kay Schaumber, Peter Schaumber, Mary Seelander, Shannon Jordan Skousgaard, Stephen Skousgaard, Father Joseph Sobierajski, Father Bob Spitzer, the Reverend John Steinbruck, Father Jim Stormes, Mary Stump, Bob Stump, David Suley, Sister Margaret Sullivan, Carl Sylvester, Dorothy Wharton Thomas, Anna Thompson, Sister Kathy Thornton, Debbie Tindale, Mary Tschudy, Megan Tschudy, Ted Tschudy, Melanne Verveer, Phil Verveer, Janet Walsh, Jim Walsh, Kenneth Walsh, William Warner,

Neville Waters Jr., Mary Rita Weiners, Clarence Wharton, the Reverend Christine Whitaker, Marcia Wiss and Tom Zaccharias.

Finally, my wife, Elizabeth Kastor, and our two sons, Benjamin and Christopher, lived with this book for three years. It was not always a well-mannered guest. To them I owe a bottomless debt.

FOR THE BEST IN PAPERBACKS, LOOK FOR THE

In every corner of the world, on every subject under the sun, Penguin represents quality and variety—the very best in publishing today.

For complete information about books available from Penguin—including Puffins, Penguin Classics, and Arkana—and how to order them, write to us at the appropriate address below. Please note that for copyright reasons the selection of books varies from country to country.

In the United Kingdom: Please write to *Dept. JC, Penguin Books Ltd, FREEPOST, West Drayton, Middlesex UB7 0BR.*

If you have any difficulty in obtaining a title, please send your order with the correct money, plus ten percent for postage and packaging, to *P.O. Box No. 11, West Drayton, Middlesex UB7 0BR*

In the United States: Please write to *Consumer Sales, Penguin USA, P.O. Box 999, Dept. 17109, Bergenfield, New Jersey 07621-0120.* VISA and MasterCard holders call 1-800-253-6476 to order all Penguin titles

In Canada: Please write to *Penguin Books Canada Ltd, 10 Alcorn Avenue, Suite 300, Toronto, Ontario M4V 3B2*

In Australia: Please write to *Penguin Books Australia Ltd, P.O. Box 257, Ringwood, Victoria 3134*

In New Zealand: Please write to *Penguin Books (NZ) Ltd, Private Bag 102902, North Shore Mail Centre, Auckland 10*

In India: Please write to *Penguin Books India Pvt Ltd, 706 Eros Apartments, 56 Nehru Place, New Delhi 110 019*

In the Netherlands: Please write to *Penguin Books Netherlands bv, Postbus 3507, NL-1001 AH Amsterdam*

In Germany: Please write to *Penguin Books Deutschland GmbH, Metzlerstrasse 26, 60594 Frankfurt am Main*

In Spain: Please write to *Penguin Books S. A., Bravo Murillo 19, 1° B, 28015 Madrid*

In Italy: Please write to *Penguin Italia s.r.l., Via Felice Casati 20, I-20124 Milano*

In France: Please write to *Penguin France S. A., 17 rue Lejeune, F–31000 Toulouse*

In Japan: Please write to *Penguin Books Japan, Ishikiribashi Building, 2–5–4, Suido, Bunkyo-ku, Tokyo 112*

In Greece: Please write to *Penguin Hellas Ltd, Dimocritou 3, GR–106 71 Athens*

In South Africa: Please write to *Longman Penguin Southern Africa (Pty) Ltd, Private Bag X08, Bertsham 2013*